THE HUMAN ATLAS

OF EUROPE

A continent united in diversity

Dedicated to Jo Cox (1974–2016),
Member of UK Parliament for Batley and
Spen, and in memory of all the refugees
who have lost their lives trying to reach
Europe in recent years

DIMITRIS BALLAS | DANNY DORLING | BENJAMIN HENNIG

First published in Great Britain in 2017 by

Policy Press   North America office:
University of Bristol   Policy Press
1–9 Old Park Hill   c/o The University of Chicago Press
Bristol   1427 East 60th Street
BS2 8BB   Chicago, IL 60637, USA
UK   t: +1 773 702 7700
t: +44 (0)117 954 5940   f: +1 773 702 9756
pp-info@bristol.ac.uk   sales@press.uchicago.edu
www.policypress.co.uk   www.press.uchicago.edu

© Policy Press 2017

British Library Cataloguing in Publication Data
A catalogue record for this book is available from the British Library

Library of Congress Cataloging-in-Publication Data
A catalog record for this book has been requested

ISBN 978 1 44731 354 0 paperback
ISBN 978 1 44733 290 9 epdf

The right of Dimitris Ballas, Danny Dorling and Benjamin Hennig to be
identified as authors of this work has been asserted by them in accordance
with the Copyright, Designs and Patents Act 1988.

Typeset and cover design by Soapbox, www.soapbox.co.uk
Printed and bound in Great Britain by Cambrian Printers, Ceredigion, Wales.
Policy Press uses environmentally responsible print partners.

Contents

Acknowledgements

We would like to thank all staff at Policy Press for all their fantastic support for this project. We would particularly like to express our gratitude to the Director, Alison Shaw, for her constant encouragement, feedback and support throughout all stages of this project. We are extremely grateful to Senior Production Editor, Jo Morton, who enthusiastically and at the same time meticulously and patiently read through, copy-edited and corrected several versions of the proofs and provided very helpful comments, amendments and excellent suggestions. We would also like to thank Dawn Rushen for copy-editing earlier versions of the manuscript and for her very helpful comments and suggestions. Thanks are also due to the design and typesetting team at Soapbox for all their hard work and support.

We are extremely grateful to David Dorling for proof-reading and for his very helpful comments and great suggestions at each stage of this project.

We would also like to thank Laurent Chalard for his constructive comments and very helpful suggestions and Álvaro Martinez-Perez for comments, advice and help with some of the data sources.

Thanks are also due to all providers of the data used in this atlas. They are mentioned in endnotes at the back of the book, but without the work of hundreds of mostly anonymous European statisticians we would not know much about where we are living. We would also like to acknowledge that the EU-SILC data set was provided by Eurostat.

The results of all data processing and analyses we conducted and the interpretations are ours and not those of Eurostat, the European Commission or any of the national authorities and other organisations whose data we have been using. Any remaining errors or misunderstandings are, of course, our own responsibility.

Dimitris Ballas is ever so grateful to Vicky Yiagopoulou who has long been an amazing source of inspiration, constant support and encouragement. Danny Dorling would like to thank Alison Dorling for allowing him not yet to slow down. Benjamin Hennig is deeply grateful to Tina Gotthardt, who has built many bridges over the borders that are mapped in this book.

A – Introduction

A 'human' atlas

What does it mean to be European today? To what extent do the people of Europe feel that they are citizens of something larger than their own country?

This is an atlas that explores geography and identity, an atlas in which we offer a very human geographical contribution to debates about many issues, bringing together many dozens of maps and facts about Europe and its people. Our approach is underpinned by the view that Europe is something much more than just a world region or a collection of nation states. Instead, we see it as a continent of people united not just by common interest but by a shared commitment to common values and ideals.

The common ideals embraced by Europe include establishment of democratic institutions, respect for human rights (including abolition of the death penalty) and the protection of minorities. These are values that need to be met before an application by any country to join the European Union (EU) will even be considered.

The EU is also based on ideals of solidarity and social cohesion, freedom of movement, equality, democracy and peace. These ideals underpin the founding treaties and documents that created the European Union, as well as more recent revisions and treaties, and provide a basis for European governments and politicians to be held to account for their actions. These ideals also inspire many ordinary Europeans, who have been supporting or engaging in voluntary activities, showing humanity and compassion, welcoming refugees and demanding safe passage and the protection of human rights to an extent that until now has not been necessary in peacetime.

The motto of the EU, 'United in diversity', signifies the intentions and efforts of Europeans to work together for peace and prosperity, while at the same time highlights that Europe's many different cultures, traditions and languages are a key asset, benefit and legacy.

Europe today

This atlas is about to come out at a time when Europe is experiencing the worst global refugee crisis in recent history, following a prolonged severe economic crisis and austerity measures that have disproportionately and brutally hit the most disadvantaged people in Europe. There has been an apparent revival of old nationalisms and divisions, coupled with the rise of extremist and populist parties across Europe. Although such parties and populist movements are far from being the majority in almost any country, they seem to have a disproportionately large influence on setting the policy agenda and media coverage and on determining what is presented to us as reality. For example, politicians and media reports have tended to approach the ongoing refugee and migration crisis as a failure of immigration control, adopting a toxic discourse rather than seizing the opportunity to celebrate humanity and uphold ideological and humanitarian responsibilities that were until very recently considered to be European or, indeed, universal ideals.

For progress to be made there is a need to rethink European social identity. To what extent can we see Europe as an ideal which protects our common rights and curtails the excesses of local politicians, of xenophobia and of fear?

We argue that the EU needs to be thought of as an entity that is more than just a union of member states, more than just a common market or just a potential monetary or fiscal union. It is also not simply a union that works mainly in the interests of big business, although it has rightly drawn much criticism for that.

Our approach to mapping Europe

One way to move towards thinking of a 'European people' instead of simply preserving the idea of a collection of 'nation-states' is to think of Europe and its economy, culture, history and geography as it actually physically exists, as a single large area, stretching from Iceland to Turkey. This may already be happening to some extent, especially among the rapidly increasing numbers of Europeans who live, study and/or work in a country other than their country of birth, including two of the authors of this atlas (the third having returned home to work within a mile of where he was born – also a common trait among many Europeans). The maps presented in this atlas show just how different the separate countries, regions and great cities of this continent are, but also the ways in which they are often so similar. *The Human Atlas of Europe* highlights the notion of Europe as a single entity by looking at its physical and population geography simultaneously in new ways, using up-to-date statistics, state-of-the-art Geographical Information Systems (GIS) and novel human cartography techniques. Looking at the maps in this atlas you can begin to believe that you are indeed looking at the geography of a single large group of people – a human atlas of Europe.

The countries included in this atlas

We include in this atlas all states that have demonstrated a strong commitment to a common European future by being closely associated with the EU, either as current members or as official candidate states (or official potential candidates for EU accession) and/or as states which are signed up to any of the following agreements: the European Economic Area, the Schengen Zone (a group of countries that have, although at times falteringly, abolished border controls for travel between them), and the European Monetary Union.

The maps

We present maps and graphics covering a wide range of themes and using data from a variety of sources such as the European Values Survey, Eurostat (including data from surveys such as the European Union Statistics on Income and Living Conditions), the United Nations, the International Labour Organisation, the World Bank and the World Health Organization. All the maps are accompanied by a commentary, usually by top and bottom five ranking tables, and in some cases by infographics showing additional complementary information.

Chapters may be read in sequence, but it is also possible to refer to particular chapters or maps of interest. We hope that you will enjoy this atlas, or, at the very least, find it interesting to see Europe in a way you've probably not seen it before.

Mapping techniques

The maps presented here differ from traditional maps in that countries are sized in proportion to particular social statistics rather than reflecting land area. (Often even traditional map projections do not reflect land area accurately because they may, for example, maintain compass directions, which has the effect of making the North of Europe appear much larger than it really is.)

Different variables relating to the population are often used, which can result in some very unusual maps being created. In some ways these are a little like pie charts, where the size of each slice of the pie is proportional to the number of people in each country having a particular characteristic. However, on these maps countries are still always drawn touching their original neighbours and so it is far easier to get an overview of the entire distribution in one glance. Pie charts cannot show the fundamental geographical connections. Furthermore, when population is used as the basic variable, other variables can be used to determine how to shade each region on these maps. The reader then has their attention automatically drawn to the places where there are most people, and to what is happening in those places – what is happening to most people is highlighted, but no one is left out.

How to identify the countries

A list of all the countries included on the maps in this atlas is given in Table A1, with their estimated population as recorded in 2014. Reference Map A1 shows a traditional land area map of these countries, using a colour scale that starts with dark red indicating those countries with the most recent association with Europe, moving through the rainbow to violet for the oldest members of the EU. Additionally, within each group of countries taking the same colour the intensity of shading is varied depending on the total population of each country. Germany, for example, is a darker violet than France, with both being founding members of today's EU but Germany being larger in population size than France. Italy, Belgium and the Netherlands, also founding member states, are even lighter with their smaller populations.

Reference Map A1:
Land area map of Europe

Colours denote years of
accession or current status
in relation to EU

- 1952
- 1973
- 1981
- 1986
- 1995
- 2001
- 2004
- 2007
- 2008
- 2011
- 2013
- Candidate country
- Potential candidates

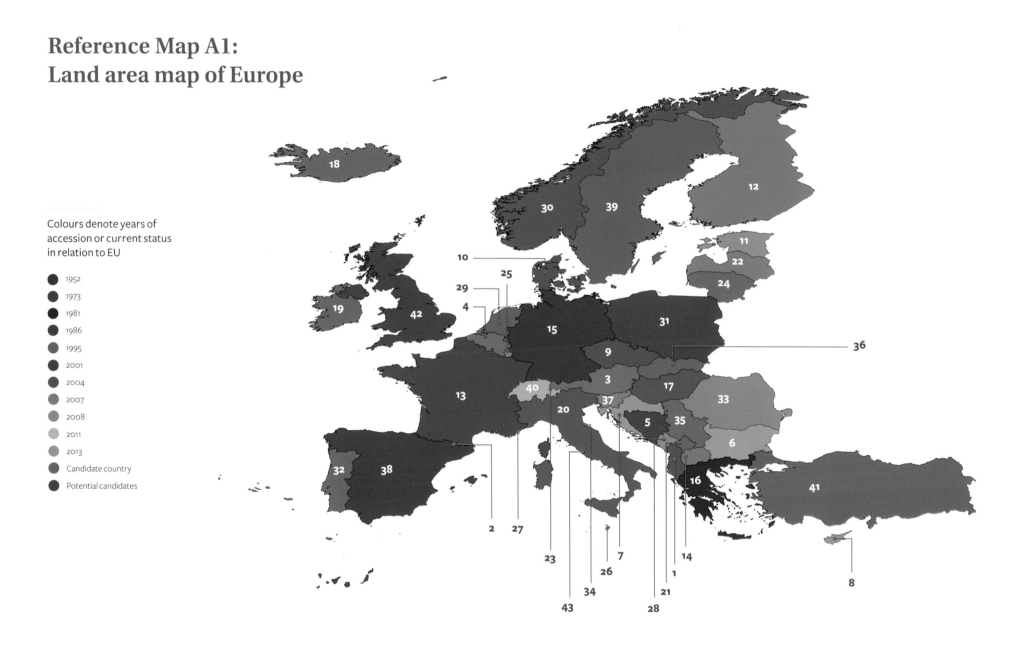

	Country name	Abbreviation used in this atlas	Official name	Population 2014
1	Albania	AL	Republic of Albania	2,894,475
2	Andorra	AD	Principality of Andorra	80,153
3	Austria	AT	Republic of Austria	8,534,492
4	Belgium	BE	Kingdom of Belgium	11,225,207
5	Bosnia-Herzegovina	BA	Bosnia-Herzegovina	3,824,746
6	Bulgaria	BG	Republic of Bulgaria	7,226,291
7	Croatia	HR	Republic of Croatia	4,236,400
8	Cyprus	CY	Republic of Cyprus	1,153,058
9	Czech Republic	CZ	Czech Republic	10,510,566
10	Denmark	DK	Kingdom of Denmark	5,639,565
11	Estonia	EE	Republic of Estonia	1,313,645
12	Finland	FI	Republic of Finland	5,463,596
13	France	FR	French Republic	66,201,365
14	FYR Macedonia	MK	Former Yugoslav Republic of Macedonia	2,108,434
15	Germany	DE	Federal Republic of Germany	80,889,505
16	Greece	GR	Hellenic Republic	10,957,740
17	Hungary	HU	Republic of Hungary	9,861,673
18	Iceland	IS	Republic of Iceland	327,589
19	Ireland	IE	Republic of Ireland	4,612,719
20	Italy	IT	Italian Republic	61,336,387
21	Kosovo	KV	Kosovo (under UN Security Council Resolution 1244/99)	1,823,149
22	Latvia	LV	Republic of Latvia	1,990,351
23	Liechtenstein	LI	Principality of Liechtenstein	37,194
24	Lithuania	LT	Republic of Lithuania	2,929,323
25	Luxembourg	LU	Grand Duchy of Luxembourg	556,074
26	Malta	MT	Republic of Malta	427,404
27	Monaco	MC	Principality of Monaco	38,066
28	Montenegro	ME	Montenegro	621,800
29	Netherlands	NL	Kingdom of the Netherlands	16,854,183
30	Norway	NO	Kingdom of Norway	5,136,475
31	Poland	PO	Republic of Poland	37,995,529
32	Portugal	PT	Portuguese Republic	10,397,393
33	Romania	RO	Romania	19,910,995
34	San Marino	SM	Republic of San Marino	31,637
35	Serbia	RS	Republic of Serbia	7,129,428
36	Slovak Republic	SK	Slovak Republic	5,418,506
37	Slovenia	SI	Republic of Slovenia	2,062,218
38	Spain	ES	Kingdom of Spain	46,404,602
39	Sweden	SE	Kingdom of Sweden	9,689,555
40	Switzerland	CH	Swiss Confederation	8,190,229
41	Turkey	TR	Republic of Turkey	75,837,020
42	United Kingdom	UK	United Kingdom of Great Britain and Northern Ireland	64,510,376
43	Vatican	VA	State of the Vatican City	842

This colour scheme is followed throughout this atlas so that on all the country cartograms (see below), the same country is always shown in the same colour.

Types of maps

There are three different types of maps in this atlas. The most common are the **country cartograms** – country-level maps where countries are sized in proportion to a variable of interest. Reference Map A2 is a population cartogram, which shows the countries resized according to their total population (listed in Table 1): the larger the population of a member state the larger the area it occupies on the map. Germany, the largest country and home (at the time of writing) to 82 million people, occupies the largest area, followed by Turkey, France, the UK and Italy, whereas the space occupied by relatively sparsely populated countries like Iceland and the Scandinavian countries is much smaller on the population cartogram in Map A2 than it is on Map A1, the land area map.

The mapping technique used is an approximation so as not to produce results that are too hard to interpret. Thus, areas with a value of zero shrink but do not disappear entirely, and countries should still be generally recognisable from their shape and position even after their size is changed. In this atlas we have typically used this type of map when there was data available for all our reference states (with the exception of Chapter J, where this type of map is used to explore variables for current EU members only) and where that data added up to a meaningful total at the European level. This usually involved a count of people (e.g. the number of people unemployed) but it could also be any other number that summed to a meaningful total (e.g. total Gross Domestic Product in euros or total carbon dioxide emissions in kilotons).

The second type of map is based on the **population cartogram** shown in Reference Map A2, but uses shading to show the value of the variable being discussed in each country. This type of map is used when data was not available for all the states covered in this atlas (e.g. the maps showing total numbers of people working in different kinds of occupations, using data from the EU Statistics on Income and Living Conditions: see Ch F, pp 117–121) and/or when the variable mapped was not one which added up to a meaningful total at the European level (e.g. the maps showing inequality and human development measures: see Ch C, pp 60–62). These are still population cartograms, but the cartogram is now simply a base map, and it is the shading in the cartogram which represents the distribution that is being discussed. It can be difficult to understand this abstractly as we describe it here, but hopefully it will become clear as you read through the atlas as to which kind of map is which and when the variable of interest is being used to shade areas rather than size them.

The third type of map found in this atlas uses a **gridded-population cartogram** approach (developed by one of the authors of this atlas). Here, the whole territory to be mapped is first divided into a grid of cells of equal size. The next step is to apply the density equalising method to resize each cell in proportion to the number of people living within it, while ensuring that the cell touches only its original eight neighbouring cells. The size of each of the grid cells therefore reflects the number of people living in this area; and the projection means that the base map itself reflects the real population distribution on a coherent geographical reference (and not the population based on artificial administrative units like the nation states that appear in Map A2).

Reference Map A3 shows a gridded-population cartogram of the countries mapped in Maps A1 and A2. This cartogram uses finer-level geographical information about where people live and gives an even better representation of the distribution of Europe's population than Map A2, as it shows variation within the countries and therefore highlights more clearly where most people are concentrated – mostly in cities. For instance, Madrid, Paris, Istanbul and London are huge, while the whole of Scandinavia is small. Countries and regions that are more densely populated (for example most of the UK, Italy, Poland, and Romania) are more visible on the map whereas the large rural areas in the north of the Europe appear considerably smaller. The Rhine-Ruhr metropolitan region in Western Europe, including the areas of Cologne, Dortmund and other urban areas that appear to be expanding towards the Netherlands, is much more prominent on this projection than it is on a conventional map or even a nation-state population cartogram.

More information can be represented by adding shading and, indeed, the gridded-population cartograms in this atlas mostly use a scale ranging from yellow for the lowest value through shades of green and blue to dark navy blue for the highest value (e.g. the maps showing percentages of working-age adults, children and older people: see Ch B, pp 19–21).

Using the mapping techniques described above we created over 140 maps covering topics ranging from life expectancy, the refugee crisis, greenhouse gas emissions and Gross Domestic Product to Eurovision voting in order to create a human atlas of Europe that addresses fundamental questions around social cohesion and sustainable growth. These maps matter because they show key features of the actual experience of the people of Europe, regardless of the physical size of the country they live in. To understand these maps it may help to imagine that they are the product of a satellite hovering in stationary orbit over the continent but containing a special lens which magnifies the areas where people live, and minimises the wilderness just to the precise extent needed to give everyone equal representation.

It can be argued that visualising and mapping Europe like this makes it easier for Europeans not only to make more sense of their home area's physical and human geography but also to think of Europe as a single entity being the place they belong to, or their 'homeland', rather than their nation state. The boundaries defining nation states are, after all, generally not much more than the (often frequently changing) historic boundaries of the realms of royal houses with particular religious affiliations that became fossilised at particular moments in time. Natural and man-made disasters, from the Chernobyl radiation cloud through to the refugee crisis, show little regard for state borders.

The adoption of the mapping approach employed in this book may make it more likely for people to care about an environmental disaster or social unrest or hardship affecting others elsewhere in Europe and further afield: in other words to feel solidarity with other people and places and to enhance a sense of common identity.

We hope that *The Human Atlas of Europe* offers a fresh perspective and a new way of thinking about Europe as a continent of cities rather than states, a continent of people rather than power, and one of hope rather than decline, reminding its people how much they have in common and highlighting that there is now, more than ever, a need to carry on working together rather than to pull apart.

Reference Map A2:
Population cartogram of Europe

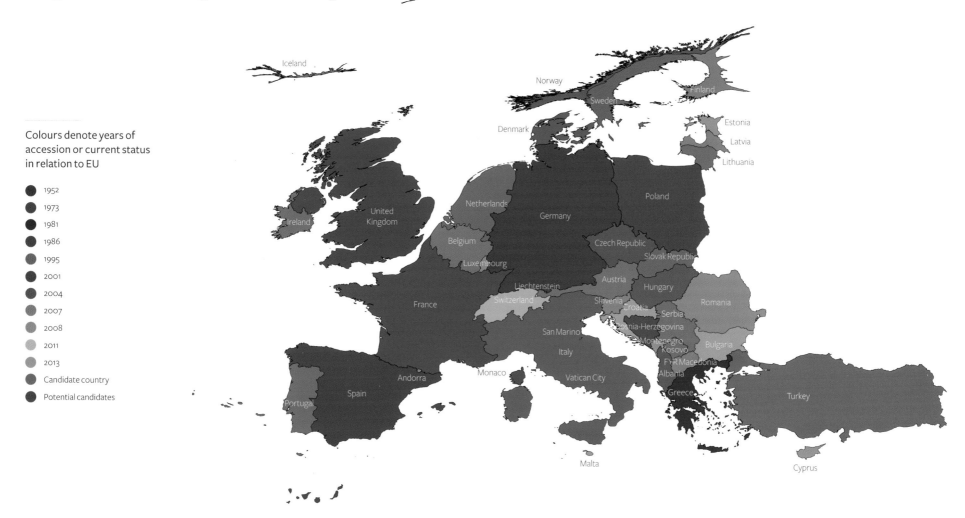

Colours denote years of
accession or current status
in relation to EU

- 1952
- 1973
- 1981
- 1986
- 1995
- 2001
- 2004
- 2007
- 2008
- 2011
- 2013
- Candidate country
- Potential candidates

Reference Map A3:
Gridded population cartogram of Europe

Colours denote years of
accession or current status
in relation to EU (capital cities
are underlined)

- 1952
- 1973
- 1981
- 1986
- 1995
- 2001
- 2004
- 2007
- 2008
- 2011
- 2013
- Candidate country
- Potential candidates

B – Population

There are 616 million people living within European boundaries (as used in this atlas). This chapter presents how they are distributed across the continent's cities, regions and countries.

- We give a flavour of how serious the **demographic and pensions crisis** may be, showing the regions where the most children, adults of working age and older people live.

- In 2015 1 million refugees crossed the Mediterranean Sea using unseaworthy vessels, and nearly 4,000 drowned. We show the **numbers of refugees and asylum-seekers across Europe**.

- We show where **people who live in a different country from that of their birth** are living, and which countries are most visited by **international tourists**.

- With the theme of minority groups, we show the **geographical distribution of the Roma people**, one group of Europeans who are still persecuted.

- We include **maps of population change over the past 20 years**, and of **births** across Europe and **future population estimates**. With fertility levels below what is required for population replacement, Europe will rely on in-migration for many decades to come.

- We also look at **geographical inequalities in life expectancy**, the countries with the most and fewest **prisoners** and the number of **homicides** in Europe, all examples of what may, in turn, be part of the impact of differing levels of economic inequality across Europe.

Population by age and sex

2014

EUROPEAN UNION

2014, POPULATION: 506.8 MILLION, SEX RATIO (M/F): 0.953

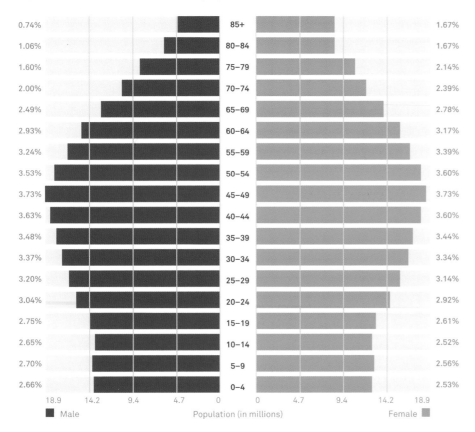

Male	Age	Female
0.74%	85+	1.67%
1.06%	80–84	1.67%
1.60%	75–79	2.14%
2.00%	70–74	2.39%
2.49%	65–69	2.78%
2.93%	60–64	3.17%
3.24%	55–59	3.39%
3.53%	50–54	3.60%
3.73%	45–49	3.73%
3.63%	40–44	3.60%
3.48%	35–39	3.44%
3.37%	30–34	3.34%
3.20%	25–29	3.14%
3.04%	20–24	2.92%
2.75%	15–19	2.61%
2.65%	10–14	2.52%
2.70%	5–9	2.56%
2.66%	0–4	2.53%

18.9 14.2 9.4 4.7 0   0 4.7 9.4 14.2 18.9

■ Male   Population (in millions)   Female ■

EUROPEAN UNION	GERMANY	ALBANIA
247,321,451 / 259,503,058	40,206,663 / 41,637,080	1,568,611 / 1,580,358

■ Males
■ Females

GERMANY

2012, POPULATION: 81.9 MILLION, SEX RATIO (M/F): 0.966

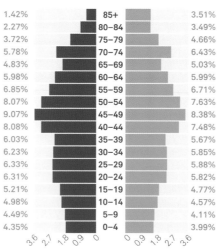

Male	Age	Female
1.42%	85+	3.51%
2.27%	80–84	3.49%
3.72%	75–79	4.66%
5.78%	70–74	6.43%
4.83%	65–69	5.03%
5.98%	60–64	5.99%
6.85%	55–59	6.71%
8.07%	50–54	7.63%
9.07%	45–49	8.38%
8.08%	40–44	7.48%
6.03%	35–39	5.67%
6.23%	30–34	5.85%
6.33%	25–29	5.88%
6.31%	20–24	5.82%
5.21%	15–19	4.77%
4.98%	10–14	4.57%
4.49%	5–9	4.11%
4.35%	0–4	3.99%

3.6 2.7 1.8 0.9 0   0 0.9 1.8 2.7 3.6

Population (in millions)

ALBANIA

2012, POPULATION: 3.1 MILLION, SEX RATIO (M/F): 0.993

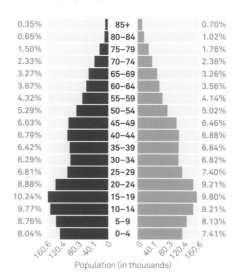

Male	Age	Female
0.35%	85+	0.70%
0.65%	80–84	1.02%
1.50%	75–79	1.76%
2.33%	70–74	2.38%
3.27%	65–69	3.26%
3.67%	60–64	3.56%
4.32%	55–59	4.14%
5.29%	50–54	5.02%
6.63%	45–49	6.46%
6.79%	40–44	6.88%
6.42%	35–39	6.84%
6.29%	30–34	6.82%
6.81%	25–29	7.40%
8.88%	20–24	9.21%
10.24%	15–19	9.80%
9.77%	10–14	9.21%
8.76%	5–9	8.13%
8.04%	0–4	7.41%

160.6 120.4 80.3 40.1 0   0 40.1 80.3 120.4 160.6

Population (in thousands)

The main diagram, known as a population pyramid, shows how the 507 million men and women who were estimated to be living in the European Union in 2014 were distributed by age. Adults aged 15–65 account for 334 million. Nearly one fifth of the total population is over 65 years old. There are only 79 million children aged 0–15. Even though more boys than girls are born, most Europeans are women as women now live longer.

The pyramids of most European countries look similar to that of the EU, but some countries like Albania have a more traditional 'pyramid-like' shape, suggesting relatively higher outmigration rates in the recent past and a lower life expectancy. Fertility has not been much higher than the EU average in poorer countries. Countries like Germany have more than average elderly populations, or at least did when these national statistics were collected and before many younger people from Syria and other countries arrived.

Adults (working age)

REGIONAL MAP, 2014

73.5% of the population of Inner London are adults of working age

Adults aged 15–65 (%)

- <62.5
- 62.5–65
- 65–67.5
- 67.5–70
- >70
- no data

Population cartogram

UK

- Children
- Adults of working age
- Older people

Top

Region	%
Fuerteventura (ES)	74.8
Eivissa, Ibiza and Formentera (ES)	73.9
Pološki (MK)	73.8
Inner London (UK) / Jugozapaden (MK)	73.5

Bottom

Region	%
Siirt (TR)	57.3
Ağri (TR)	57.1
Şirnak (TR)	55.6
Evrytania (GR)	55.5
Şanliurfa (TR)	55.3

Low working-age populations are found either where there are many children (Şanlıurfa, Turkey) or where many people are older, such as in Dorset (only 58% of working age) and the Isle of Wight (59%) in the UK, and in other predominantly rural and coastal areas across Europe.

The highest percentage is found in the Spanish islands of Fuerteventura and Ibiza. There are usually higher shares of working-age populations in urban areas, where there are fewer elderly people as well as fewer children, including in Inner London, which has the fourth highest rate of any region in Europe, and in Poland, Slovak Republic and Croatia.

Within Turkey working-age people tend to migrate westwards, sometimes leaving children behind with grandparents.

Children

REGIONAL MAP, 2014

Children under 15 (%)

- <12.5
- 12.5–15
- 15–17.5
- 17.5–20
- >20
- ◯ no data

Population cartogram

Children make up **20.2%** of the population in Dublin

Top

Region	%
Şirnak (TR)	41.5
Şanlıurfa (TR)	41.2
Ağri (TR)	39.1
Siirt (TR)	38.5
Mus (TR)	38.4

Bottom

Region	%
Wurzburg (DE)	10.0
Zamora (ES)	9.9
Lugo (ES) / Ourense (ES)	9.7
Suhl (DE)	9.2

25.9%
Turkey has the highest proportion of children in Europe

Given that the story of the Pied Piper comes from Hamelin, Germany, it is perhaps appropriate that the lowest proportion of children as a share of the local population in Europe is found not too far away, in the city of Suhl (at 9.2%), although this is closely followed by Ourense, Lugo and Zamora in northwestern Spain. Other areas with few children are also mostly found in Italy,

Bulgaria and Greece, where the fewest children are currently being born. The regions with the highest proportions of children are found in Eastern Turkey. In the Mid-East region of the Republic of Ireland, comprised of the counties Kildare, Meath and Wicklow, and bordering the greater Dublin region, 25% of the population are currently aged 0–15.

The regions with the highest and lowest percentages of children in the UK are Bradford (22%) and Edinburgh (14%).

Older people

REGIONAL MAP, 2014

Older people over 65 (%)

- <15
- 15–17.5
- 17.5–20
- 20–22.5
- >22.5
- no data

Population cartogram

In Evrytania, **33%** of the population are 65 or older

Top

Region	%
Evrytania (GR)	33.0
Ourense (ES)	30.0
Zamora (ES)	29.2
Ioannina (GR)	29.0
Dessau-Rosslau (DE)	28.9

Bottom

Region	%
Ağri (TR)	3.8
Şanlıurfa (TR)	3.5
Van (TR)	3.2
Şırnak (TR)	3.0
Hakkâri (TR)	2.8

The regions with the smallest proportion of people aged 65 and over are found in Eastern Turkey. Of the 54 regions with less than 10% older people, 46 are in Turkey. In Inner London East, only 7.8% of the population are now aged 65 or over.

The region with the largest percentage of older people is in the mountainous region of Evrytania in Central Greece (33%).

Older people in Europe are found in greater than average proportions in the North of Italy and Germany, along the Mediterranean coast and in the interior of France, in Northern Spain, South West England and North Wales. Many of these areas include popular retirement destinations.

In the cities of Paris, Warsaw and Budapest, slightly fewer older people live in the suburbs than in the centre, while Berlin, London and Milan show the opposite trend.

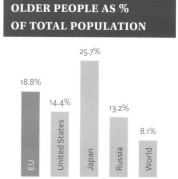

OLDER PEOPLE AS % OF TOTAL POPULATION

- EU 18.8%
- United States 14.4%
- Japan 25.7%
- Russia 13.2%
- World 8.1%

Gender

REGIONAL MAP, 2014

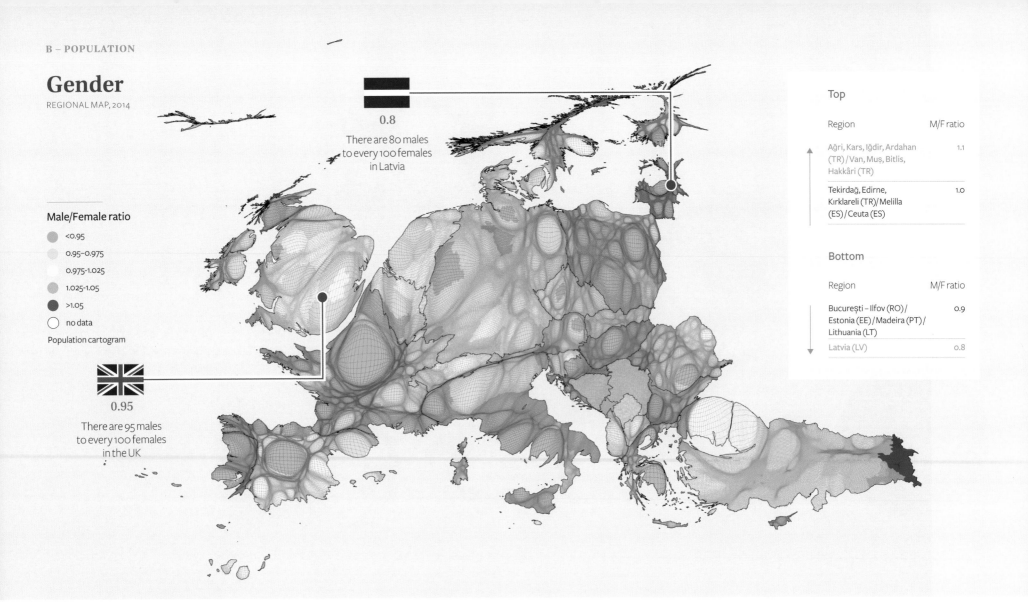

0.8

There are 80 males
to every 100 females
in Latvia

0.95

There are 95 males
to every 100 females
in the UK

Male/Female ratio

- <0.95
- 0.95–0.975
- 0.975–1.025
- 1.025–1.05
- >1.05
- no data

Population cartogram

Top

Region	M/F ratio
Ağri, Kars, Iğdir, Ardahan (TR) / Van, Muş, Bitlis, Hakkâri (TR)	1.1
Tekirdağ, Edirne, Kırklareli (TR)/ Melilla (ES) / Ceuta (ES)	1.0

Bottom

Region	M/F ratio
Bucureşti – Ilfov (RO) / Estonia (EE) / Madeira (PT) / Lithuania (LT)	0.9
Latvia (LV)	0.8

Women outnumber men most significantly in Latvia. Other regions with more women than men are mostly found in Eastern Europe, but also in many parts of France (especially Paris), Italy, Greece, Portugal and Spain. Areas in the UK with more women include Merseyside, Cornwall and most of Scotland. This imbalance can occur where more men have left an area, often in search of work elsewhere.

It is almost always the case that more boys are born than girls and so where there are more children there are more males. But in regions of Eastern Turkey where the highest ratios are found, both men and women may also be leaving the region to find work, keeping the overall population younger and thus more male.

Other regions with fewer women than men are found throughout Turkey, as well as in some of the Greek island regions in the Aegean Sea and the rural, mountainous and coastal areas, mostly in Spain, but also in parts of northern Europe.

Asylum-seekers

2015

This map shows how the numbers of persons who have applied for international protection in Europe varied between the EU member states in 2015. Only countries of the European Union are shown here and they are resized according to the total number of asylum applicants throughout 2015. Most of these people crossed the Mediterranean Sea in desperation, travelling in dinghies or other unseaworthy vessels, and often in extremely dangerous weather conditions. At least 3,695 people died in their attempt to reach Europe in this way and this figure includes babies and young children.

Colour key, see Reference map A1, p 10

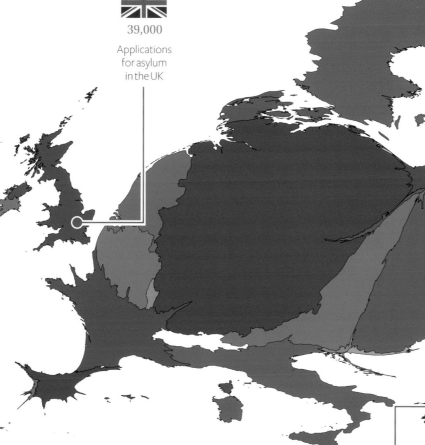

39,000

Applications
for asylum
in the UK

Top

Country	Total
Germany	476,620
Hungary	177,135
Sweden	162,550
Austria	88,180
Italy	84,085

Bottom

Country	Total
Latvia	330
Lithuania	315
Slovenia	275
Estonia	230
Croatia	210

13,205

Applications
for asylum
in Greece

**ASYLUM
APPLICATIONS**

1,321,560

**IN THE EUROPEAN
UNION**

**DEAD OR MISSING
REFUGEES IN 2015**

3,695

**IN THE
MEDITERRANEAN**

**REFUGEE ARRIVALS
BY SEA IN 2015**

956,456

**ACROSS THE
MEDITERRANEAN**

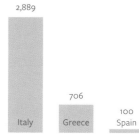

**DEATHS IN THE
MEDITERRANEAN SEA 2015**

2,889

706

100

Italy   Greece   Spain

Populations of concern

2013

People fleeing war and persecution can now be found everywhere in Europe, but mostly in countries that have been affected by war in recent years, such as the countries that used to be part of the former Yugoslavia, or in countries near war zones, such as Turkey, bordering Syria.

In this map countries are sized in relation to the number of people defined by the UN as 'populations of concern' (refugees, asylum-seekers, stateless and internally displaced persons).

Recently, considerable numbers of displaced persons have fled to the Baltic countries from the 2014 war and tension in Ukraine, while countries such as Greece and Italy have recently become hotspots in the worst global refugee crisis since the Second World War. When this map can be updated these countries are very likely to have increased in size significantly due to the large number of recent arrivals.

Colour key, see Reference map A1, p 10

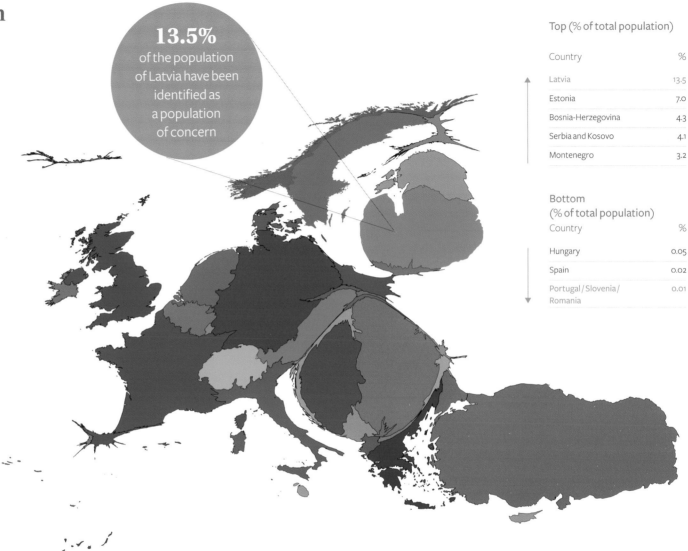

13.5% of the population of Latvia have been identified as a population of concern

Top (% of total population)

Country	%
Latvia	13.5
Estonia	7.0
Bosnia-Herzegovina	4.3
Serbia and Kosovo	4.1
Montenegro	3.2

Bottom (% of total population)

Country	%
Hungary	0.05
Spain	0.02
Portugal / Slovenia / Romania	0.01

Top (total numbers)

Country	Total
Turkey	804,372
Germany	335,562
Serbia and Kosovo	291,139
France	285,468
Latvia	268,143

Bottom (total numbers)

Country	Total
Luxembourg	2,116
Portugal	1,357
Iceland	477
Slovenia	249
Liechtenstein	116

Asylum holders

2013

According to the UNHCR there were 1,763,262 people officially recognised as refugees living in Europe in 2013. There are large numbers of displaced people in countries that are likely to be their first destination in Europe, such as Turkey, but refugees also settle in regions in Europe where they may have cultural or family links.

As with populations of concern, the numbers here are likely to have increased significantly due to the exacerbation of the refugee crisis in 2015 (with further increases expected in the near future).

The EU has recently put forward emergency plans to relocate migrants and refugees across the continent. However, there remains an urgent need for a more substantial and comprehensive response to welcome refugees in a way that would be consistent with European and universal ideals. This is the very least that would be appropriate, given the huge resources that European states have at their disposal.

This page shows the numbers of people who had been granted asylum in a European country at any time previously and were thought to be still living in that country in 2013.

Colour key, see Reference map A1, p10

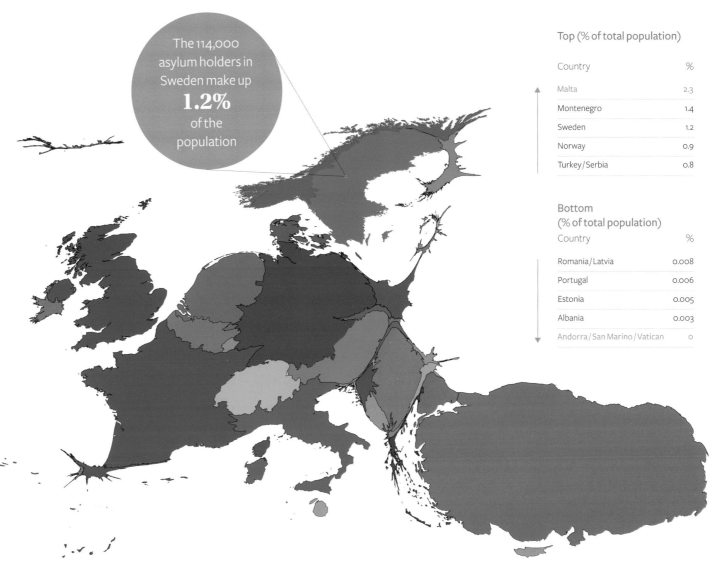

The 114,000 asylum holders in Sweden make up **1.2%** of the population

Top (% of total population)

Country	%
Malta	2.3
Montenegro	1.4
Sweden	1.2
Norway	0.9
Turkey / Serbia	0.8

Bottom (% of total population)

Country	%
Romania / Latvia	0.008
Portugal	0.006
Estonia	0.005
Albania	0.003
Andorra / San Marino / Vatican	0

Top (total numbers)

Country	Total
Turkey	609,938
France	232,487
Germany	187,567
United Kingdom	126,055
Sweden	114,175

Bottom (total numbers)

Country	Total
Albania	93
Iceland	79
Estonia	70
Monaco	34
Andorra / San Marino / Vatican	0

Born abroad

2010

In 2010, the number of people in Europe born in a different country from the one they were living in was stated by the World Bank to be over 52 million – 8.5% of the total population of all European states included in this atlas.

Until the middle of the 19th century the dominant trend was for Europe to send people to other continents and not to receive many migrants. This changed in the second half of the 20th century as European countries like Greece, Italy, Spain and Portugal, which had been regions of emigration to Northern Europe and the Americas, became areas of return migration as well as of immigration.

These numbers are likely to rise further in the future as a result of increased travel and mobility between all European countries, with rapidly growing numbers of people deciding to study, work and settle in a country other than that of their birth.

When the UK voted to leave the EU in 2016 the number of people applying for citizenship increased. Threats or attempts to impose migration controls often increase inward migration, as occurred before in the UK in the 1960s.

Colour key, see Reference map A1, p 10

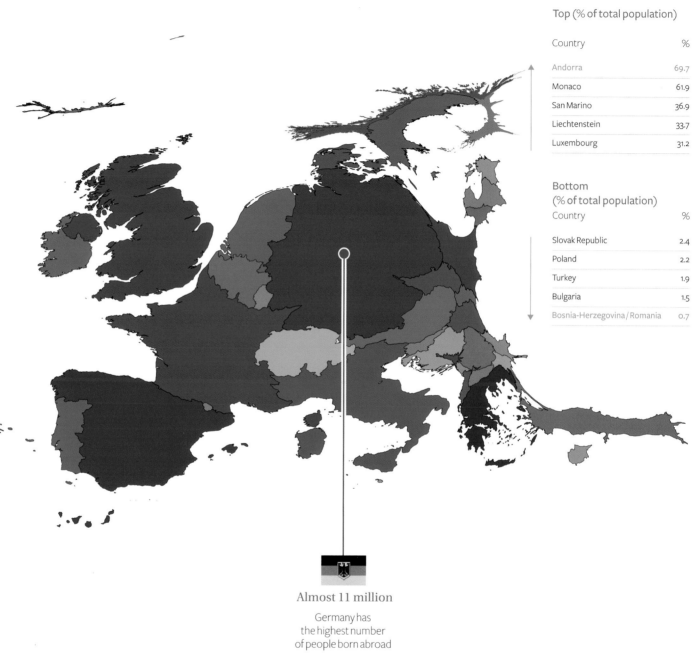

Almost 11 million

Germany has
the highest number
of people born abroad

Top (% of total population)

Country	%
Andorra	69.7
Monaco	61.9
San Marino	36.9
Liechtenstein	33.7
Luxembourg	31.2

Bottom (% of total population)

Country	%
Slovak Republic	2.4
Poland	2.2
Turkey	1.9
Bulgaria	1.5
Bosnia-Herzegovina / Romania	0.7

Born abroad, increase

2000–10

This map shows where the number of residents born abroad was increasing over the first decade of the 21st century. The number of immigrants as a percentage of total population tends to be higher in more affluent countries due to 'pull factors' such as better job opportunities or higher pay rates.

Immigrants themselves also contribute to the economic growth and prosperity of destination countries, using skills and education often acquired at the expense of taxpayers in their home country. Many destination countries have ageing populations and desperately need immigrants, as they support pension systems by paying in contributions to social insurance and pension schemes, and in many cases take up jobs which involve looking after the elderly and working in hospitals. Immigrants are frequently employed in jobs that local people do not want to do.

Migrants also bring benefits in non-monetary ways that are more difficult to quantify, such as enriching their new country by exposure to different cultures.

Colour key, see Reference map A1, p 10

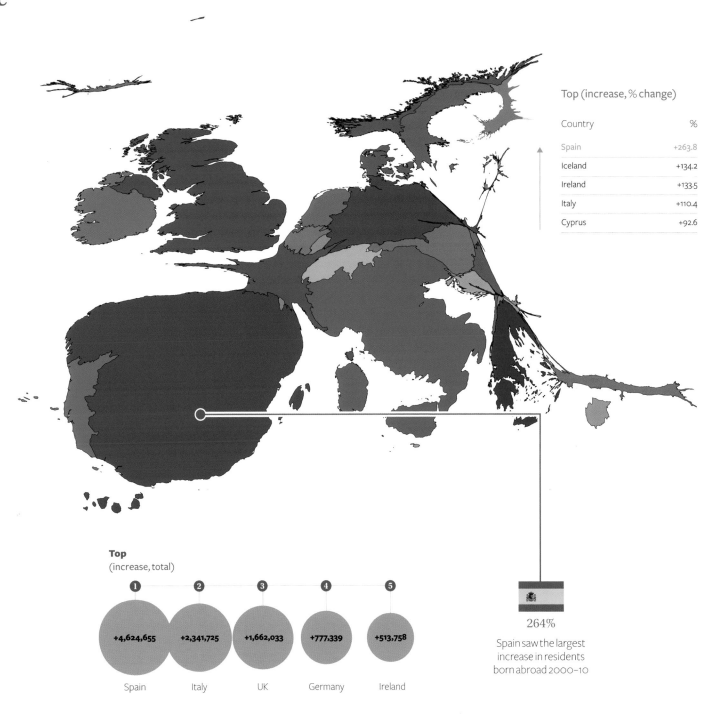

Top (increase, % change)

Country	%
Spain	+263.8
Iceland	+134.2
Ireland	+133.5
Italy	+110.4
Cyprus	+92.6

Top
(increase, total)

1	2	3	4	5
+4,624,655	+2,341,725	+1,662,033	+777,339	+513,758
Spain	Italy	UK	Germany	Ireland

264%

Spain saw the largest increase in residents born abroad 2000–10

Born abroad, decrease

2000–10

Nine countries experienced a decline in numbers of residents born abroad between 2000 and 2010.

Commentators rarely consider that rates of immigration fall as well as rise. As rates of mobility tend to increase over time, there will generally be ever higher proportions of people born in one nation state living in another.

Occasionally, when economic disaster, war or a similar calamity strikes, rates of immigration decline, and fewer people born abroad live in a place than previously. It has always been the most economically depressed areas that have lost migrants, and when a country becomes less attractive as a migration destination, economic and social decline tend to escalate.

Colour key, see Reference map A1, p 10

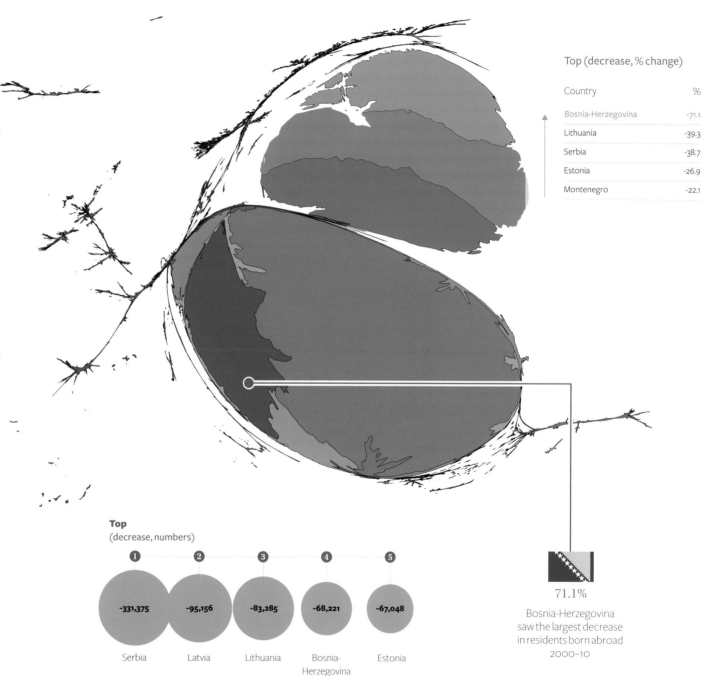

Top (decrease, % change)

Country	%
Bosnia-Herzegovina	-71.1
Lithuania	-39.3
Serbia	-38.7
Estonia	-26.9
Montenegro	-22.1

Top
(decrease, numbers)

❶	❷	❸	❹	❺
-331,375	-95,156	-83,285	-68,221	-67,048
Serbia	Latvia	Lithuania	Bosnia-Herzegovina	Estonia

71.1%

Bosnia-Herzegovina saw the largest decrease in residents born abroad 2000–10

Foreign citizens

REGIONAL MAP, 2014

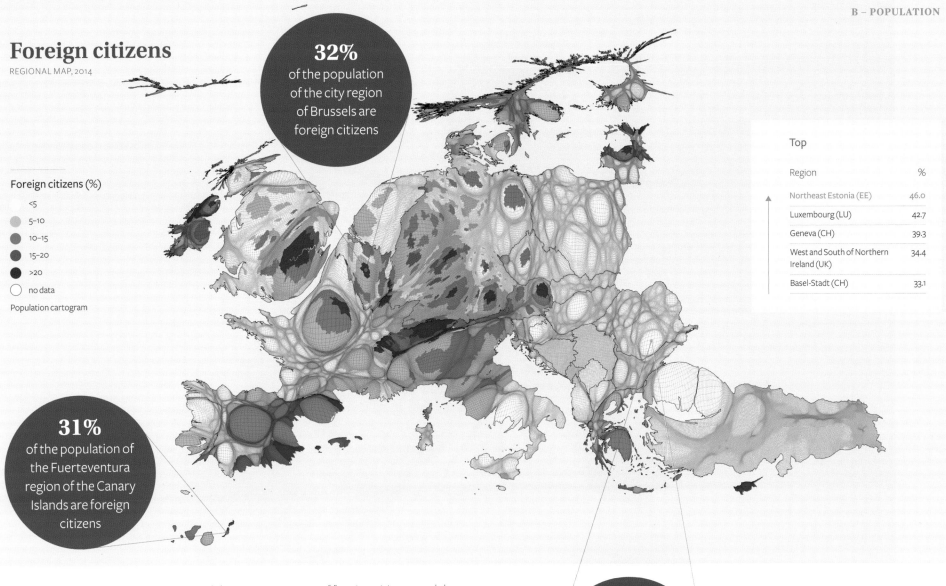

32% of the population of the city region of Brussels are foreign citizens

31% of the population of the Fuerteventura region of the Canary Islands are foreign citizens

In many regions of Romania less than **0.1%** of residents are foreign citizens

Foreign citizens (%)

- <5
- 5–10
- 10–15
- 15–20
- >20
- no data

Population cartogram

Top

Region	%
Northeast Estonia (EE)	46.0
Luxembourg (LU)	42.7
Geneva (CH)	39.3
West and South of Northern Ireland (UK)	34.4
Basel-Stadt (CH)	33.1

Numbers of foreign residents vary widely between regions of the same country. The highest proportion as a percentage of the region's total population is found in Northeast Estonia, where there are large numbers of Russian nationals. Regions that are home to many important European and international institutions, such as Luxembourg, Geneva and Brussels welcome high proportions of foreign citizens, and the West and South of Northern Ireland receives considerable numbers of citizens of the Republic of Ireland.

The regions with the lowest proportions are mostly found in Eastern Europe, but also in the South of Italy and in some rural regions of Western Europe and most of the UK regions, other than London and Northern Ireland.

Roma people

2011–14, ESTIMATES FROM VARIOUS SOURCES

A key feature of the underpinning ideals of the EU is support for diversity and respect for human rights, encompassing the presence and tolerance of, and support for, numerous minorities across all European countries.

Roma people represent the largest and perhaps most disadvantaged minority group in the EU. Unlike other ethnic or national groups, Roma people do not have a historical homeland. They are extremely diverse, with many multiple identities based on language, history, religion and occupations.

Although the Roma population is arguably the largest minority in Europe, it is difficult to obtain reliable statistics on the exact size of the population by country. This map is based on estimates from many different sources and is probably the most reliable map of the distribution of Roma people that can currently be drawn.

Colour key, see Reference map A1, p 10

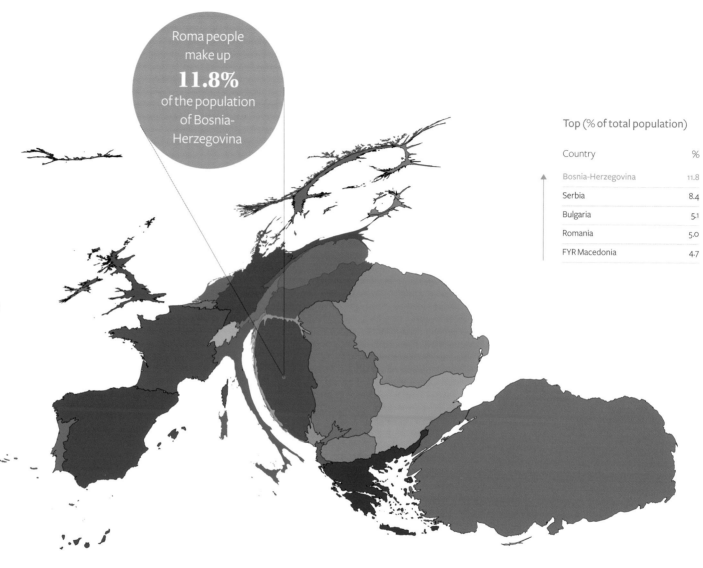

Roma people make up **11.8%** of the population of Bosnia-Herzegovina

Top (% of total population)

Country	%
Bosnia-Herzegovina	11.8
Serbia	8.4
Bulgaria	5.1
Romania	5.0
FYR Macedonia	4.7

ROMA HOUSEHOLDS LIVING IN DEEP POVERTY

71%

IN EASTERN EUROPE

Top (estimated numbers)

Country	Estimated number
Turkey	2,500,000
Romania	1,000,000
Spain	650,000
Serbia	600,000
France	500,000

Bottom (estimated numbers)

Country	Estimated number
Ireland	3,000
Denmark	1,750
Cyprus	650
Estonia	456
Luxembourg	125

International tourist arrivals

2013

The top tourist destinations in Europe are countries that have large populations, but the map also highlights smaller countries that are major tourist destinations, such as Austria, Croatia, Cyprus, Greece and Malta.

The number of Europeans visiting other countries for recreation has been rapidly increasing due to improved and more frequent air, rail and ferry connections across Europe, including the growth of low-cost airlines.

This increased movement has been an important driver for the strengthening of European identity and cohesion, but more environmentally sustainable modes of transport need to be promoted, such as rail and ferry services instead of air travel, consistent with European goals relating to sustainable development. It is not always necessary to travel great distances to visit interesting and exciting places. Avoiding the 'tourist traps' can be just as rewarding, less expensive and more environmentally sustainable.

Colour key, see Reference map A1, p 10

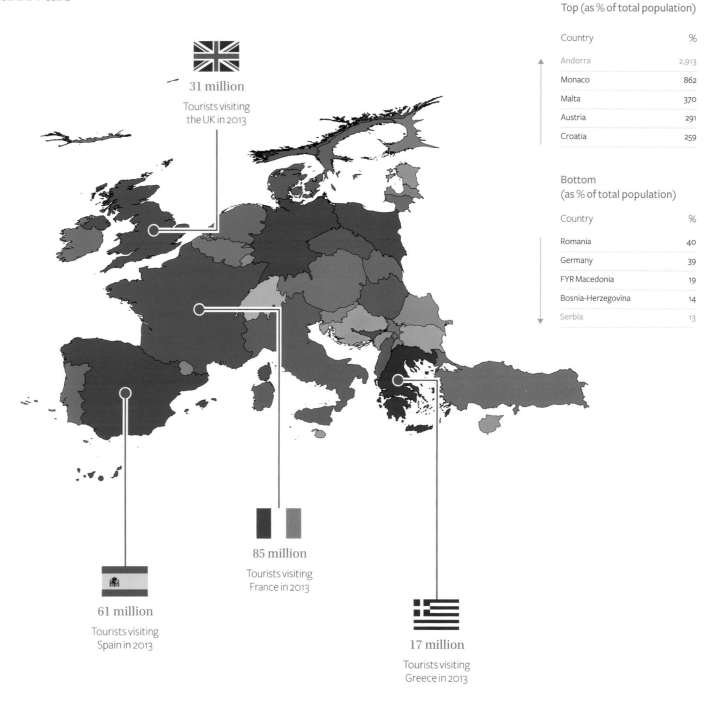

31 million

Tourists visiting the UK in 2013

85 million

Tourists visiting France in 2013

61 million

Tourists visiting Spain in 2013

17 million

Tourists visiting Greece in 2013

Top (as % of total population)

Country	%
Andorra	2,913
Monaco	862
Malta	370
Austria	291
Croatia	259

Bottom (as % of total population)

Country	%
Romania	40
Germany	39
FYR Macedonia	19
Bosnia-Herzegovina	14
Serbia	13

Population increase

1990–2014

The total population of the European countries mapped in this atlas increased from 563 million in 1990 to 616 million in 2014. Some 30 out of the 43 countries mapped saw their population rise, and this map shows where this growth was highest.

Most of the increases are due to in-migration and increased life expectancy, but initially in some countries, such as Turkey, there were also relatively high fertility rates that have now fallen back, mostly below replacement level. Ageing, as a result of increased life expectancy, means that for the same number of people born there are far more people living at any one time, and this is the reason why global populations may reach or even exceed 10 billion in future – it is not due to people having more children.

Ageing, however, eventually slows down, as is currently happening in Japan, for example – people cannot carry on living for longer and longer, forever.

Colour key, see Reference map A1, p 10

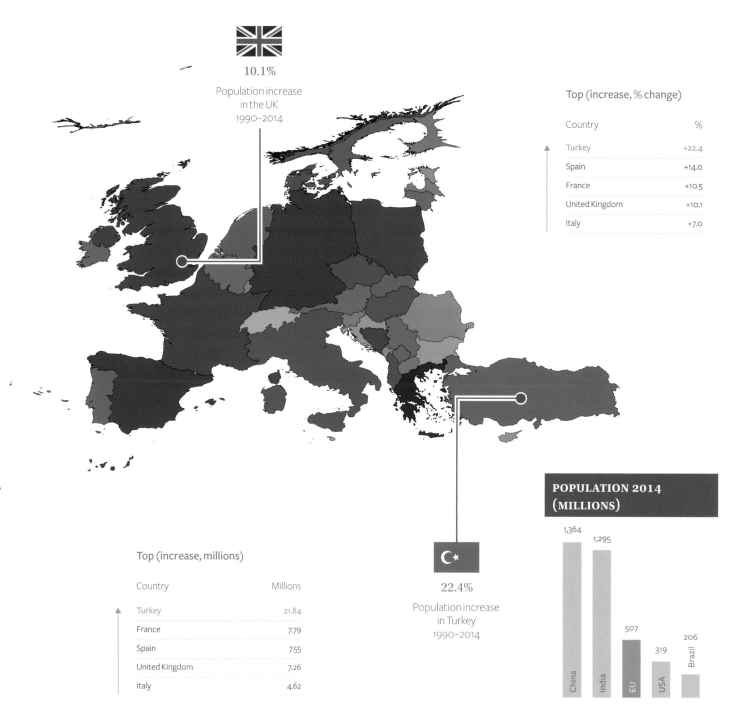

10.1%
Population increase
in the UK
1990–2014

22.4%
Population increase
in Turkey
1990–2014

Top (increase, % change)

Country	%
Turkey	+22.4
Spain	+14.0
France	+10.5
United Kingdom	+10.1
Italy	+7.0

Top (increase, millions)

Country	Millions
Turkey	21.84
France	7.79
Spain	7.55
United Kingdom	7.26
Italy	4.62

POPULATION 2014 (MILLIONS)

China	India	EU	USA	Brazil
1,364	1,295	507	319	206

Population decline

1990–2014

Population decline is mostly the result of out-migration due to economic disasters, which were especially acute in Eastern European countries such as Romania and Bulgaria following the collapse of communism after 1989, when the Baltic States also experienced rapid population declines as people were able to leave following the break-up of the Soviet Union, and as people had far fewer children in the ensuing economic chaos. The elderly also died in much greater numbers in Eastern Europe following the tearing down of the Berlin Wall in 1989, although this trend may have begun earlier, and that may have even been a factor in the collapse of communism.

Forced migration as a result of war and conflict in the former Yugoslavia exacerbated the declines in the populations of some countries, especially what is now Bosnia-Herzegovina.

What is certain is that a population catastrophe occurred thereafter – many towns and villages became ghost towns, many homes were abandoned, and there was even an increase in the population of wild wolves, which had spread as far west as Hamburg (formerly in West Germany) by 2015.

Colour key, see Reference map A1, p 10

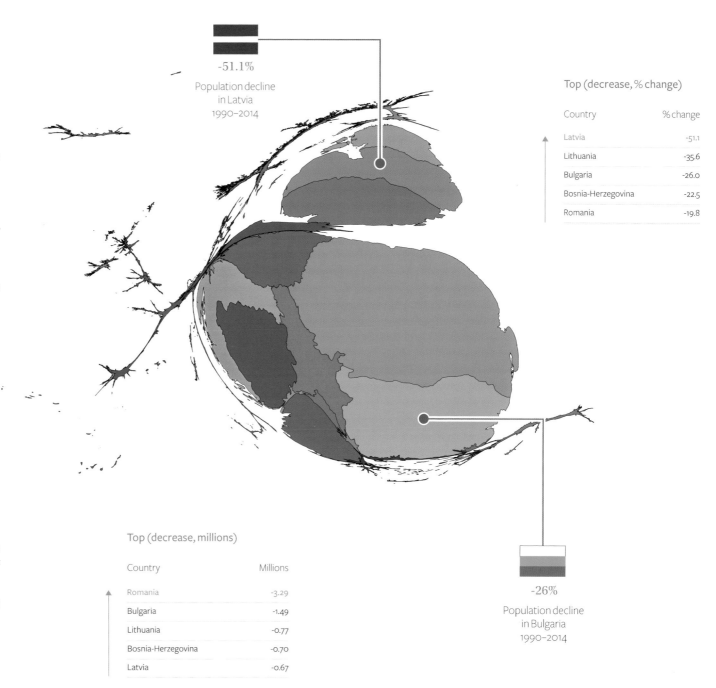

-51.1%
Population decline
in Latvia
1990–2014

-26%
Population decline
in Bulgaria
1990–2014

Top (decrease, % change)

Country	% change
Latvia	-51.1
Lithuania	-35.6
Bulgaria	-26.0
Bosnia-Herzegovina	-22.5
Romania	-19.8

Top (decrease, millions)

Country	Millions
Romania	-3.29
Bulgaria	-1.49
Lithuania	-0.77
Bosnia-Herzegovina	-0.70
Latvia	-0.67

Projected population 2050

2014

The UN's Population Division estimates that world population growth is slowing down. The population of the European countries mapped in this atlas is projected to increase from 616 million to 630 million by 2050, which is much less than the actual increase that has occurred over the past 25 years.

In 2014 the most populous country in Europe was Germany, followed by Turkey, France, the UK and Italy, but this ranking was projected to change, with Turkey and the UK taking first and second places by 2050. However, the recent influx of generally young refugees from Syria and other countries into Germany make such a turnaround now far less likely.

There may also possibly be more migration from Turkey towards the centre of Europe since, even if formal integration with the EU is not improved, there is still a rising demand for more younger people to live in Central Europe as the population ages. But the future is always hard to predict, even just 34 years ahead.

Colour key, see Reference map A1, p 10

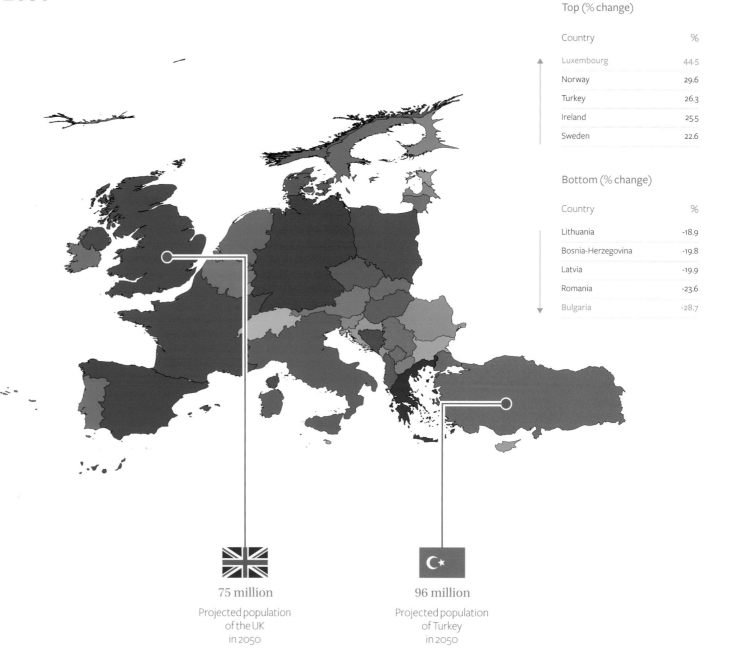

75 million

Projected population
of the UK
in 2050

96 million

Projected population
of Turkey
in 2050

Top (% change)

Country	%
Luxembourg	44.5
Norway	29.6
Turkey	26.3
Ireland	25.5
Sweden	22.6

Bottom (% change)

Country	%
Lithuania	-18.9
Bosnia-Herzegovina	-19.8
Latvia	-19.9
Romania	-23.6
Bulgaria	-28.7

Total births

2014

This map shows where the 6.7 million babies registered in Europe in 2014 were born.

From the late 1960s onwards there has been a dramatic fall in global fertility rates, especially in the most affluent countries.

Many countries in Europe are possibly soon going to face a demographic and pension crisis as there will be fewer people of working age, and therefore fewer taxpayers, making it impossible – without changes to current arrangements – to maintain levels of support, especially in areas where young people are leaving and fertility rates are low.

People can work for longer, and pensionable ages are rising in several parts of Europe, most noticeably in the UK, but also in Greece and other nations currently facing tough austerity measures.

Colour key, see Reference map A1, p 10

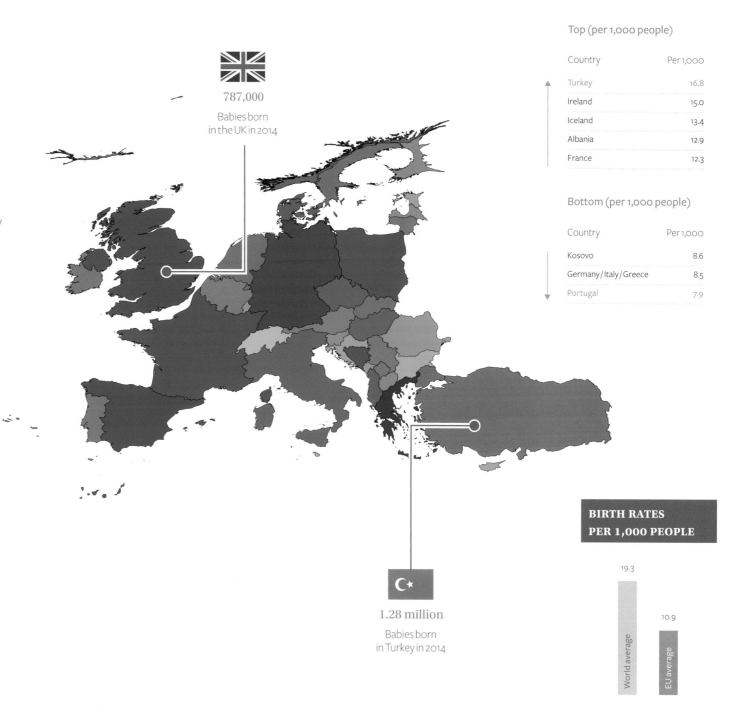

787,000

Babies born
in the UK in 2014

1.28 million

Babies born
in Turkey in 2014

Top (per 1,000 people)

Country	Per 1,000
Turkey	16.8
Ireland	15.0
Iceland	13.4
Albania	12.9
France	12.3

Bottom (per 1,000 people)

Country	Per 1,000
Kosovo	8.6
Germany / Italy / Greece	8.5
Portugal	7.9

**BIRTH RATES
PER 1,000 PEOPLE**

19.3

10.9

World average

EU average

Life expectancy (national)

2013

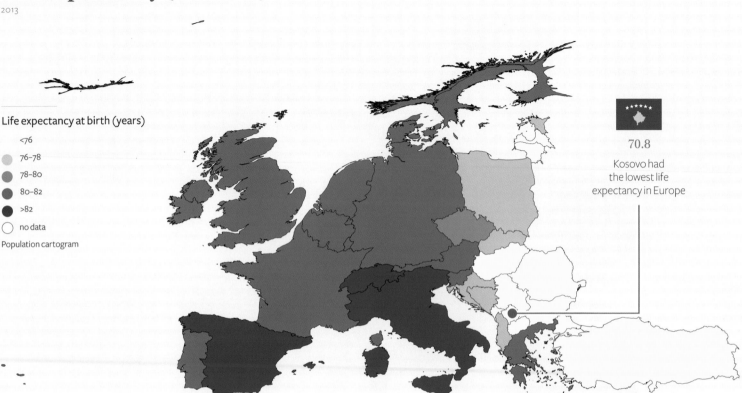

Life expectancy at birth (years)

- <76
- 76–78
- 78–80
- 80–82
- >82
- no data

Population cartogram

70.8

Kosovo had the lowest life expectancy in Europe

Top

Country	Years
Iceland	83.1
Switzerland	82.7
Spain/Liechtenstein	82.4
Italy	82.3

Bottom

Country	Years
Bulgaria/Romania	74.5
Lithuania	74.2
Latvia	74.0
Kosovo	70.8

Life expectancy and life chances, both worldwide and within Europe, vary greatly according to where you live and your social status.

There are considerable disparities within Europe, with a very obvious East–West divide. A growing number of studies suggest a strong link between factors relating to life expectancy and other aspects of population health,

and income and wealth inequality, especially in more affluent societies and in response to growing austerity. The most disadvantaged groups within some European countries have seen elderly life expectancy decreasing in recent years: 2015 was the worst in decades for rising deaths among older people in England, and it was even worse in Scotland. Despite these issues, however,

national life expectancies remain high in Spain and Italy.

Across Europe life expectancy may be rising, but healthy life expectancy is not rising as quickly. One of the most effective ways of addressing this crisis is to encourage migration from elsewhere, including welcoming more refugees.

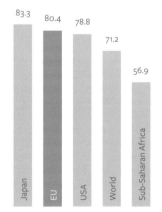

AVERAGE LIFE EXPECTANCY

Japan	EU	USA	World	Sub-Saharan Africa
83.3	80.4	78.8	71.2	56.9

EU countries have an average life expectancy rate among the highest in the world

Life expectancy (regional)

REGIONAL MAP, 2013

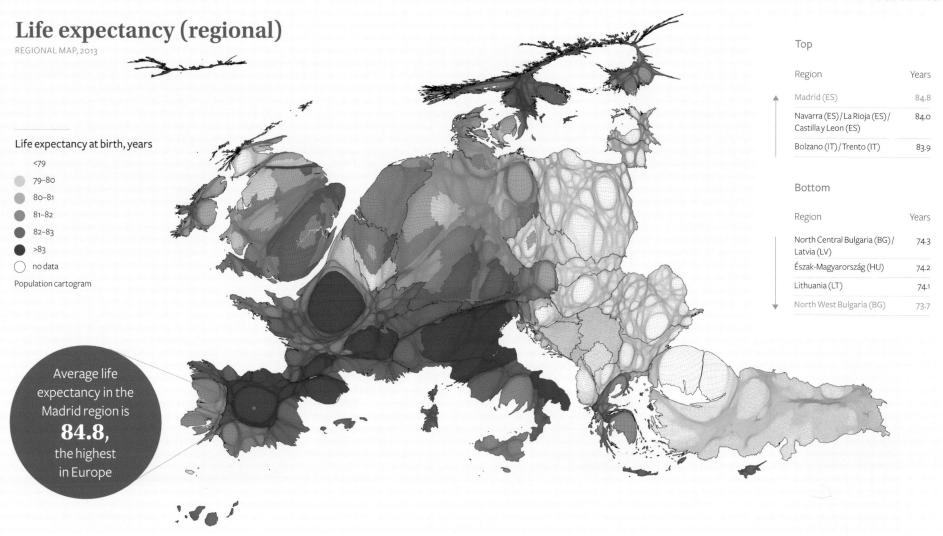

Life expectancy at birth, years

- <79
- 79–80
- 80–81
- 81–82
- 82–83
- >83
- no data

Population cartogram

Average life expectancy in the Madrid region is **84.8**, the highest in Europe

Life expectancy varies greatly across European regions. There are 23 regions where life expectancy at birth is 83 years or more. Of these, nine are in Spain, three are in France (including the capital city region of Paris), one is in Iceland and ten are in Italy.

Nearly all of the 84 regions with life expectancy at birth less than 79 years are in Eastern Europe; the others are in Belgium (Hainaut, 78.3 years and Namur 78.7 years) and southwestern Scotland in the UK, where life expectancy remains at just 78.3. This region includes Glasgow.

It is not the coastal regions of Mediterranean countries that enjoy the highest life expectancies, but the more prosperous inland areas, including Madrid, much of Catalonia, and northern Italy around Milan.

People who are more likely to experience poor health often move out of more expensive areas. At the same time, people with better health more often leave poorer areas causing those areas to then record even worse levels of health.

Prisoners

2013

There are currently over 800,000 people imprisoned across all of Europe, and the vast majority of these are young men.

Turkey and the UK, between them, hold nearly a third of Europe's prison population. Several Eastern European countries have relatively large numbers of prisoners in relation to their total populations. In Western Europe, the highest rate of imprisonment is recorded by the UK, while in Eastern Europe, the highest rate is in Lithuania, where courts and legislators are highly likely to impose custodial sentences for crimes.

The proportion of the population in prison is spectacularly low in the four principalities of Andorra, Monaco, Liechtenstein and San Marino. It is possible that those convicted of a crime in these places may hold other nationalities and serve their sentence in prisons in neighbouring countries. This is not the case in Iceland, which imprisons a tiny fraction per capita, of the numbers of people imprisoned in Latvia or Lithuania.

The definition of who is classed as a prisoner and how prisoners are actually held varies greatly between countries, with many countries having very open prison arrangements.

Colour key, see Reference map A1, p 10

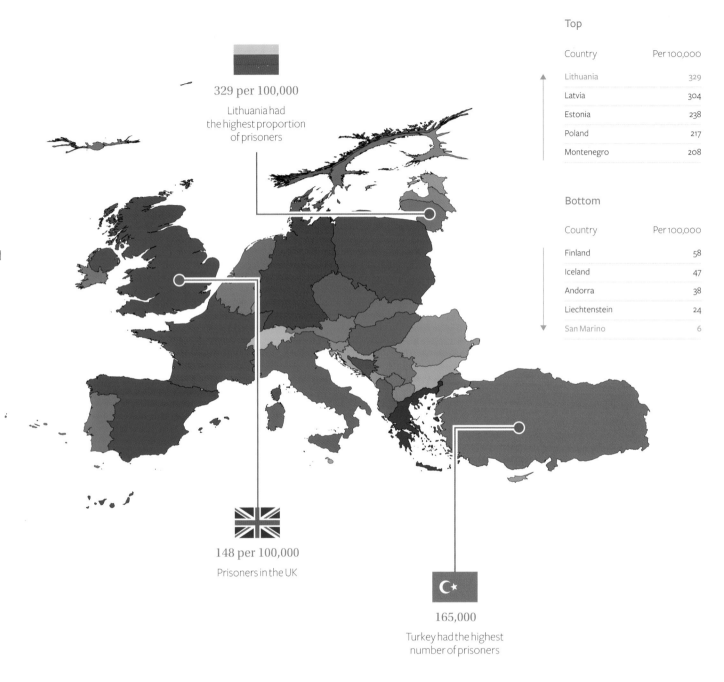

329 per 100,000
Lithuania had the highest proportion of prisoners

148 per 100,000
Prisoners in the UK

165,000
Turkey had the highest number of prisoners

Top

Country	Per 100,000
Lithuania	329
Latvia	304
Estonia	238
Poland	217
Montenegro	208

Bottom

Country	Per 100,000
Finland	58
Iceland	47
Andorra	38
Liechtenstein	24
San Marino	6

Homicides

2012

There were 8,082 homicides in Europe in 2012, less than half the number in the US. Nearly a quarter of European homicides occurred in Turkey, although Eastern European countries also recorded large numbers, and high rates in relation to total population. The world's highest homicide rate was recorded in Honduras (90.4 per 100,000 people).

Not all deaths that might be considered as homicides are always officially prosecuted as such. In North West England a few years ago, the deaths of cockle pickers on a beach were all recorded as 'murder' because the gang in charge of the pickers were negligent. However, hundreds of elderly people killed by one doctor, Harold Shipman, were also regarded as 'murders', but formally only a handful were officially classified as such (had Shipman not been caught, they would not have been counted at all, and had the cockle pickers' deaths been attributed to an accident, they would not have been recorded as homicides).

One man can alter the murder rate of a country, as happened in Norway in 2011, when a mass murderer killed 69 young people on the island of Utøya as well as eight people in Oslo.

While murders are generally becoming less common, isolated atrocities may be increasing.

Colour key, see Reference map A1, p 10

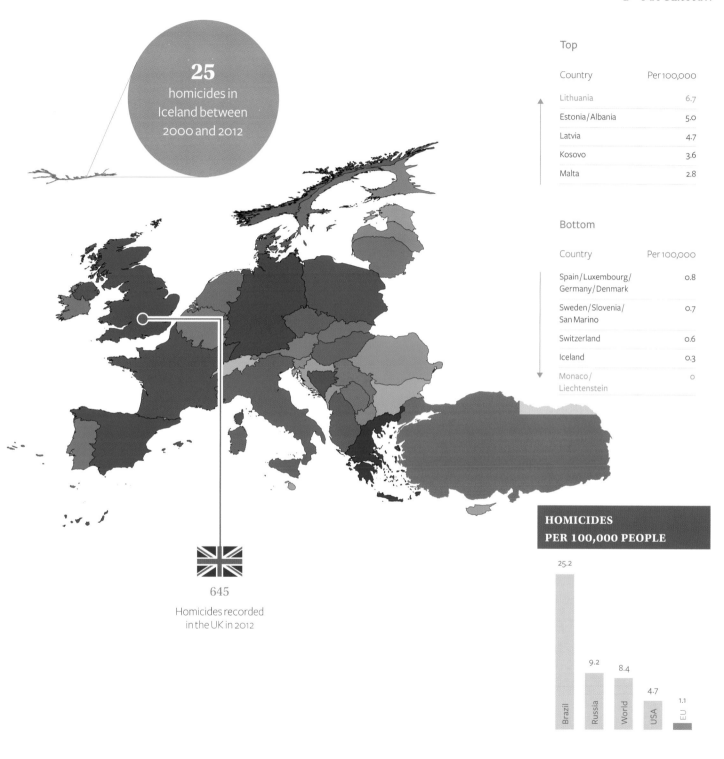

25 homicides in Iceland between 2000 and 2012

645

Homicides recorded in the UK in 2012

Top

Country	Per 100,000
Lithuania	6.7
Estonia / Albania	5.0
Latvia	4.7
Kosovo	3.6
Malta	2.8

Bottom

Country	Per 100,000
Spain / Luxembourg / Germany / Denmark	0.8
Sweden / Slovenia / San Marino	0.7
Switzerland	0.6
Iceland	0.3
Monaco / Liechtenstein	0

HOMICIDES PER 100,000 PEOPLE

Brazil	25.2
Russia	9.2
World	8.4
USA	4.7
EU	1.1

C – Wealth and Poverty

Europe is one of the most affluent and prosperous places in the world, although there are significant social and spatial inequalities in its distribution of income and wealth. As the numbers of vulnerable and socially excluded populations living precarious lives have been rising considerably following recent years of turmoil and severe austerity measures, this atlas includes both countries that are in the top 10 richest in the world, as well as some of the world's less wealthy nations.

- The themes covered in this chapter include: traditional measures of **economic prosperity** such as GDP, disposable household income and numbers of households living in **poverty**; income inequality, and the UN **Human Development** Index.
- Other themes include **government debt** and **stocks traded**, as well as **internet use** and mobile telephone connections.
- The maps and infographics explore **what changed** so quickly **nationally** and **regionally** in the economic circumstances of Europeans in the years following the 2008 economic crisis.
- In 2015 more than half of the states mapped in this atlas had at least one resident with a personal fortune of at least US$1 billion. There were a total of 420 **billionaires** living across all of Europe with their assets valued at US$1.6 trillion.

Gross Domestic Product (GDP)

2014

A country's GDP is the market value of goods and services produced by all sectors of its economy in a year, usually measured in US dollars (US$). It takes no account of much vital unpaid work, for example caring, teaching and childrearing.

None of the countries with the highest total GDP (Germany, the UK, France, Italy and Spain) are in the top five for GDP per capita. This is topped by three very small but extremely affluent states – Monaco, Liechtenstein and Luxembourg – followed by Norway and Switzerland – which are medium-sized countries in terms of population, but which also have the lowest unemployment rates among the world's richest nations, some of the highest life expectancies, and much greater than average rates of economic equality.

GDP per person is not average annual personal income. In those European countries where income inequalities are lower, and where shareholders and the rich take less profit, GDP per capita is nearer to median incomes.

Colour key, see Reference map A1, p 10

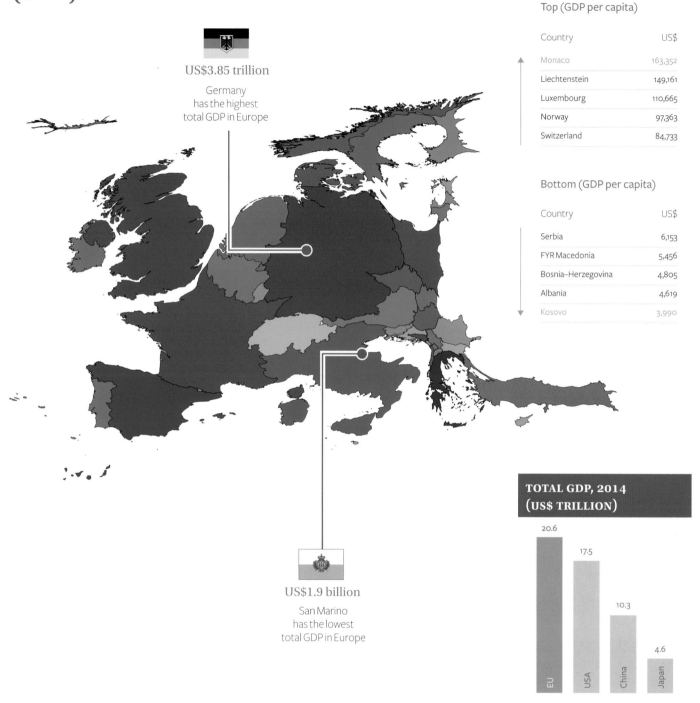

US$3.85 trillion

Germany
has the highest
total GDP in Europe

US$1.9 billion

San Marino
has the lowest
total GDP in Europe

Top (GDP per capita)

Country	US$
Monaco	163,352
Liechtenstein	149,161
Luxembourg	110,665
Norway	97,363
Switzerland	84,733

Bottom (GDP per capita)

Country	US$
Serbia	6,153
FYR Macedonia	5,456
Bosnia–Herzegovina	4,805
Albania	4,619
Kosovo	3,990

TOTAL GDP, 2014 (US$ TRILLION)

EU	20.6
USA	17.5
China	10.3
Japan	4.6

GDP increase

2007–14

Twenty-eight of the countries mapped in this atlas experienced an increase in their GDP during the period from the start of the economic crisis in 2007/08 to 2014. These were mostly in Central and Eastern Europe, but Germany and Switzerland also stand out.

Growth in GDP doesn't necessarily mean growth in wages. For example, in the UK median wages had not yet returned to their 2007 levels by 2014/15. Most of what growth there had been was only reflected in greater wealth for a few, mostly a minority of those living in the South of England, where housing inflation has resulted in a debt-fuelled mini-boom, and worsening living conditions for renters.

Rising GDP also does not necessarily mean less unemployment. In France GDP has risen but unemployment remains high because people are not pressured into taking any job on offer. In the UK the expansion of welfare sanctions (with over 1 million people being sanctioned in 2013) has forced poorer people to take any job they can find.

Colour key, see Reference map A1, p 10

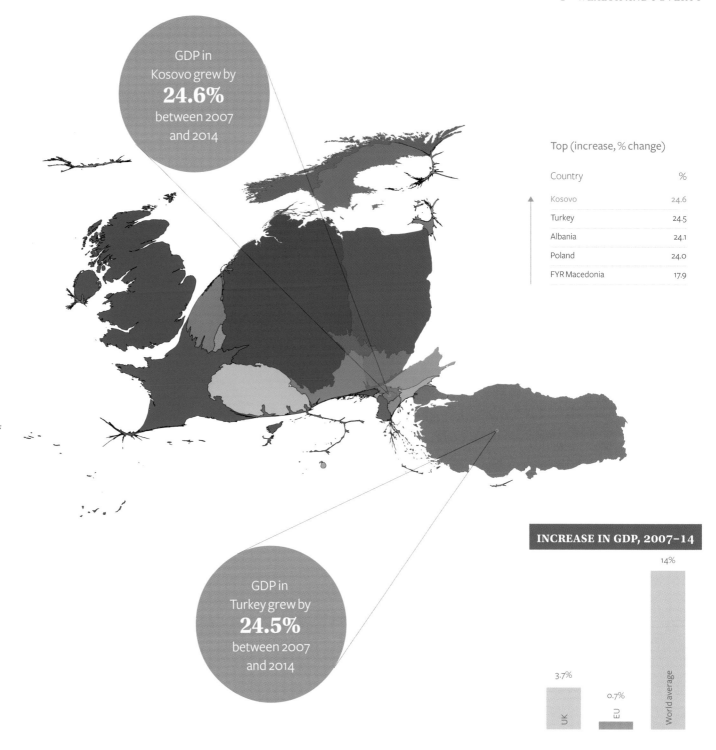

GDP in Kosovo grew by **24.6%** between 2007 and 2014

GDP in Turkey grew by **24.5%** between 2007 and 2014

Top (increase, % change)

Country	%
Kosovo	24.6
Turkey	24.5
Albania	24.1
Poland	24.0
FYR Macedonia	17.9

INCREASE IN GDP, 2007–14

UK 3.7%
EU 0.7%
World average 14%

GDP decline

2007–14

Between 2007/08 when the economic crisis began and 2014, there were 14 countries that experienced a reduction in the value of goods and services being produced and sold.

The countries in the South of Europe stand out. These massive negative changes in GDP are also reflected in the rise of unemployment in these countries.

Italy dominates the map, as its fall in GDP has been greater than in all of the next four countries with the largest absolute falls combined. However, in relation to the initial size of its economy, Italy has only experienced the fourth-largest fall.

In the first edition of this atlas, which reflected the position at 2012, it was the UK that had experienced the greatest absolute fall. By 2014, GDP had recovered slightly in the UK, but not by as much as in many other countries.

Colour key, see Reference map A1, p 10

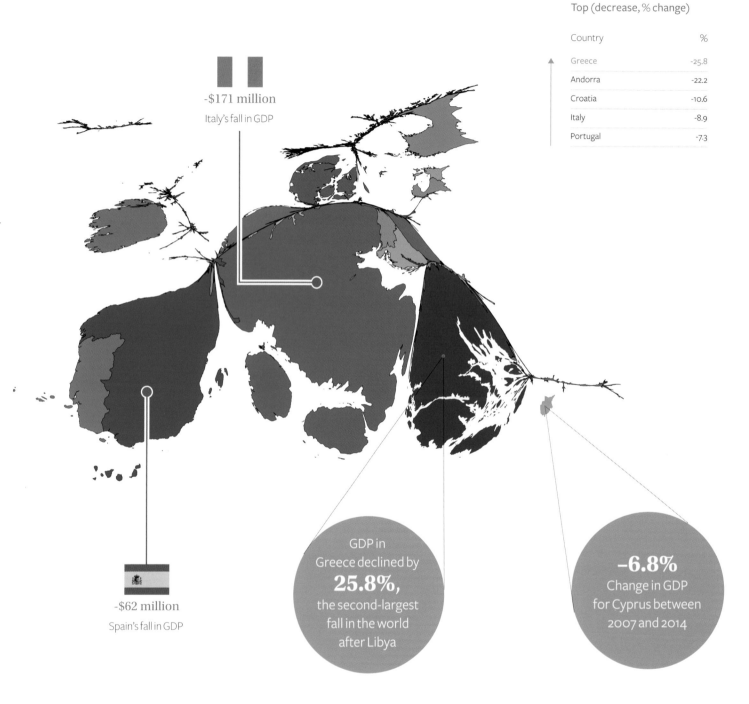

-$171 million

Italy's fall in GDP

-$62 million

Spain's fall in GDP

GDP in Greece declined by **25.8%**, the second-largest fall in the world after Libya

−6.8% Change in GDP for Cyprus between 2007 and 2014

Top (decrease, % change)

Country	%
Greece	-25.8
Andorra	-22.2
Croatia	-10.6
Italy	-8.9
Portugal	-7.3

GDP per inhabitant

REGIONAL MAP, 2013

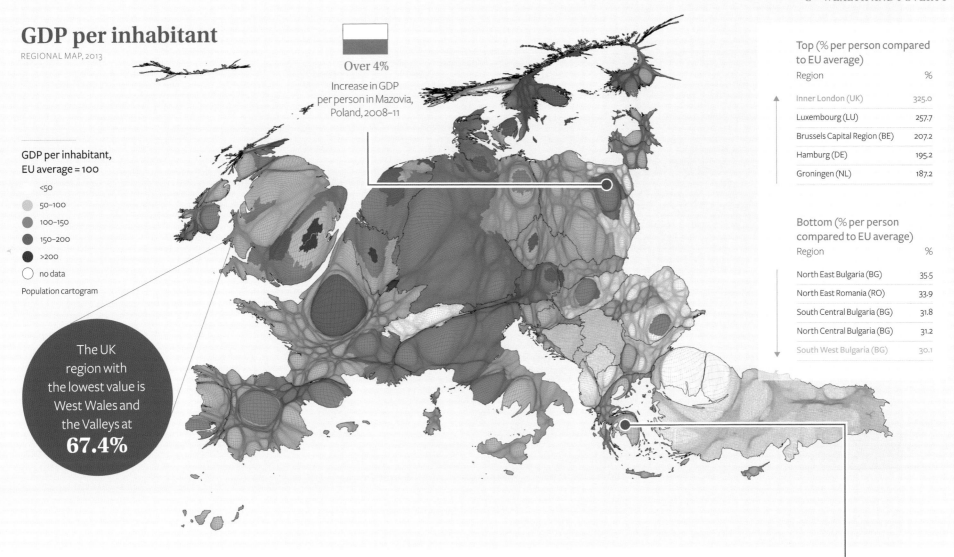

Over 4%

Increase in GDP
per person in Mazovia,
Poland, 2008–11

GDP per inhabitant,
EU average = 100

- <50
- 50–100
- 100–150
- 150–200
- >200
- no data

Population cartogram

The UK
region with
the lowest value is
West Wales and
the Valleys at
67.4%

Top (% per person compared to EU average)

Region	%
Inner London (UK)	325.0
Luxembourg (LU)	257.7
Brussels Capital Region (BE)	207.2
Hamburg (DE)	195.2
Groningen (NL)	187.2

Bottom (% per person compared to EU average)

Region	%
North East Bulgaria (BG)	35.5
North East Romania (RO)	33.9
South Central Bulgaria (BG)	31.8
North Central Bulgaria (BG)	31.2
South West Bulgaria (BG)	30.1

This map reveals how much better or worse off each area is compared to the EU average (set to equal 100%) and using Purchasing Power Standards. The European regions are resized in proportion to the population living within them. Areas are then classified as 'rich' (deep blue), 'better-off' (blue), 'average' (light blue and green) and 'poor' (yellow).

Regions in Turkey and the Western Balkan countries would almost certainly have been among the poorest if regional data had been available for these countries.

The map reveals an East–West divide, but we can also see disparities within countries. More money is received by Madrid compared to most of the rest of Spain, and by Rome and Milan at the possible expense of Naples and much of the rest of Italy. Paris takes even more in comparison to almost all of the rest of France, but London is the capital that takes by far the most in comparison to the rest of the country.

5%

Fall in GDP
per person in Greece
2008–11

Disposable income

REGIONAL MAP, 2011

Disposable income of private households (€)

- <10,000
- 10,000–13,000
- 13,000–16,000
- 16,000–19,000
- >19,000
- no data

Population cartogram

The lowest disposable income in the UK was **€12,900** in the West Midlands

Top

Region	€
Luxembourg (LU)	23,800
Upper Bavaria (DE)	23,700
Inner London (UK)	23,500
Stuttgart (DE)	22,100
Île de France (FR)	21,600

Bottom

Region	€
South West – Oltenia (RO)	5,000
North West (RO)/Central (RO)	4,900
South – Muntenia (RO)	4,800
North West Bulgaria (BG)	4,700
North East (RO)	4,300

Disposable income is the income after tax from all sources, including paid employment, property rental income and welfare benefits in cash. It does not include social transfers made in kind, such as the provision of universal healthcare or education free at the point of delivery.

Regions with very high average household incomes are found in Germany, especially in the West of Germany, and in France, Austria, Northern Italy and a small slither of the South of England and Inner London.

Regions in the lowest household income category – where households survive on below €10,000 per year on average – are all in Eastern Europe, in Bulgaria, the Czech Republic, Estonia, Hungary, Latvia, Poland, Romania and Slovak Republic.

Most households will be living on less than these amounts, particularly in regions where income inequalities are high, such as in Southern England. Most people are generally not well off in richer regions.

Disposable income change

REGIONAL MAP, 2007/08–11

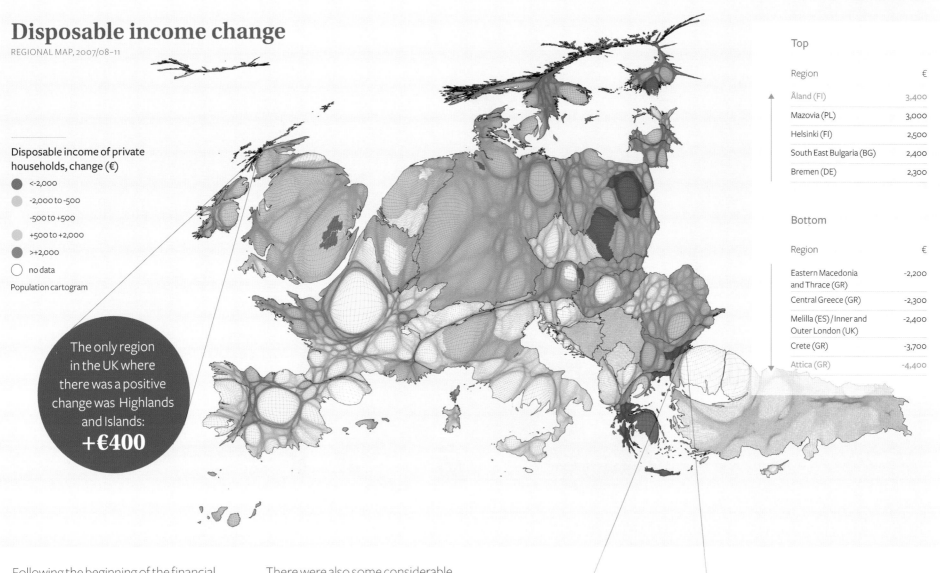

Disposable income of private households, change (€)

- ● <-2,000
- ○ -2,000 to -500
- ○ -500 to +500
- ○ +500 to +2,000
- ● >+2,000
- ○ no data

Population cartogram

The only region in the UK where there was a positive change was Highlands and Islands: **+€400**

Disposable household income increased by **€2,400** in the Black Sea region of South East Bulgaria

Top

Region	€
Åland (FI)	3,400
Mazovia (PL)	3,000
Helsinki (FI)	2,500
South East Bulgaria (BG)	2,400
Bremen (DE)	2,300

Bottom

Region	€
Eastern Macedonia and Thrace (GR)	-2,200
Central Greece (GR)	-2,300
Melilla (ES) / Inner and Outer London (UK)	-2,400
Crete (GR)	-3,700
Attica (GR)	-4,400

Following the beginning of the financial crisis and recession in Europe in 2007/08 through to 2011, the largest falls in income were seen in Greece, with the greatest decline recorded in the Athens capital city region of Attica. Considerable falls in average income were also experienced in some regions of Italy, Spain and the UK, including in London, where bankers' bonuses were cut for a few years.

There were also some considerable increases in household income, with the highest in the Åland island region of Finland, followed by the capital city regions of Poland and Finland, and South East Bulgaria, which includes the historic city of Burgas on the Black Sea.

Most of the regions where average household incomes increased are generally found in Central and Eastern Europe.

Government debt

2012

This map of government debt as a percentage of GDP is dominated by countries with large economies that also tend to have relatively large government debt in absolute terms, but there are some countries – such as Italy and Greece – that feature more prominently here than might normally have been expected, given the size of their GDP. These two countries (and especially Greece; see also 'GDP decline' map, p 44) were among the most heavily affected in Europe by the 2007/08 economic crisis and subsequent austerity measures.

The countries that appear very small are mostly in Northern and Eastern Europe. Note that countries in the Scandinavian region increased their debt rather than cut state spending.

Consider these figures for individual countries' debt levels as a proportion of GDP against those for the EU as a whole (72.9%), as well as other countries such as the US (94.3%) and Japan (196%), although in Japan the debt is largely domestic – older people lend to the government and receive an income in return.

Colour key, see Reference map A1, p 10

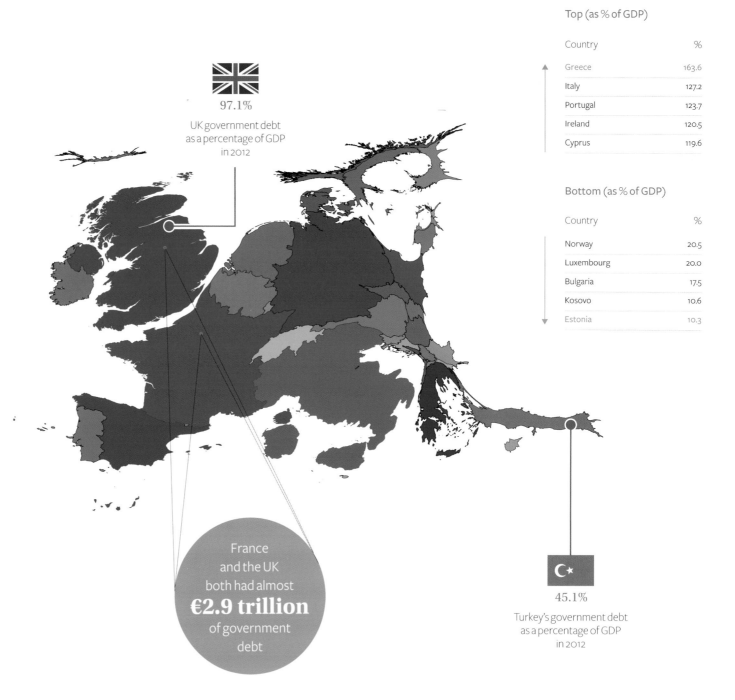

97.1%

UK government debt
as a percentage of GDP
in 2012

France and the UK both had almost **€2.9 trillion** of government debt

45.1%

Turkey's government debt
as a percentage of GDP
in 2012

Top (as % of GDP)

Country	%
Greece	163.6
Italy	127.2
Portugal	123.7
Ireland	120.5
Cyprus	119.6

Bottom (as % of GDP)

Country	%
Norway	20.5
Luxembourg	20.0
Bulgaria	17.5
Kosovo	10.6
Estonia	10.3

Stock exchange listed companies

2012

At the end of 2012 there were 12,380 domestic companies listed on Europe's stock exchanges (for the countries mapped in this atlas), compared to 4,102 in the US and 3,470 in Japan. About a quarter of all listed companies in Europe were in Spain, which also has the largest number overall.

Only those companies that have numerous shareholders are included here. Some private companies can be very large, employing thousands of people, and making billions of euros a year.

Numbers of listed companies are partly related to the differential costs of establishing companies in different countries – in Germany these costs are high, whereas in the UK they are low. Less red tape is not necessarily a good thing as it is easier to set up companies that then fail when the costs are lower. Far more companies fail in the UK compared to Germany. So areas that may have too little regulation are drawn larger here, including many of the Baltic States.

Colour key, see Reference map A1, p 10

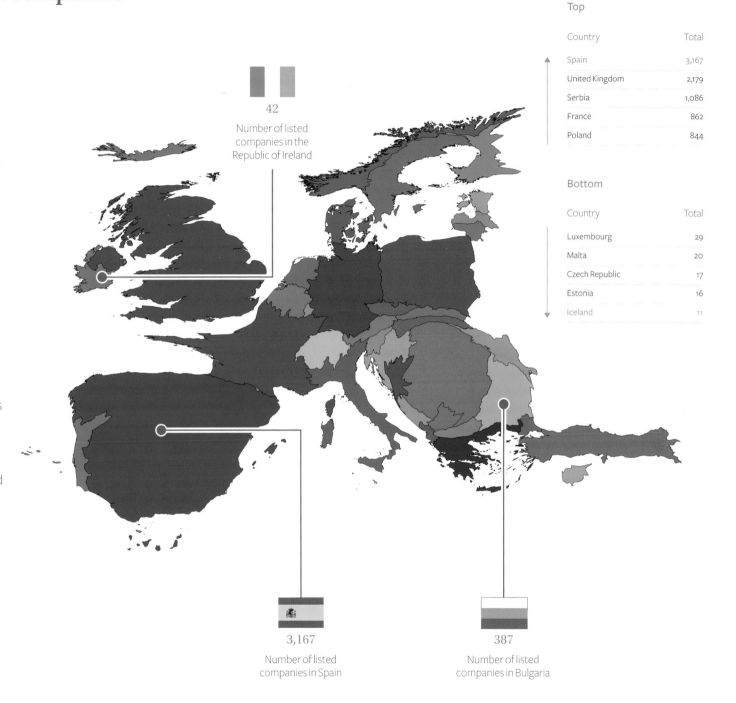

42
Number of listed companies in the Republic of Ireland

3,167
Number of listed companies in Spain

387
Number of listed companies in Bulgaria

Top

Country	Total
Spain	3,167
United Kingdom	2,179
Serbia	1,086
France	862
Poland	844

Bottom

Country	Total
Luxembourg	29
Malta	20
Czech Republic	17
Estonia	16
Iceland	11

Market value of stock exchange listed companies

2012

The estimated 'market value' of all listed 'domestic' companies calculated from their total share price at the end of 2012 was approximately US$12 trillion. About a quarter of this total was found in the UK, closely followed by France, Germany, Switzerland and Spain.

Domestic companies appear to be worth more in countries where income inequalities are greater. In such countries, those who own shares or who rent out property receive more income, and those who are employed receive less. Wages and salaries tend, for most people, to be lower when companies are valued higher, as companies tend to be worth more to shareholders when they do not have to pay so much to workers.

By one measure the UK is the most economically unequal country in Europe, as 28% of all income is taken by its best-off 10%. According to the OECD in 2015 the next most unequal countries were Portugal (where they take 26%), and then France, Greece and Italy (25%). The most equitable countries are Finland, Belgium, Denmark, Norway and Slovenia, where the best-off tenth take 20% to 21.5% of all income. See cartogram of 'Income inequality' on page 60 for the 'Gini' measure.

Colour key, see Reference map A1, p 10

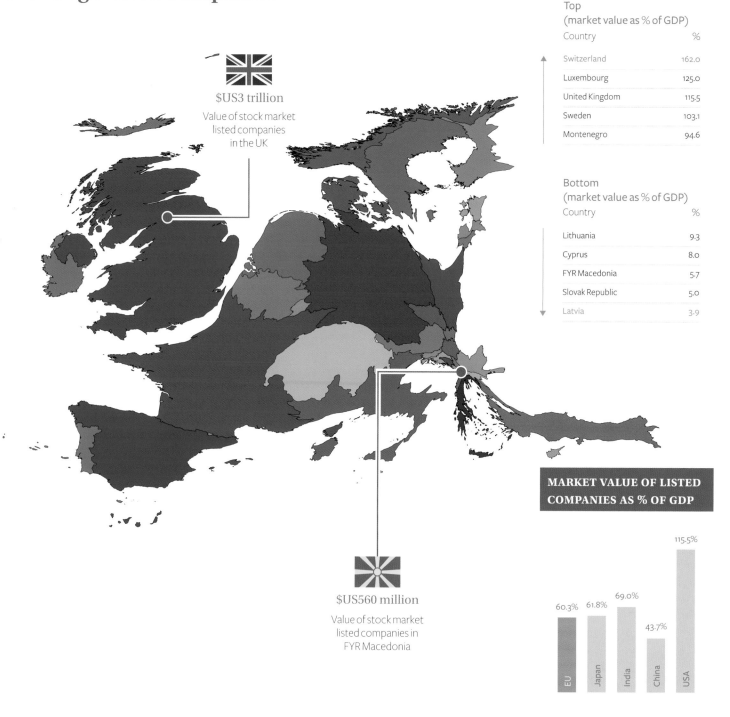

$US3 trillion

Value of stock market listed companies in the UK

$US560 million

Value of stock market listed companies in FYR Macedonia

Top
(market value as % of GDP)

Country	%
Switzerland	162.0
Luxembourg	125.0
United Kingdom	115.5
Sweden	103.1
Montenegro	94.6

Bottom
(market value as % of GDP)

Country	%
Lithuania	9.3
Cyprus	8.0
FYR Macedonia	5.7
Slovak Republic	5.0
Latvia	3.9

MARKET VALUE OF LISTED COMPANIES AS % OF GDP

EU	Japan	India	China	USA
60.3%	61.8%	69.0%	43.7%	115.5%

Stocks traded

2012

The total value of stocks traded in all countries mapped in this atlas in 2012 was just over US$9 trillion, with the largest value being in the UK (approximately US$2.5 trillion, or 93.9% of GDP).

One reason why the UK has such a large share of the European trading market is that companies and individuals may declare that they are 'not domiciled' in the UK and so avoid paying much tax in Europe while trading shares in Europe through London. Although this sometimes benefits the UK as it brings in more financial business, when there is a financial crisis the UK's over-reliance on stock markets and share trading as a source of economic wealth becomes very clear.

Switzerland appears to be similarly exposed, and yet, when the economic crisis hit, Switzerland's financial sector did not contract. Perhaps regulation is better than in the UK, or perhaps there are also other factors making Switzerland more secure, such as the gold traded being stored there, as well as stricter financial controls in general.

Colour key, see Reference map A1, p 10

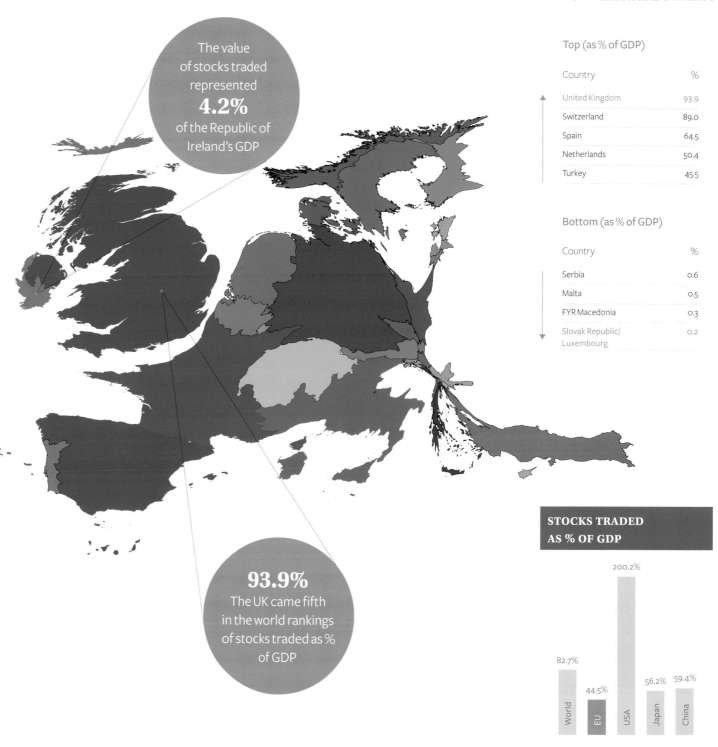

The value of stocks traded represented **4.2%** of the Republic of Ireland's GDP

93.9% The UK came fifth in the world rankings of stocks traded as % of GDP

Top (as % of GDP)

Country	%
United Kingdom	93.9
Switzerland	89.0
Spain	64.5
Netherlands	50.4
Turkey	45.5

Bottom (as % of GDP)

Country	%
Serbia	0.6
Malta	0.5
FYR Macedonia	0.3
Slovak Republic/ Luxembourg	0.2

STOCKS TRADED AS % OF GDP

	%
World	82.7%
EU	44.5%
USA	200.2%
Japan	56.2%
China	59.4%

Internet access

2014

This map of internet connections is dominated by Germany and the UK, and generally by the most populous countries in Europe, but in relative terms, smaller countries, such as Iceland, Norway and Denmark, top the list of connections per person, with 95 or more internet users per 100 people. In contrast, the UK rate in 2014 was 91.6 per 100 people.

These statistics imply incredibly dense penetration in these parts of Europe in recent years, but although it is possible that the very young or very old may be internet users it is more likely that they live in households with internet access but don't use the internet themselves.

Germany had the highest number of secure internet servers in 2014, with nearly a quarter of the European total of 436,000, followed by the UK, with nearly a fifth.

These figures are likely to change quickly, though. Increasingly, the energy costs of the internet are seen as important as people become more aware of how much energy they consume, and what kinds of pollution are created from the different sources of energy used to produce electricity. For example, Iceland is now providing more servers, part-cooled by the weather and powered by geothermal energy sources.

Colour key, see Reference map A1, p 10

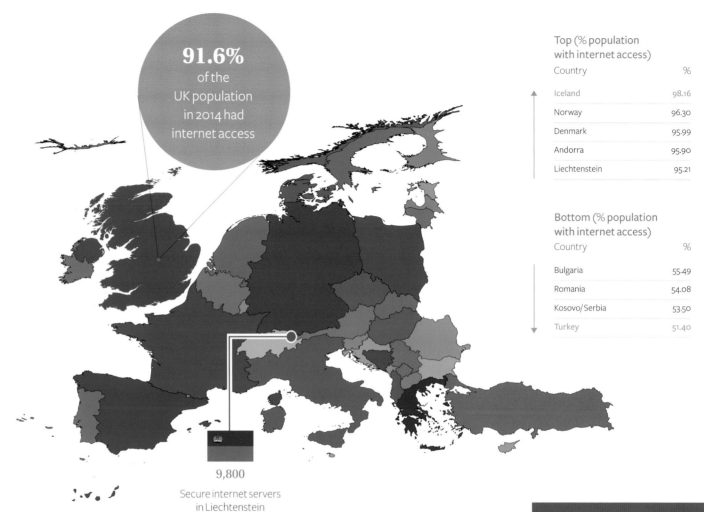

91.6% of the UK population in 2014 had internet access

9,800
Secure internet servers in Liechtenstein per million people

Top (% population with internet access)

Country	%
Iceland	98.16
Norway	96.30
Denmark	95.99
Andorra	95.90
Liechtenstein	95.21

Bottom (% population with internet access)

Country	%
Bulgaria	55.49
Romania	54.08
Kosovo/Serbia	53.50
Turkey	51.40

Top (secure internet servers per million people)

Country	Per million
Liechtenstein	9,762
Monaco	3,216
Iceland	3,214
Switzerland	2,820
Luxembourg	2,645

Bottom (secure internet servers per million people)

Country	Per million
Turkey	57
Montenegro	56
Serbia	44
Bosnia-Herzegovina	36
Albania	24

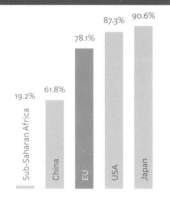

INTERNET ACCESS (% OF POPULATION)

Sub-Saharan Africa	19.2%
China	61.8%
EU	78.1%
USA	87.3%
Japan	90.6%

Telephone lines

2014

There were approximately 237 million fixed telephone lines thought to be in working order across Europe in 2014.

Fixed telephone lines have been losing importance over the years due to the proliferation of mobile phones and, more recently, alternative internet-based communications (such as Skype and Facetime). Finland, one of the countries where mobile phone technology was developed, is now found within the bottom five countries when looking at landlines per inhabitant.

Other European countries, such as Albania and Poland, which still have low landline use, may never see a great rise as mobile phones will probably be used in future in preference to installing fixed lines, and as people want fibre optic connections for the internet rather than the twisted-pair copper wire connections of old-fashioned telephone lines. However, the old telephone lines do have separate sources of power, and can often still operate for making calls when there are power cuts and where there is no mobile access.

Colour key, see Reference map A1, p 10

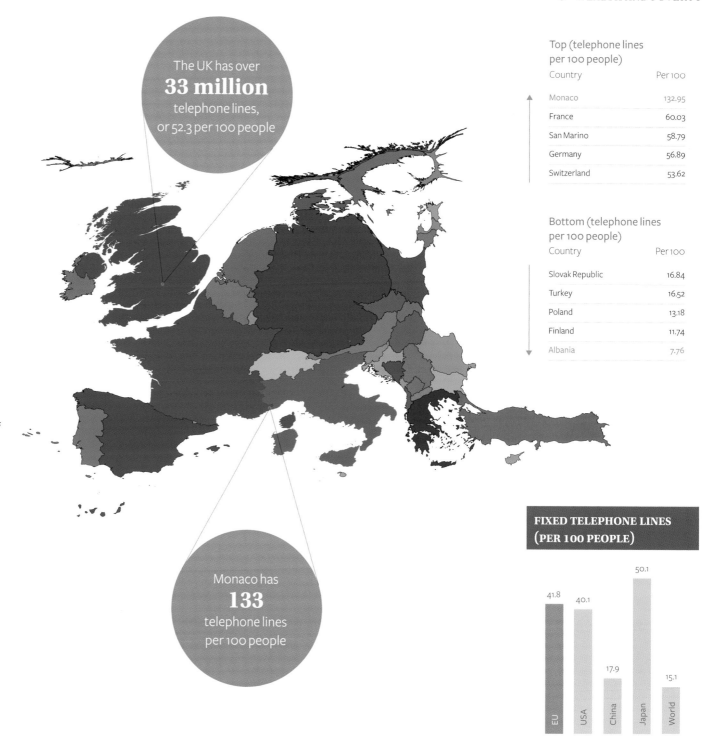

The UK has over
33 million
telephone lines,
or 52.3 per 100 people

Monaco has
133
telephone lines
per 100 people

Top (telephone lines per 100 people)

Country	Per 100
Monaco	132.95
France	60.03
San Marino	58.79
Germany	56.89
Switzerland	53.62

Bottom (telephone lines per 100 people)

Country	Per 100
Slovak Republic	16.84
Turkey	16.52
Poland	13.18
Finland	11.74
Albania	7.76

FIXED TELEPHONE LINES (PER 100 PEOPLE)

EU	USA	China	Japan	World
41.8	40.1	17.9	50.1	15.1

Mobile phones

2014

There were approximately 744 million current mobile-cellular subscriptions in working order across all the countries mapped in this atlas in 2014 – approximately 121 subscriptions per 100 people! This may partly be because if someone has two SIM cards in one phone which they can alternate between, this counts as two subscriptions. It is more likely, however, that many people have a pay-as-you-go mobile in their car in case of emergencies, and another they use more regularly, or they have an old phone that still has access to the network, as well as a new one from another provider. Others will have one phone provided by their work, and another they own, or a number of SIM cards being used in various tablets, and so on.

Given that many people still have no cellular subscription, it is likely that this count includes many subscriptions that are, in practice, inactive.

Colour key, see Reference map A1, p 10

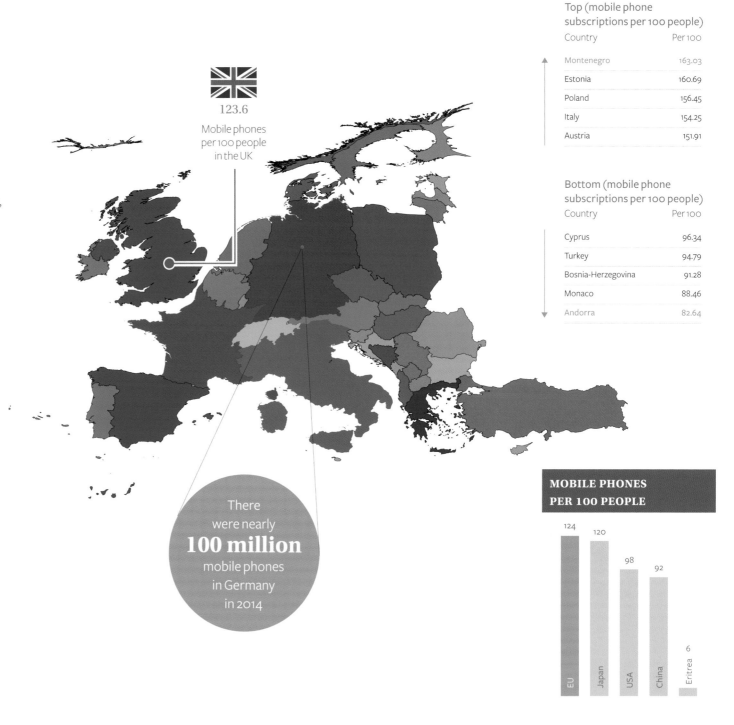

123.6

Mobile phones per 100 people in the UK

There were nearly **100 million** mobile phones in Germany in 2014

MOBILE PHONES PER 100 PEOPLE

EU	Japan	USA	China	Eritrea
124	120	98	92	6

Vulnerable employment
2013

In 2013, 14% of the total employed workforce across all the countries mapped in this atlas were 'vulnerably employed', that is, working as unpaid family workers or on their own account – i.e. self-employed without employees. They often lack formal work arrangements and access to maternity, holiday and sickness pay, have uncertain earnings and have no 'workers rights'.

Vulnerable employment is most common in Eastern and Southern Europe, with almost a third of the working population of Greece, Romania and Turkey, and over 50% of workers in Albania in vulnerable employment.

In contrast, such employment is least common in the North West of Europe.

Much employment that is not categorised as vulnerable may actually be vulnerable if contracts are short-term or zero-hours, as is increasingly the case in the UK. In recent years in Germany, as unemployment fell, precarious and temporary employment rates have risen.

Colour key, see Reference map A1, p 10

PEOPLE IN VULNERABLE EMPLOYMENT

37.3 million
IN EUROPE

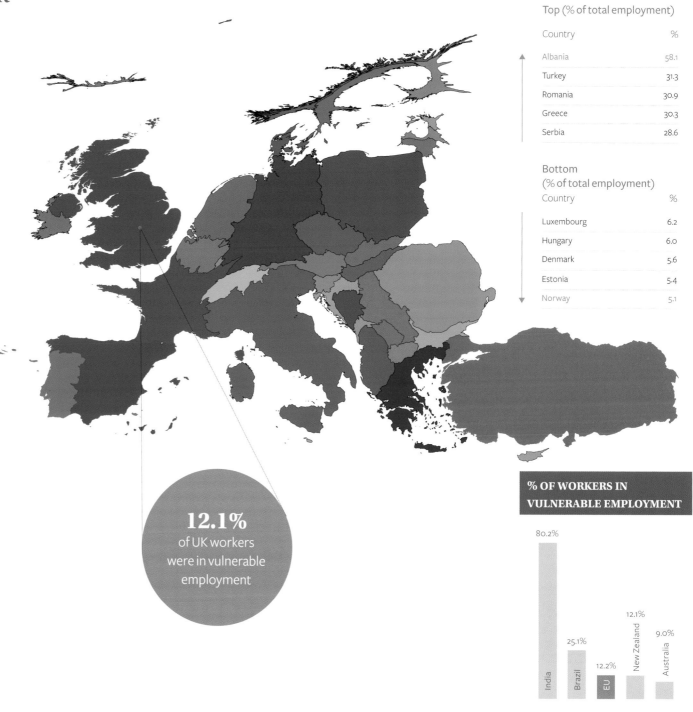

12.1%
of UK workers were in vulnerable employment

Top (% of total employment)

Country	%
Albania	58.1
Turkey	31.3
Romania	30.9
Greece	30.3
Serbia	28.6

Bottom (% of total employment)

Country	%
Luxembourg	6.2
Hungary	6.0
Denmark	5.6
Estonia	5.4
Norway	5.1

% OF WORKERS IN VULNERABLE EMPLOYMENT

- India 80.2%
- Brazil 25.1%
- EU 12.2%
- New Zealand 12.1%
- Australia 9.0%

Relative poverty (national)

POPULATION LIVING BELOW NATIONAL POVERTY LINE, 2014

A national poverty line is set at 60% of that country's median average disposable income adjusted for household type. Numbers of people living below this line have been rising considerably in some parts of Europe following years of turmoil, and austerity measures that have disproportionately hit the most disadvantaged citizens and regions.

No one would need to live on such low incomes if fewer people were living on twice the average income or higher.

More people live in poverty in the UK and Germany combined than in all of Turkey. In relative terms, there are more than three times as many people living in poverty in Turkey and most of the countries that once made up Yugoslavia, than there are in Iceland, the Czech Republic, the Netherlands, Norway and Denmark.

This measure does not take into account housing costs, especially high rents. Of all large European countries, rents are highest in the UK and so there are more people struggling to survive than just the poorest 16%.

Colour key, see Reference map A1, p 10

16%

of the UK population living below the national poverty line in 2014

There were over **20 million** people living below the national poverty line in Turkey in 2014

Top
(% of total population)

Country	%
Kosovo	29.7
Turkey	26.5
Montenegro / Serbia	24.5
FYR Macedonia	24.2

Bottom
(% of total population)

Country	%
Denmark	11.9
Norway	10.9
Netherlands	10.4
Czech Republic	8.6
Iceland	7.8

PEOPLE LIVING BELOW POVERTY LINE

111 million
IN EUROPE

Relative poverty (regional)

REGIONAL MAP, 2014

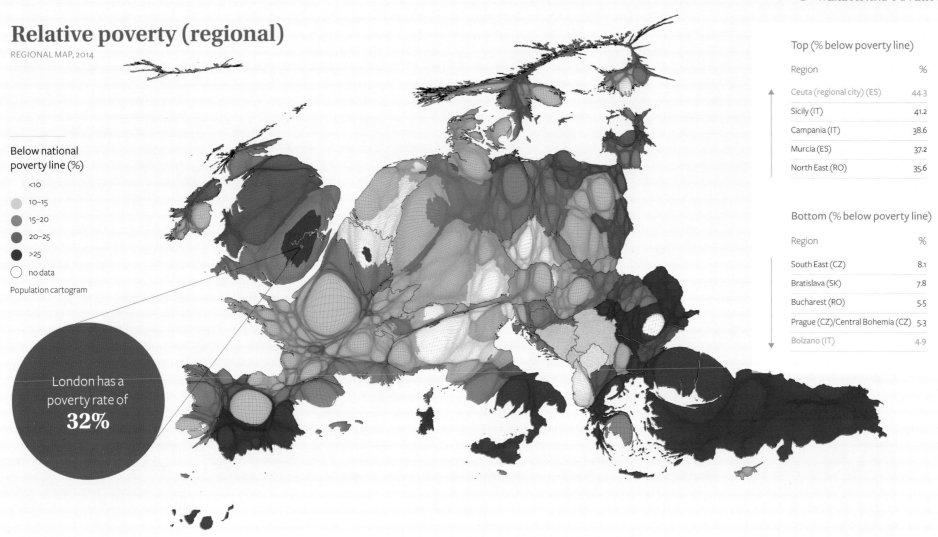

Below national poverty line (%)

- <10
- 10–15
- 15–20
- 20–25
- >25
- no data

Population cartogram

London has a poverty rate of **32%**

Top (% below poverty line)

Region	%
Ceuta (regional city) (ES)	44.3
Sicily (IT)	41.2
Campania (IT)	38.6
Murcia (ES)	37.2
North East (RO)	35.6

Bottom (% below poverty line)

Region	%
South East (CZ)	8.1
Bratislava (SK)	7.8
Bucharest (RO)	5.5
Prague (CZ)/Central Bohemia (CZ)	5.3
Bolzano (IT)	4.9

In all European countries, poverty is not spread evenly but concentrated in particular regions. High rates of poverty have been a persistent stark feature within the most affluent cities in countries with high income inequality, such as London in the UK, and Brussels in Belgium, although in other large European capitals such as Berlin, Paris, Madrid and Rome such extreme poverty is considered unacceptable.

On this map, about 40 regions have extremely high poverty rates (over 25% of their populations being poor), and all these are shaded deep blue. This includes Turkey, mapped here as a single region due to a lack of data for its smaller areas. These poorer regions are mostly in Southern and Eastern Europe, where severe economic crises and unfair austerity measures have led to much more poverty in recent years, and particularly in Bulgaria, all Greek regions except the capital city region of Athens, Southern Italy and Spain (including the Canary Islands).

Poverty below US$2 a day

2012

There are an estimated 3 million Europeans living in extreme absolute poverty (on the equivalent of less than US$2 a day), 2 million of whom live in Turkey. This means a near-subsistence lifestyle; however, people working as peasants on the land may have better access to basic foodstuffs than would be available in a US city for $2. Although by official estimates very few people in Western Europe have to subsist on this little, many destitute and homeless people across the whole continent do not appear in the statistics.

Colour key, see Reference map A1, p 10

Top
(% of total population)

Country	%
FYR Macedonia	4.20
Bulgaria	3.92
Albania	3.03
Turkey	2.56
Kosovo	2.09

4.2%
of the population
of FYR Macedonia
live on less than
$2 a day

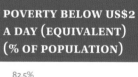

POVERTY BELOW US$2 A DAY (EQUIVALENT) (% OF POPULATION)

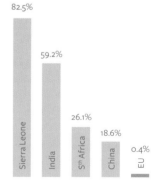

Sierra Leone	82.5%
India	59.2%
Sth Africa	26.1%
China	18.6%
EU	0.4%

Top
(total numbers)

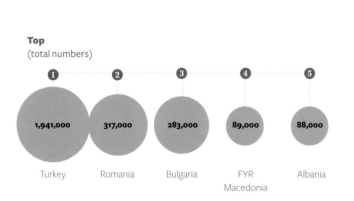

❶	❷	❸	❹	❺
1,941,000	317,000	283,000	89,000	88,000
Turkey	Romania	Bulgaria	FYR Macedonia	Albania

Billionaires

2015, DATA FROM *FORBES* MAGAZINE

In 2015 there were an estimated 420 billionaires across Europe, with their combined assets valued at US$1.6 trillion. Twenty-four of the 43 states mapped here had at least one resident with a personal fortune of US$10 billion or more.

The number of billionaires in the US in 2015 was 1,741 – far higher than the European total, despite the US having a smaller population. Far more people live in extreme and average poverty in the US.

Just over a quarter of the estimated US$1.6 trillion total wealth of Europe's US$ billionaires was found in Germany, with most of the rest in other countries of North and West of Europe.

However, these figures only show where the wealth of billionaires is officially held. In reality, many billionaires split their time between different homes across Europe and are not officially resident in any one country. For tax purposes they may say they live in, for example, the Middle East, Russia, or a small tax haven island, but they cannot spend more than 90 days in any one place to avoid being taxed on their wealth and income there.

Most of the 19 countries mapped in this atlas with no billionaires are in Eastern Europe and the Baltic States.

Colour key, see Reference map A1, p 10

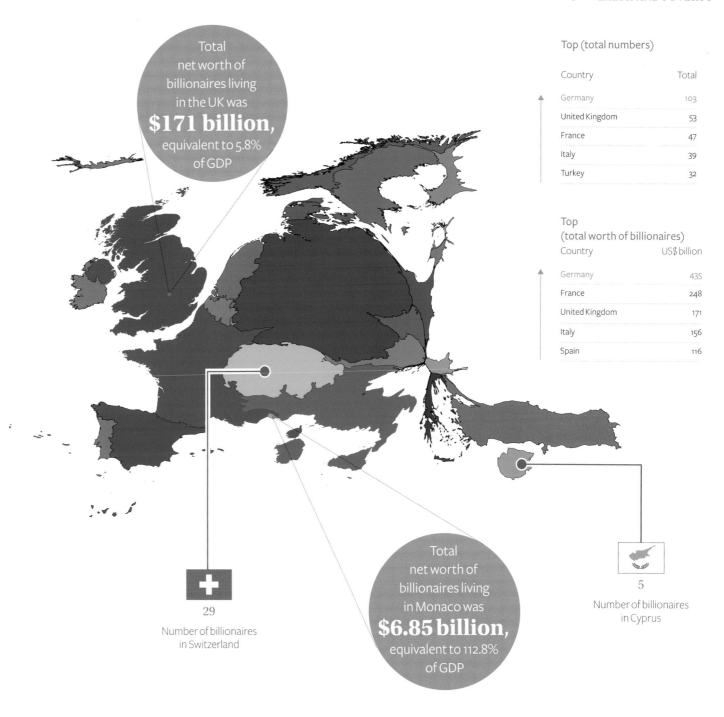

Total net worth of billionaires living in the UK was **$171 billion,** equivalent to 5.8% of GDP

29
Number of billionaires in Switzerland

Total net worth of billionaires living in Monaco was **$6.85 billion,** equivalent to 112.8% of GDP

5
Number of billionaires in Cyprus

Top (total numbers)

Country	Total
Germany	103
United Kingdom	53
France	47
Italy	39
Turkey	32

Top (total worth of billionaires)

Country	US$ billion
Germany	435
France	248
United Kingdom	171
Italy	156
Spain	116

Income inequality

VARIOUS YEARS, 2003–14

Top (Gini index)

Country	Index
Turkey	44.8
FYR Macedonia	37.0
Bosnia-Herzegovina	36.21
Latvia	35.5
Bulgaria	35.4

Bottom (Gini index)

Country	Index
Sweden	25.4
Czech Republic	25.1
Slovenia	25.0
Iceland	24.0
Norway	22.7

30.2

Gini index
for the UK

Gini index

- <25
- 25–30
- 30–35
- 35–40
- >40
- ○ no data

Population cartogram

Income inequality is measured by the Gini index, which ranges from a minimum value of 0, representing perfect equality, to 100, implying perfect inequality. This index doesn't weight the experience of any group of the population especially highly, and so the income of the best-off 1%, for example, has little effect, leaving a country like the UK, where the best-off 1% takes twice as much as, say, in Switzerland, only slightly more unequal by this measure.

In contrast, Turkey appears to be very unequal because inequalities among the bulk of the population there are higher, due to many people still working on the land and receiving a near-subsistence income.

Because the poor always outnumber the rich, when there is greater inequality among the poor, a country can appear to be more unequal overall by this measure. In contrast, if people were weighted by their incomes and inequality considered by where most of the money was going, countries like the UK would appear most unequal. According to the OECD, the best-off 10% in the UK takes 28% of all income.

Gender inequality

2013

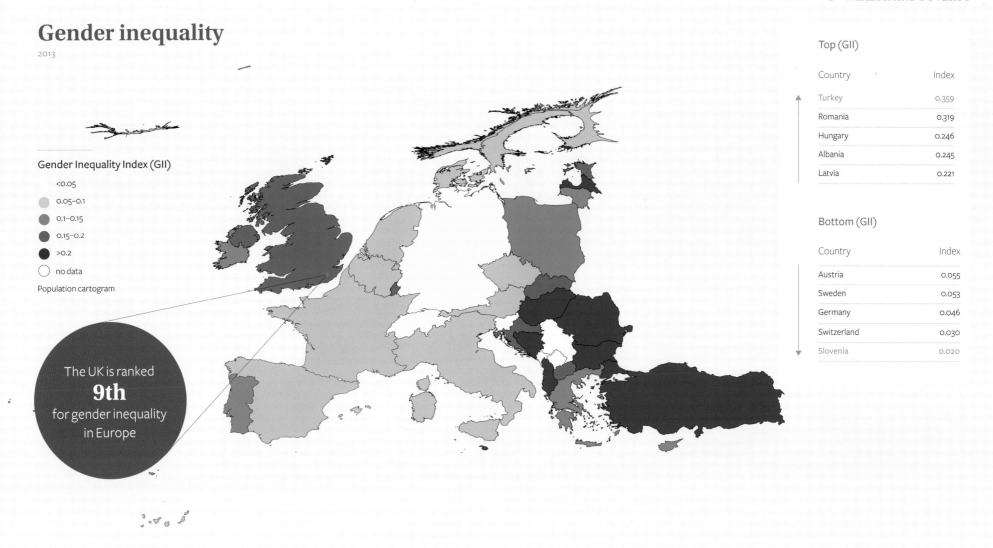

Gender Inequality Index (GII)

- <0.05
- 0.05–0.1
- 0.1–0.15
- 0.15–0.2
- >0.2
- no data

Population cartogram

The UK is ranked **9th** for gender inequality in Europe

Top (GII)

Country	Index
Turkey	0.359
Romania	0.319
Hungary	0.246
Albania	0.245
Latvia	0.221

Bottom (GII)

Country	Index
Austria	0.055
Sweden	0.053
Germany	0.046
Switzerland	0.030
Slovenia	0.020

A higher value of the UN Gender Inequality Index (GII) indicates greater gender inequality. The EU average is 0.13, world average 0.45 and Arab States average 0.55. The GII captures the disadvantages facing women and girls, and discrimination against them in health, education, political representation and the labour market. The GII measures reproductive health (maternal mortality, and adolescent birth rates), empowerment (proportion of parliamentary seats occupied by females and proportion of adult females and males aged 25 and older with at least some secondary education) and economic status (women's labour force participation).

Although similar to the Human Development Index (HDI) (see next map), it is particularly aimed at exposing differences in achievements between women and men, and at measuring the human development costs of gender inequality. The higher the value of the index, the greater the disparities between females and males, and so the greater the loss to human emancipation in general.

Men may well suffer as well as women in countries that tolerate greater levels of gender inequality, with their partners more likely to die in childbirth, the male-dominated politics of the country more aggressive, and they may be expected to take more traditional male roles rather than having greater flexibility.

Human Development Index

2013

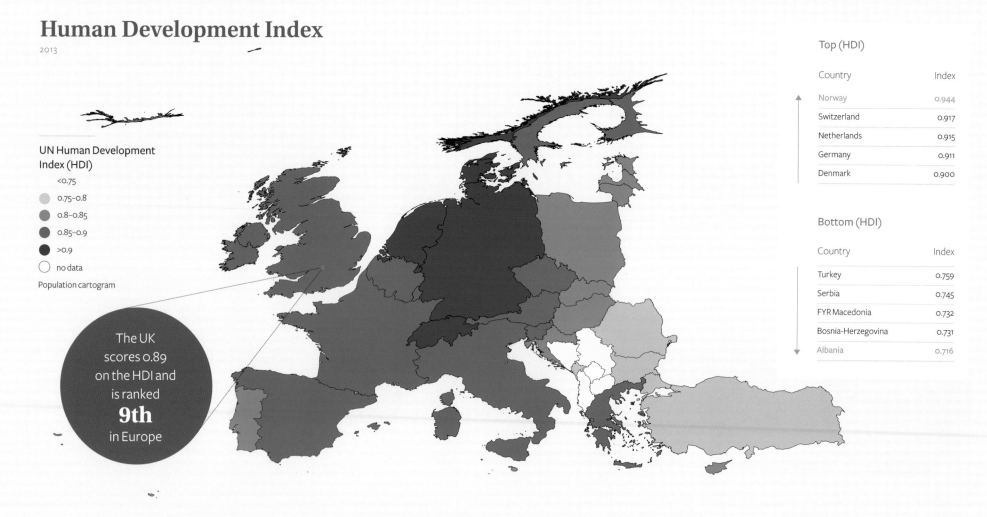

UN Human Development
Index (HDI)

- <0.75
- 0.75–0.8
- 0.8–0.85
- 0.85–0.9
- >0.9
- no data

Population cartogram

The UK scores 0.89 on the HDI and is ranked **9th** in Europe

Top (HDI)

Country	Index
Norway	0.944
Switzerland	0.917
Netherlands	0.915
Germany	0.911
Denmark	0.900

Bottom (HDI)

Country	Index
Turkey	0.759
Serbia	0.745
FYR Macedonia	0.732
Bosnia-Herzegovina	0.731
Albania	0.716

The Human Development Index (HDI) measures achievement in three key dimensions of human development: a long and healthy life, being knowledgeable, and having a decent standard of living. It was based on Professor Amartya Sen's work and is aimed at highlighting human capabilities to help assess the development of a country rather than focusing on economic growth alone.

The UN classifies nearly all countries within Europe as having very high human development (with values more than 0.8). Norway has the highest level, not only in Europe but across the world. The world's top five rankings also include Switzerland and the Netherlands, Australia (2nd) and the US (5th).

The UK as a whole does not score particularly highly, though, because it is very divided, with several Northern and Western regions experiencing poor and worsening mortality rates, educational standards that are not improving in real terms, and low or stagnant wages and benefit rates. Iceland scores higher than the UK, even after factoring in the recent economic crises experienced there.

It also does very well considering that countries nearer the centre of Europe generally fare better than those on the edges.

D – Health

Everyone has a right to health, and the European ideals of social solidarity and cohesion have been fundamental in ensuring free or cheap access to healthcare across Europe for all. Looking at health across Europe and beyond, this chapter explores mortality rates, diseases, lifestyle factors, health spending and staffing/access to healthcare.

- The EU enjoys very low **mortality rates** by world standards – much lower than the US.
- There have been significant reductions in **health inequalities** between European regions, although an apparent East–West division remains, with war, society breakdown and economic turmoil having lasting effects.
- There are national and regional variations in **health risk factors and lifestyles** across Europe – for instance, the likelihood of smoking is greatly influenced by whether it is considered to be normal to smoke in the country in which you live.
- The amount of public and private **spending on health** varies considerably between countries.
- There are also **social and spatial inequalities in health service provision**, meaning large differences in the type of provision and numbers of medical professionals available.

Mortality rate

2012

All-cause mortality rate

- <350
- 350–400
- 400–450
- 450–500
- >500

Population cartogram

409

Mortality rate
in the UK

397

Mortality rate
in the Republic of Ireland

Top

Country	Per 100,000
Albania	766
Serbia	709
Bulgaria	708
Latvia	704
Romania	691

Bottom

Country	Per 100,000
France	369
Spain	360
Iceland	355
Italy	339
Switzerland	331

These mortality rates measure the annual number of deaths occurring for every 100,000 people.

The shading in this map starkly reveals the old underlying East–West division within Europe. Mortality rates often reflect past conditions, such as war or war-like situations or living under authoritarian and oppressive regimes, with poverty rates rising rapidly in much of Eastern Europe after 1989, harming health in those regions greatly.

Mortality rates in Russia rose in absolute terms in the 1990s, as they also did in the countries that make up the former Yugoslavia during the wars of the 1990s. War, society breakdown and economic turmoil continue to have effects on overall population health outcomes for many years after the initial events.

This map shows the most recent data available for all countries. In some countries mortality rates have risen in more recent years, most dramatically in the UK in 2015, but also (to a lesser extent) in France that year.

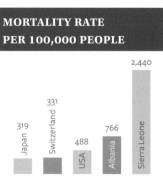

MORTALITY RATE PER 100,000 PEOPLE

- Japan 319
- Switzerland 331
- USA 488
- Albania 766
- Sierra Leone 2,440

Deaths from non-communicable diseases

2012

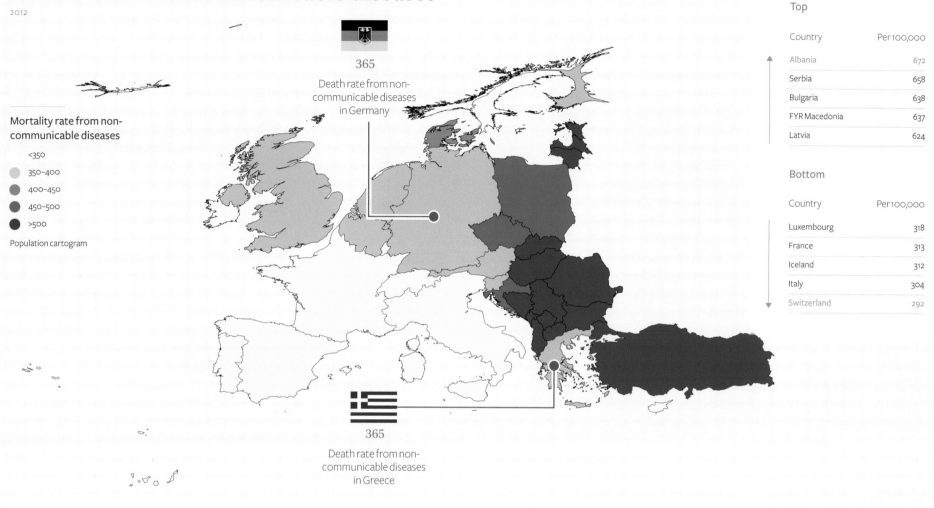

Mortality rate from non-communicable diseases

- <350
- 350–400
- 400–450
- 450–500
- >500

Population cartogram

365

Death rate from non-communicable diseases in Germany

365

Death rate from non-communicable diseases in Greece

Top

Country	Per 100,000
Albania	672
Serbia	658
Bulgaria	638
FYR Macedonia	637
Latvia	624

Bottom

Country	Per 100,000
Luxembourg	318
France	313
Iceland	312
Italy	304
Switzerland	292

The commonest types of non-communicable diseases considered here are cardiovascular (such as heart attacks and strokes), chronic respiratory diseases, cancers and diabetes. They are not transmitted from person to person, and often have a long duration and may be fatal.

Among the risk factors for non-communicable diseases are lifestyle variations such as having a poor diet or smoking, or lack of physical activity, and environmental factors such as exposure to air pollution. To some extent, genetic factors also play a part.

There is an East–West division within Europe, but also most Mediterranean and Scandinavian countries have considerably lower rates than much of the rest of Western Europe.

According to the World Health Organization, in 2015 non-communicable diseases were the cause of death for 38 million people worldwide – almost three-quarters of these occurred in low and middle-income countries. Nearly half of these deaths (17.5 million) were caused by cardiovascular diseases, 8.5 million by cancer, 4 million by respiratory diseases and 1.5 million by diabetes.

DEATH RATE PER 100,000 PEOPLE

Turkmenistan	1025
Russia	790
USA	413
UK	359
Japan	244

Deaths from injuries

2012

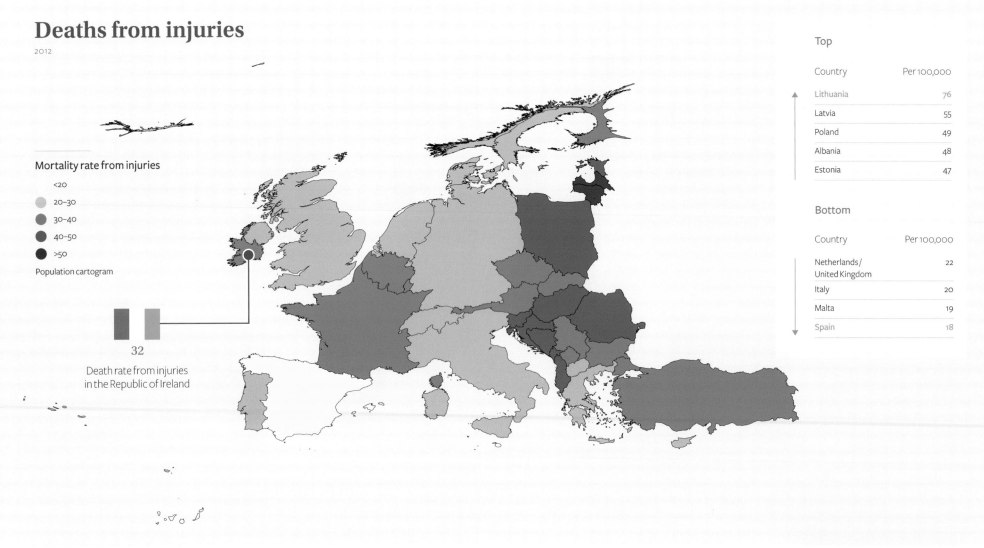

Mortality rate from injuries

- <20
- 20–30
- 30–40
- 40–50
- >50

Population cartogram

32

Death rate from injuries
in the Republic of Ireland

Top

Country	Per 100,000
Lithuania	76
Latvia	55
Poland	49
Albania	48
Estonia	47

Bottom

Country	Per 100,000
Netherlands / United Kingdom	22
Italy	20
Malta	19
Spain	18

The numbers of deaths in 2012 from injuries (including those caused by traffic crashes, drowning, poisoning, falls as well as violence and suicide) are shown here per 100,000 of the population. Throughout most of Europe injuries are the commonest cause of death between ages 5 and 40.

Lithuania stands out, with a mortality rate from injuries more than four times higher than Spain, the country with the lowest rate (which also had the second lowest rate of deaths from injuries in the world).

According to the World Health Organization, such injuries lead to over 5 million deaths worldwide every year, accounting for 9% of global mortality. The lowest rate in the world was recorded in Singapore (17.5 deaths per 100,000 people), whereas the highest, not surprisingly, were recorded in countries affected by war and conflict: Syria had the highest rate (308 deaths per 100,000 people) followed by Somalia (189), Mozambique (175) and Afghanistan (169).

INJURIES – DEATH RATE PER 100,000 PEOPLE

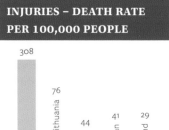

Syria	Lithuania	USA	Japan	Iceland
308	76	44	41	29

Deaths from communicable diseases

2012

Mortality rate from communicable diseases

- <15
- 15–20
- 20–25
- 25–30
- >30

Population cartogram

22

Death rate from communicable diseases in the Republic of Ireland

29

Death rate from communicable diseases in the UK

150 times as many deaths from these diseases in Sierra Leone (world highest) as in Finland (world lowest)

Top

Country	Per 100,000
Albania	47
Turkey	44
Portugal	40
Romania	39
Slovak Republic	35

Bottom

Country	Per 100,000
Switzerland	15
Iceland	14
Austria	13
Croatia	12
Finland	9

Communicable and other infectious diseases include hepatitis, HIV/AIDS, influenza and tuberculosis. Shown here are the annual number of deaths per 100,000 of the population.

Finland, Croatia and Austria have the lowest rates in Europe and also worldwide. Iceland, which has the fourth lowest rate in Europe, is fifth in the world, after Australia. Italy, Switzerland and Cyprus are also in the bottom 10 countries worldwide.

Compare Europe with other countries and world regions, such as the US (31 deaths per 100,000 people), Japan (34), China (41), India (253) and Brazil (93). Europe's highest rates of deaths, higher than the average for China, are found in Albania (47) and Turkey (44).

With better healthcare systems and public health measures, almost all deaths from these causes are preventable.

16

Death rate from communicable diseases in Cyprus

Deaths from diseases of the circulatory system

REGIONAL MAP, 2011

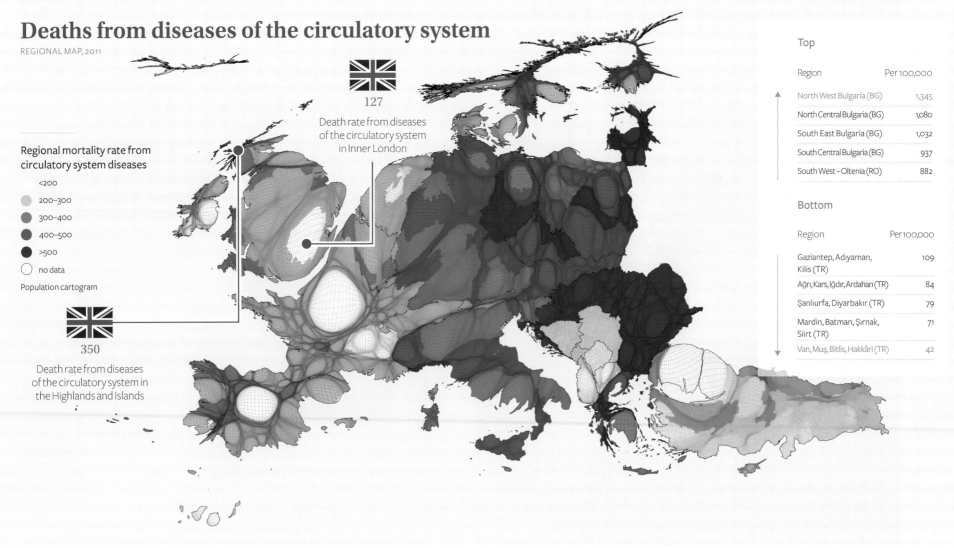

Regional mortality rate from circulatory system diseases

- <200
- 200–300
- 300–400
- 400–500
- >500
- no data

Population cartogram

350

Death rate from diseases of the circulatory system in the Highlands and Islands

127

Death rate from diseases of the circulatory system in Inner London

Top	
Region	Per 100,000
North West Bulgaria (BG)	1,345
North Central Bulgaria (BG)	1,080
South East Bulgaria (BG)	1,032
South Central Bulgaria (BG)	937
South West – Oltenia (RO)	882

Bottom	
Region	Per 100,000
Gaziantep, Adıyaman, Kilis (TR)	109
Ağrı, Kars, Iğdır, Ardahan (TR)	84
Şanlıurfa, Diyarbakır (TR)	79
Mardin, Batman, Şırnak, Siirt (TR)	71
Van, Muş, Bitlis, Hakkâri (TR)	42

The numbers of deaths from diseases of the circulatory system (including coronary heart disease, strokes and heart failure) are shown here per 100,000 of the population.

There is a very clear East–West distinction, although Turkey is an obvious exception. Higher rates of smoking and air pollution towards the East as well as stresses caused by war and the turmoil that followed the fall of the Berlin Wall in 1989 matter, but other geographical patterns are also evident.

Rates of mortality are much lower in South West Europe, other than in Portugal, which doesn't experience as low a rate as might be expected given its geography. Iceland and Norway report very low rates, as do the city regions of Paris, Madrid, London, Dublin and Istanbul.

Smoking, obesity, diet and exercise influence the patterns seen here, as well as the quality and availability of health services, including direct screening for risk factors.

Migration may play a role, as healthier people are more mobile, resulting in higher rates of mortality being recorded in the areas from which the healthy migrants move away.

DEATHS FROM DISEASES OF THE CIRCULATORY SYSTEM

368

EU AVERAGE PER 100,000 PEOPLE

Deaths from cancer

REGIONAL MAP, 2011

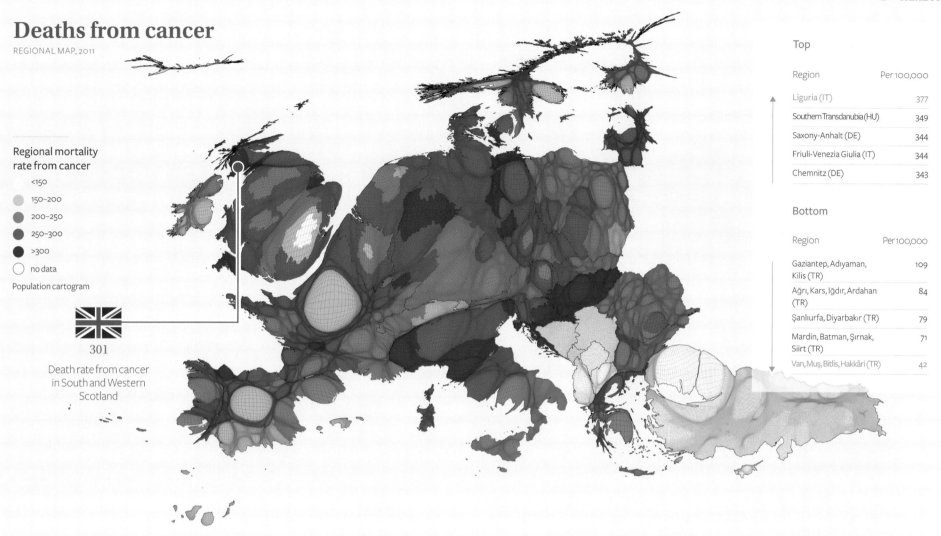

Regional mortality rate from cancer

- <150
- 150–200
- 200–250
- 250–300
- >300
- no data

Population cartogram

301

Death rate from cancer
in South and Western
Scotland

Top

Region	Per 100,000
Liguria (IT)	377
Southern Transdanubia (HU)	349
Saxony-Anhalt (DE)	344
Friuli-Venezia Giulia (IT)	344
Chemnitz (DE)	343

Bottom

Region	Per 100,000
Gaziantep, Adıyaman, Kilis (TR)	109
Ağrı, Kars, Iğdır, Ardahan (TR)	84
Şanlıurfa, Diyarbakır (TR)	79
Mardin, Batman, Şırnak, Siirt (TR)	71
Van, Muş, Bitlis, Hakkâri (TR)	42

Regions with cancer death rates of over 300 deaths per 100,000 people are found in seven countries: Croatia, France, Germany, Hungary, Italy, Spain and the UK. In the UK, these include the Highlands and Islands (318), Cumbria (313), Cornwall and the Isles of Scilly (310), South and Western Scotland (304), Lincolnshire (303), Devon (303) and Dorset and Somerset (300).

The regions with the lowest rates include all the regions of Turkey, the autonomous Spanish city region of Ceuta in North Africa, Cyprus, as well as Inner London. Different regional and historical patterns of smoking and industrial pollution will have played a part in creating the patterns seen here.

These are crude death rates and are not adjusted to take account of the resident profile. Areas with relatively elderly populations will be likely to have a higher incidence of cancer, and so Inner London appears low (142) because many of the people living there are young adults. Once the healthy migrant effect is also considered, some of the urban patterns may be easier to understand. Treatment may also be faster or more effective in cities than in rural areas.

DEATHS FROM CANCER

253

EU AVERAGE PER 100,000 PEOPLE

Deaths from diseases of the respiratory system

REGIONAL MAP, 2011

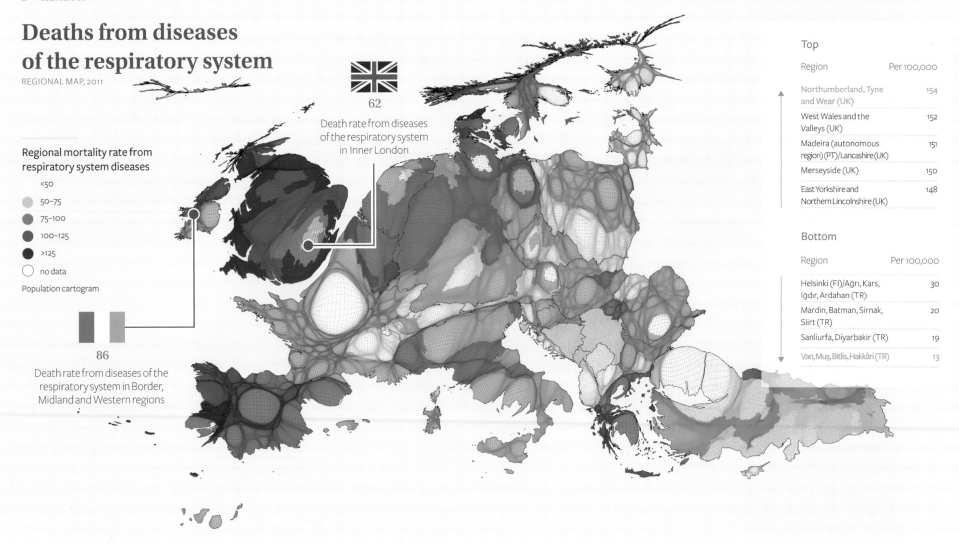

Regional mortality rate from respiratory system diseases

- <50
- 50–75
- 75–100
- 100–125
- >125
- no data

Population cartogram

86

Death rate from diseases of the respiratory system in Border, Midland and Western regions

62

Death rate from diseases of the respiratory system in Inner London

Top

Region	Per 100,000
Northumberland, Tyne and Wear (UK)	154
West Wales and the Valleys (UK)	152
Madeira (autonomous region) (PT)/Lancashire (UK)	151
Merseyside (UK)	150
East Yorkshire and Northern Lincolnshire (UK)	148

Bottom

Region	Per 100,000
Helsinki (FI)/Ağrı, Kars, Iğdır, Ardahan (TR)	30
Mardin, Batman, Sirnak, Siirt (TR)	20
Sanliurfa, Diyarbakir (TR)	19
Van, Muş, Bitlis, Hakkâri (TR)	13

The regions with the highest death rates from respiratory diseases (over 125 deaths per 100,000) are all found in Denmark, Portugal, and especially in the UK, although the pattern shown in the UK is more complex compared to patterns of more common diseases.

There are differences in diagnosis and death certification between countries and between doctors.

For example, doctors in the UK used to, and many probably still do, put down pneumonia as the primary cause of death when it was only the final event of a more long-standing condition, like dementia. Nevertheless, it is worth noting that susceptibility to diseases of the respiratory system is thought to be higher in areas with higher rates of traffic-caused air pollution, which may explain part of the pattern seen here.

This does not explain the high rates in much of the UK, where excess winter deaths are often attributed to respiratory disease, presumably because the population is not as well protected from the cold in winter as people tend to be in other Northern European countries.

DEATHS FROM DISEASES OF THE RESPIRATORY SYSTEM

75

EU AVERAGE PER 100,000 PEOPLE

Deaths from alcohol use

2008

Death rate from alcohol use

- <1
- 1–2
- 2–3
- 3–4
- >4
- no data

Population cartogram

1.4
The death rate from alcohol use in the UK was the same as the world average

10.5
Litres of alcohol consumed per person per year in the UK

Top (deaths from alcohol use)

Country	Per 100,000
Estonia	8.8
Denmark	6.9
Germany	4.3
France	4.2
Slovenia	4.1

Bottom (deaths from alcohol use)

Country	Per 100,000
Spain	0.6
Andorra	0.4
Bosnia-Herzegovina/ Italy/Malta	0.2
Albania/Greece	0.1
Cyprus/Slovak Republic	0

Top (alcohol consumption, litres per head)

Country	Litres
Andorra	13.3
Lithuania	12.9
Ireland	12.8
Czech Republic	12.7
Austria	12.1

Bottom (alcohol consumption, litres per head)

Country	Litres
Iceland	6.3
Italy	6.1
Albania	5.0
Bosnia-Herzegovina	4.3
Turkey	1.5

The numbers of deaths from alcohol use are shown here per 100,000 people.

As alcohol consumption is high and increasing among young people, and as other causes of death (such as smoking and some infectious diseases) become less common, these alcohol-use related causes will become more important in time.

The highest rates of alcohol-use related deaths were mostly found in Northern and Eastern Europe, but do not correspond to annual (absolute) alcohol consumption per head.

The lowest rates were mostly found in Southern Europe, but the Netherlands, Iceland and Lithuania also had very low rates (less than 1 death per 100,000).

The more affluent countries tend to have higher death rates. According to the United Nations Human Development Index, the mortality rate in countries classified as having 'very high human development' was 1.9 per 100,000, whereas those with 'low human development' had a rate of 0.9; the average rate worldwide was 1.4.

Comparing Europe with other countries around the world, the mortality rate in the US in the same year was 2.1, in Japan 0.3 and in China 0.9.

Deaths from drug use

2008

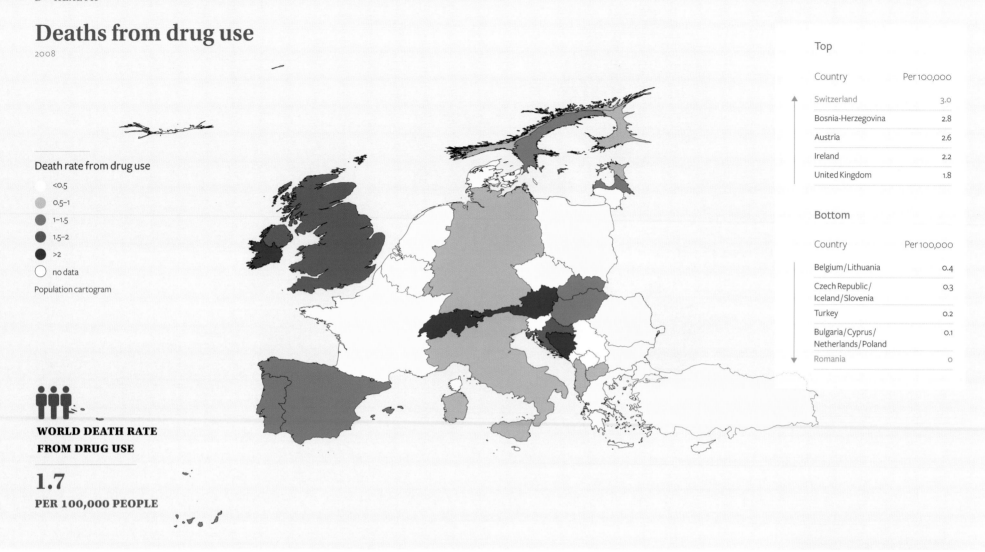

Death rate from drug use

- ⬤ <0.5
- ⬤ 0.5–1
- ⬤ 1–1.5
- ⬤ 1.5–2
- ⬤ >2
- ○ no data

Population cartogram

WORLD DEATH RATE FROM DRUG USE

1.7

PER 100,000 PEOPLE

Top

Country	Per 100,000
Switzerland	3.0
Bosnia-Herzegovina	2.8
Austria	2.6
Ireland	2.2
United Kingdom	1.8

Bottom

Country	Per 100,000
Belgium / Lithuania	0.4
Czech Republic / Iceland / Slovenia	0.3
Turkey	0.2
Bulgaria / Cyprus / Netherlands / Poland	0.1
Romania	0

The numbers of deaths from drug use are shown here per 100,000 of the population.

The highest rates were mostly found in Central Europe, but also in the Republic of Ireland and the UK. Although the latest data available were for 2008, we should not expect to see a fall in numbers of these deaths, especially after the economic crash of that year.

The average for countries classified as having 'very high human development' (according to the United Nations Human Development Index) was 1.0, and for those classified as having 'low human development', 2.9.

In the US the rate was 1.6, whereas in Japan and China the recorded rate was negligible. The highest rate worldwide was found in Afghanistan (33.1).

Of the five large highly populated countries of Europe, the UK has the highest rate of deaths from drugs, at 1.8 per 100,000 people per year.

Deaths from drug use may be more reliably reported than those due directly or indirectly to alcohol.

DEATH RATE PER 100,000 PEOPLE

6.6	3.2	1.4	0.8	0.4
Arab States	South Asia	Europe and Central Asia	Latin America and the Caribbean	East Asia and the Pacific

Obesity

2008

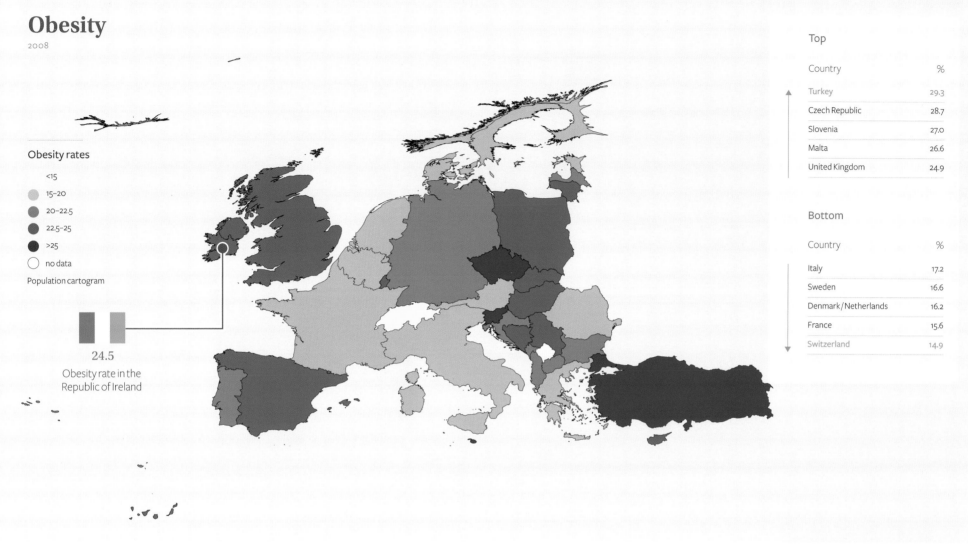

Obesity rates

- <15
- 15–20
- 20–22.5
- 22.5–25
- >25
- ◯ no data

Population cartogram

24.5

Obesity rate in the
Republic of Ireland

Top

Country	%
Turkey	29.3
Czech Republic	28.7
Slovenia	27.0
Malta	26.6
United Kingdom	24.9

Bottom

Country	%
Italy	17.2
Sweden	16.6
Denmark / Netherlands	16.2
France	15.6
Switzerland	14.9

The obesity rate is measured as the proportion of the adult population aged 20 and over having a body mass index of 30 or above.

In comparison with other world regions and countries, the overall obesity rate in countries with 'very high human development', according to United Nations data, was 22%, whereas in countries with 'very low human development' it was 2.9%.

The highest rate in the world was found in the island state of Palau (47.6%) in the Western Pacific Ocean.

All European countries have lower rates than that of the US, which was 33.7%.

Of the five large highly populated countries of Europe (Germany, France, the UK, Spain and Italy), the UK has the highest rate. However, for Europe as a whole, the rate is now highest in Turkey.

Within affluent countries obesity is most commonly associated with high rates of poverty and its associated stresses.

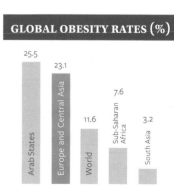

GLOBAL OBESITY RATES (%)

- Arab States 25.5
- Europe and Central Asia 23.1
- World 11.6
- Sub-Saharan Africa 7.6
- South Asia 3.2

Female smokers

2015

Female smokers (%)

- <20
- 20–30
- 30–40

Population cartogram

18%

Female smoking rate
in the UK

28%

Female smoking rate
in Germany

Top

Country	%
Serbia	40
Austria	35
Croatia	34
Greece	33
Bosnia-Herzegovina	30

Bottom

Country	%
Denmark	16
Iceland	15
Portugal	14
Turkey	12
Albania	8

Smoking rates for women and men are recorded separately because of the historical differences between men and women's tobacco use. Throughout Europe very few women smoked 60 or 70 years ago, whereas many men did smoke; women then began to take up smoking but in some countries more than in others.

Estimated numbers of female smokers are shown here as a percentage of the total adult female population.

The countries with the highest rates were mostly found in South East Europe, but there is a much more varied geographical pattern of countries that have the lowest rates, from countries in the West, such as Portugal and the UK, to Italy, Finland, Albania and Turkey. However, Turkey and Albania had very high numbers of male smokers.

Lower rates may be the result of successful health campaigns as well as the effective ban on smoking in public spaces, but cultural factors may make it less likely for females to smoke in some countries.

Smoking rates tend to be falling everywhere now, but there is a legacy of excess deaths in countries where they were once highest.

Male smokers

2015

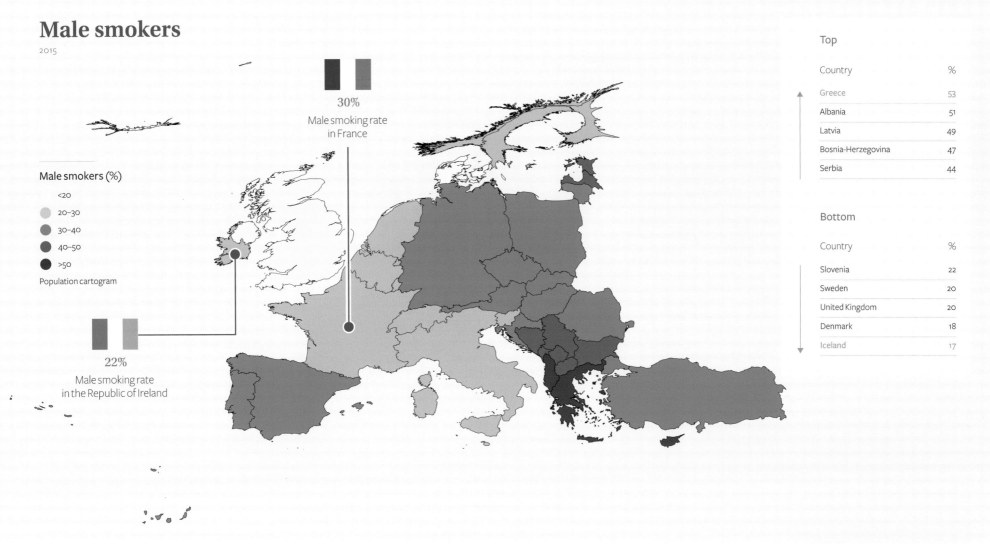

Male smokers (%)

- <20
- 20–30
- 30–40
- 40–50
- >50

Population cartogram

30%
Male smoking rate
in France

22%
Male smoking rate
in the Republic of Ireland

Top

Country	%
Greece	53
Albania	51
Latvia	49
Bosnia-Herzegovina	47
Serbia	44

Bottom

Country	%
Slovenia	22
Sweden	20
United Kingdom	20
Denmark	18
Iceland	17

Estimated numbers of male smokers are shown here as a percentage of the total adult male population.

The highest rates are found in Central and Eastern Europe, but also in Spain and Portugal.

The lowest rates are mostly found in countries that have historically had relatively low numbers of smokers, but also stronger and more effective health campaigns and smoking ban policies.

Denmark used to have one of the highest smoking rates in Western Europe until quite recently. Only Denmark and Iceland now have a lower rate of smoking among their male population than the US rate (19.5%).

The highest male smoking rate worldwide is found in Indonesia (76%), followed by Jordan (70%). The lowest rate is found in Panama (11%).

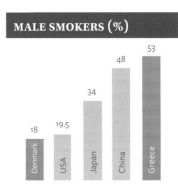

MALE SMOKERS (%)

Denmark	USA	Japan	China	Greece
18	19.5	34	48	53

Suicides

2012

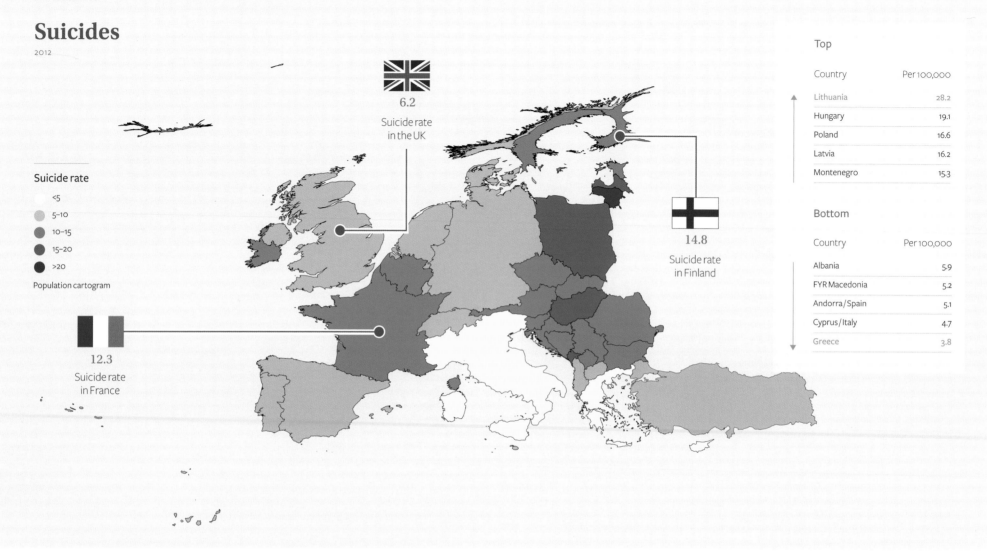

Suicide rate

- <5
- 5–10
- 10–15
- 15–20
- >20

Population cartogram

6.2
Suicide rate
in the UK

14.8
Suicide rate
in Finland

12.3
Suicide rate
in France

Top

Country	Per 100,000
Lithuania	28.2
Hungary	19.1
Poland	16.6
Latvia	16.2
Montenegro	15.3

Bottom

Country	Per 100,000
Albania	5.9
FYR Macedonia	5.2
Andorra / Spain	5.1
Cyprus / Italy	4.7
Greece	3.8

Estimated numbers of suicides are shown here per 100,000 people for each country.

The highest rates are generally found in Northern and Eastern Europe, including the Baltic States and in particular Lithuania, which has the highest rate. These tend to be places that have been affected by severe austerity measures in the early 2010s. Rates have also been higher in France for many years compared to nearby countries.

Greece, Italy and Cyprus had the lowest rates in Europe, despite being severely affected by the economic recession and austerity measures since 2009, although it is likely that these rates have been rising since 2012, particularly among the poorest and most disadvantaged.

According to media reports at the time of writing, there has been a considerable increase in the number of suicides in the UK, which may be linked to the government's review of work capability assessments for sick and disabled people.

Religious belief may make suicide less common, or suicides may be under-reported due to lack of acceptance in religious countries.

Total health spending

2014

An estimated total of US$1.9 trillion was spent on health across all countries included in this atlas in 2014.

One-fifth of this expenditure was in Germany, followed by France, the UK and Italy. In relative terms (per capita), however, none of these countries is in the top five for expenditure, which includes some of the most affluent countries in Europe and in the world, such as Norway.

The countries with the lowest per capita expenditure are mostly found in Eastern Europe.

Colour key, see Reference map A1, p 10

Health spending in the UK was equivalent to

9.1%

of GDP

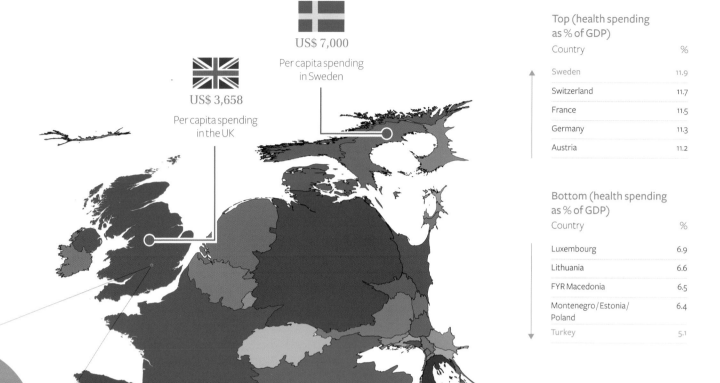

US$ 7,000
Per capita spending in Sweden

US$ 3,658
Per capita spending in the UK

Top (health spending as % of GDP)

Country	%
Sweden	11.9
Switzerland	11.7
France	11.5
Germany	11.3
Austria	11.2

Bottom (health spending as % of GDP)

Country	%
Luxembourg	6.9
Lithuania	6.6
FYR Macedonia	6.5
Montenegro/Estonia/Poland	6.4
Turkey	5.1

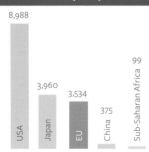

HEALTH SPENDING PER CAPITA (US$)

USA	Japan	EU	China	Sub-Saharan Africa
8,988	3,960	3,534	375	99

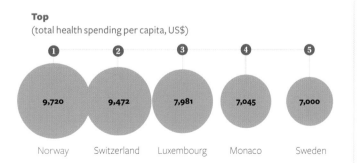

Top
(total health spending per capita, US$)

❶	❷	❸	❹	❺
9,720	9,472	7,981	7,045	7,000
Norway	Switzerland	Luxembourg	Monaco	Sweden

Bottom
(total health spending per capita, US$)

❺	❹	❸	❷	❶
535	454	449	316	253
Romania	Montenegro	Bosnia-Herzegovina	FYR Macedonia	Albania

Public/private share of health spending

2013

Public/private health spending as % of total health spending

● ● Public
○ ○ Private

	11.8 Monaco 88.2	12.2 San Marino 87.8	14.5 Norway 85.5	14.6 Denmark 85.4
	16.3 Luxembourg 83.7	16.5 UK 83.5	22.5 France 77.5	39.5 Serbia 60.5
	40.7 Bulgaria 59.3	42.7 Montenegro 57.3	48.4 Albania 51.6	46.3 Cyprus 53.7

$

HEALTH SPENDING IN PUBLIC SECTOR

US$1.5 trillion

IN EUROPE

$

HEALTH SPENDING IN PRIVATE SECTOR

US$0.45 trillion

IN EUROPE

The proportion of health spending in the public sector varies widely. Despite the reputation of the UK's public National Health Service, many other countries, including those shown here, as well as the other Scandinavian countries and Switzerland, spent a higher proportion of total health spending in the public sector.

Lower public health spending tends to be a feature of poverty and/or of more individualistic and less well-planned societies.

In Albania and Cyprus private spending accounts for more than 50% of total health expenditure, significantly above the EU average (22%) and the world average (40%), and similar to the level of private spending in the US (52%).

The relative level of private health expenditure tends to be low (much less than 50% of the total) in countries with 'very high human development' (according to the United Nations), such as Japan, where it was 18%.

In some countries, although spending may be classified as private, there can often be strong public control over how this private spending is regulated. In contrast, in other countries such as the UK, private healthcare firms may be far less well regulated, and there are often concerns about mortality rates in private hospitals for essentially low-risk procedures.

Doctors (national)

2010

The number of doctors in each country is shown here per 100,000 of the population.

There are an estimated 1,900,000 doctors in Europe, and about 300,000 of them work and live in Germany, which has the highest absolute number. However, in relative terms, the most doctors are found in San Marino (4,735 per 100,000 population), followed by Greece (617).

Within any one country access to doctors will vary. In some countries doctors will be relatively evenly spread across the population, available roughly equally to all potential patients, or may be located where more people tend to be ill. In other countries they will be more concentrated in more affluent areas, and so those who are better off will find accessing a doctor easier. In this case, we would expect mortality rates to be higher in countries where access to health services is harder to secure, and where there are fewer services (in this case, doctors) available.

Another factor to consider is the number of doctors working in primary care and the numbers based in hospitals, as well as the contribution made by other medical personnel. In some countries, for example, doctors are hardly ever involved in childbirth, which is midwife-led.

Colour key, see Reference map A1, p 10

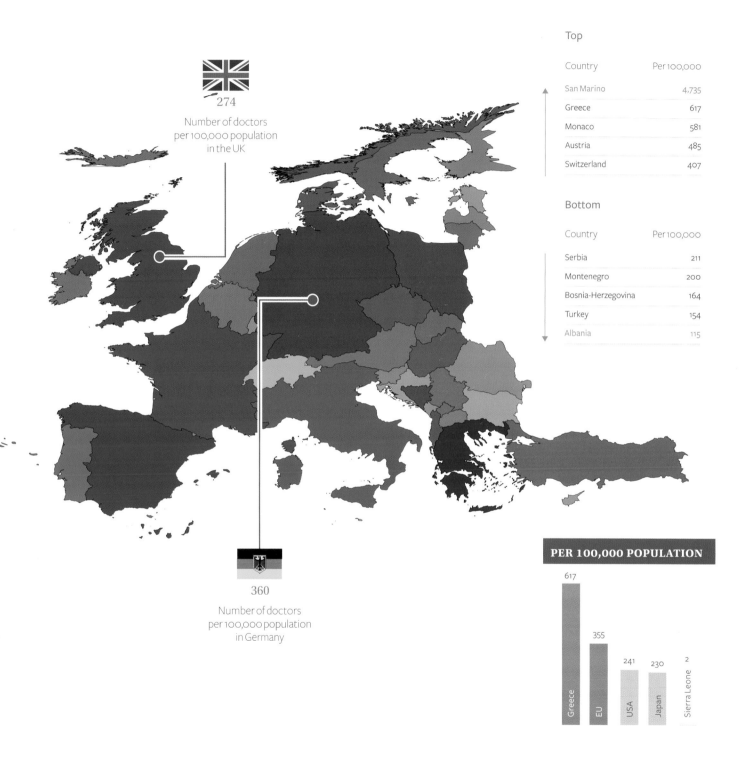

274

Number of doctors
per 100,000 population
in the UK

360

Number of doctors
per 100,000 population
in Germany

Top

Country	Per 100,000
San Marino	4,735
Greece	617
Monaco	581
Austria	485
Switzerland	407

Bottom

Country	Per 100,000
Serbia	211
Montenegro	200
Bosnia-Herzegovina	164
Turkey	154
Albania	115

PER 100,000 POPULATION

Greece	EU	USA	Japan	Sierra Leone
617	355	241	230	2

Dentists

2009/10

There were an estimated 350,000 dentistry personnel working in Europe in 2010, and these were mostly dentists.

Dentists appear more evenly distributed than nurses and midwives, but less so than doctors.

Different countries have different traditions of what aspects of healthcare they prioritise, and this map largely reflects these historical factors. Again, within any country, provision may not be even – wealthier people may find it easier to gain access to dentists than others, and where this is the case many dentists may be working mostly on cosmetic treatment.

However, when there is a saturation of dentists, such as in Greece, you would hope that the overall high level of availability means that fewer people suffer from lack of access, whereas in Montenegro you would expect the few dentists there to concentrate mostly on emergencies, but this may not be the case.

Dental costs and quality of treatment can vary dramatically between countries, which may result in the ridiculous but ever more common example of people flying to another country for dental treatment.

Colour key, see Reference map A1, p 10

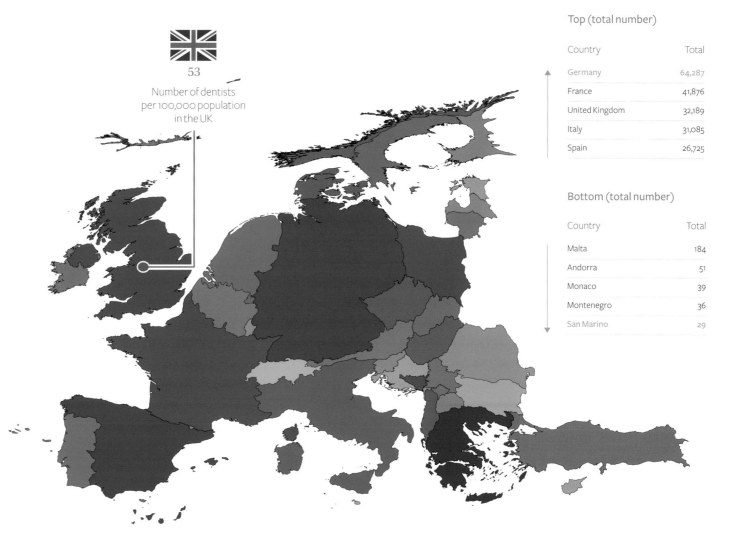

53

Number of dentists
per 100,000 population
in the UK

Top (total number)

Country	Total
Germany	64,287
France	41,876
United Kingdom	32,189
Italy	31,085
Spain	26,725

Bottom (total number)

Country	Total
Malta	184
Andorra	51
Monaco	39
Montenegro	36
San Marino	29

Top (dentists per 100,000)

Country	Per 100,000
Greece	132
Iceland	102
Cyprus	92
Estonia	91
Norway	89

Bottom (dentists per 100,000)

Country	Per 100,000
Poland	32
Turkey	27
Serbia	23
Bosnia-Herzegovina	17
Montenegro	6

Health professionals

2014

Top (nurses and midwives)

Country	Per 100,000
Norway	1,744
Luxembourg	1,232
Ireland	1,193
Sweden	1,192
Germany	1,139

Bottom (nurses and midwives)

Country	Per 100,000
Slovenia	251
Greece	206
Croatia	157
Serbia	113
Romania	73

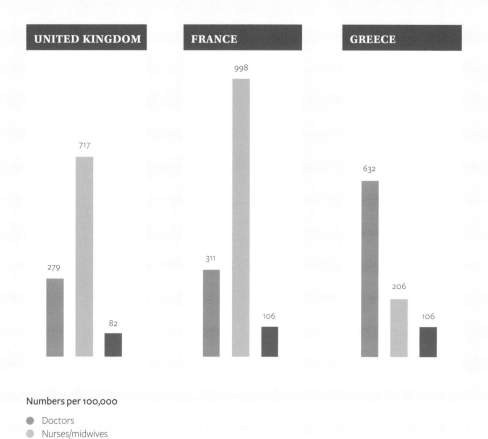

UNITED KINGDOM   **FRANCE**   **GREECE**

United Kingdom: 279, 717, 82
France: 311, 998, 106
Greece: 632, 206, 106

Numbers per 100,000

- Doctors
- Nurses/midwives
- Pharmacists

Top (pharmacists)

Country	Per 100,000
Finland	127
Belgium	120
Ireland	118
Spain	117
Malta	115

Bottom (pharmacists)

Country	Per 100,000
Turkey	35
Serbia	33
Netherlands	27
Cyprus	22
Montenegro	17

In 2014, Germany had the highest number of practising nurses (900,000), followed by France (640,000) and the UK (430,000). The highest number of midwives was to be found in the UK (32,000).

In relative terms, the highest ratio of nurses and midwives is found in Northern Europe. Some smaller countries with more doctors have fewer nurses, and doctors may deliver babies rather than midwives, but other factors that may explain this pattern include: income and wealth; an older, frailer population needing more care; whether care tends to be provided in hospitals or in the community; and how primary healthcare is provided (numbers of nurses based in local health centres).

Where nurse and doctor numbers are low, pharmacists might be taking a bigger role in helping families to access medicines and advice.

There were over 440,000 pharmacists working in the EU in 2014, with the largest numbers in France (70,000) and Italy (65,000).

Different definitions of 'pharmacist' may apply in different jurisdictions, and pharmacist qualifications may still vary quite widely across Europe, especially for older practitioners.

Doctors (regional)

REGIONAL MAP, 2012

Practising doctors per 100,000 people

- ○ <200
- ○ 200–300
- ● 300–400
- ● 400–500
- ● >500
- ○ no data

Population cartogram

275

Practising doctors per 100,000 population in the UK

622

Practising doctors per 100,000 people in Crete

Top (practising doctors)

Region	Per 100,000
Ceuta (ES)	871
Attica (GR)	834
Bratislava (SK)	681
Prague (CZ)	679
Vienna (AT)	664

Bottom (practising doctors)

Region	Per 100,000
Hatay, Kahramanmaraş, Osmaniye (TR)	122
Van, Muş, Bitlis, Hakkâri (TR)	112
Ağrı, Kars, Iğdır, Ardahan (TR)	106
Mardin, Batman, Şırnak, Siirt (TR)	99

The number of practising doctors across the European regions is shown here per 100,000 of the population.

The regions with the highest rates comprise the tiny Spanish territory in Northern Africa, Ceuta, followed by four capital city regions.

The number of physicians working in the UK, a richer country than much of Europe, is very low when measured per person, especially in England (and even in London now). While not as low as in Turkey or in other parts of Eastern Europe, the low numbers in the UK contrast with better provision in neighbouring affluent countries.

One reason that some countries have fewer doctors may be that more nurses and (in particular) midwives take on more specialised tasks that are carried out by doctors in other countries.

Note also that the numbers of physicians in some capital cities are often higher than in the surrounding regions.

Hospital beds

REGIONAL MAP, 2012

281

Hospital beds
per 100,000
in the UK

**Hospital beds
per 100,000 people**

- ⬜ <250
- ⬜ 250–500
- ⬜ 500–750
- ⬛ 750–1000
- ⬛ >1000
- ⭕ no data

Population cartogram

Top

Region	Per 100,000
Mecklenburg-Vorpommern (DE)	1,276
West Pomeranian (PL)	1,194
Thuringia (DE)	999
Bucharest (RO)	982
Salzburg (AT)	959

Bottom

Region	Per 100,000
Van, Muş, Bitlis, Hakkâri (GR)	195
Central Greece (GR) / Hatay, Kahramanmaraş, Osmaniye (TR)	189
Ağrı, Kars, Iğdır (TR)	181
Mardin, Batman, Şırnak, Siirt (TR)	99

The numbers of hospital beds provided per 100,000 people in the local population are shown across European regions, at coarser levels in Germany, and only at national level in the UK and the Netherlands.

The regions with higher levels than the EU average (534 hospital beds per 100,000) are mostly found in Germany, France, Poland, Romania and Austria.

The regions with the lowest levels are mostly found in Southern Europe, particularly in Turkey, Greece, Italy and Spain.

Throughout Europe, there is a general urban/rural divide that could be explained to some extent by the presence of specialised hospitals in the big cities. Rates are especially low in Southern Spain, in Istanbul and

Eastern Turkey, and in Stockholm, which may provide more support for people to be treated at home.

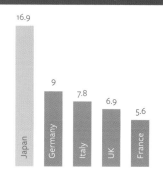

AVERAGE LENGTH OF STAY IN HOSPITAL BED (ALL CAUSES, DAYS)

Japan	Germany	Italy	UK	France
16.9	9	7.8	6.9	5.6

E – Education

Promoting equity in education and training is consistent with the European welfare state model, with part of the Europe 2020 Strategy aiming to significantly reduce numbers of early leavers from education and increase numbers of graduates with a university degree, for example. The maps that follow give a flavour of social and spatial disparities in educational attainment and learning across Europe's countries and regions.

- A **general picture of education levels** across the whole population is provided, showing that opportunities for (and benefits from) learning are far from equally distributed. As the **chances of attending university** remain socially and spatially divided, in some countries like the UK these disparities have been increased with the introduction of significantly high levels of tuition fees and the perseverance of private schooling.
- **Participation in early years education** is explored by looking at the numbers of children attending some form of pre-school education, such as kindergarten, nursery, playgroup or other form of early educational activity.
- With geographical inequalities increasing as a result of highly qualified Europeans migrating from regions hit hardest by the economic crisis towards regions with lower unemployment (mostly in Northern and Western Europe), and investments in higher education made by more Eastern and Southern countries in the past decades now benefiting Europe as a whole, **outcomes** for young people are paramount.
- As growing numbers of young people are **studying abroad**, including exchange students, their mobility contributes to the formation and bolstering of a European identity, both in the receiving countries as well as among the migrating populations.

No schooling

2010

This map analyses the numbers of people living in each country who have had little or no formal education ('no schooling').

The meaning of 'no schooling' can range from 'arrived from outside Europe having never been to school' to 'hardly ever attended school', which will be the case for many older people in many parts of Europe where farming was a major employment sector, through to 'attended school but achieved so little that in terms of educational benefit, it is as if the person never attended'.

Turkey dominates the map as it has the highest number of people with no formal schooling, followed by Italy, Germany, Portugal and Spain. However, in relative terms, Portugal has the most people with no schooling as a percentage of the total population aged 15 and over.

Colour key, see Reference map A1, p 10

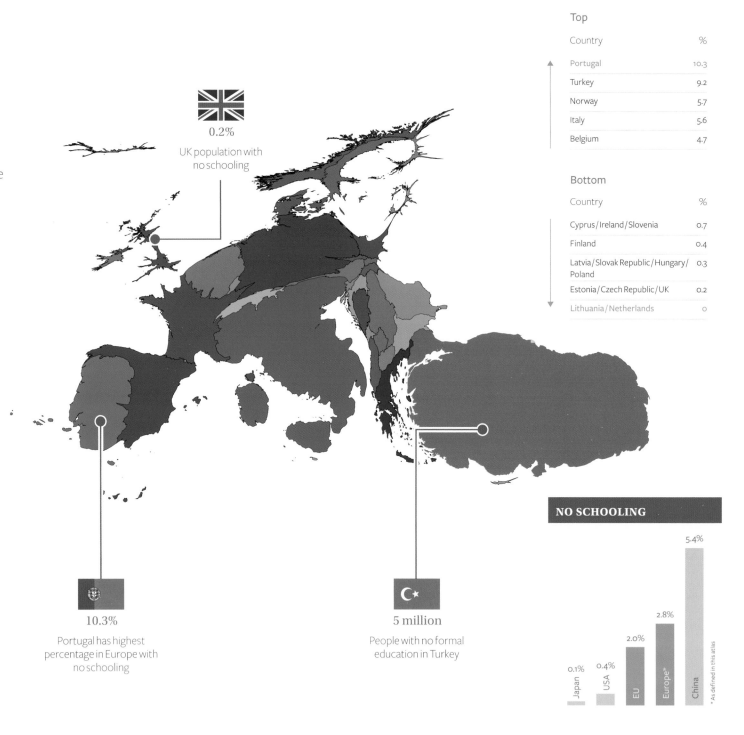

0.2%

UK population with no schooling

10.3%

Portugal has highest percentage in Europe with no schooling

5 million

People with no formal education in Turkey

Top

Country	%
Portugal	10.3
Turkey	9.2
Norway	5.7
Italy	5.6
Belgium	4.7

Bottom

Country	%
Cyprus / Ireland / Slovenia	0.7
Finland	0.4
Latvia / Slovak Republic / Hungary / Poland	0.3
Estonia / Czech Republic / UK	0.2
Lithuania / Netherlands	0

NO SCHOOLING

- Japan 0.1%
- USA 0.4%
- EU 2.0%
- Europe* 2.8%
- China 5.4%

* As defined in this atlas

Primary only education

2010

This map shows how the estimated 73 million Europeans aged 15 and over who had only benefited from, at most, a primary school education were spread across the continent.

Most will now be elderly, and as they die, the total numbers should be expected to fall. In relative terms, the highest rates of people receiving only primary school education were mostly found in the South of Europe, but Finland and Iceland were also in the top five countries due to the poor provision of education there many decades ago.

Secondary education will have been made more widely available earlier in those countries with the lowest proportions of people who did not progress beyond a primary education.

Turkey has the highest number in absolute terms (nearly 21 million) followed by Italy, France and Spain (7 to 8 million) and the UK (6 million).

Worldwide the highest rates are found in Sub-Saharan Africa, in particular Tanzania (50.2%).

Colour key, see Reference map A1, p 10

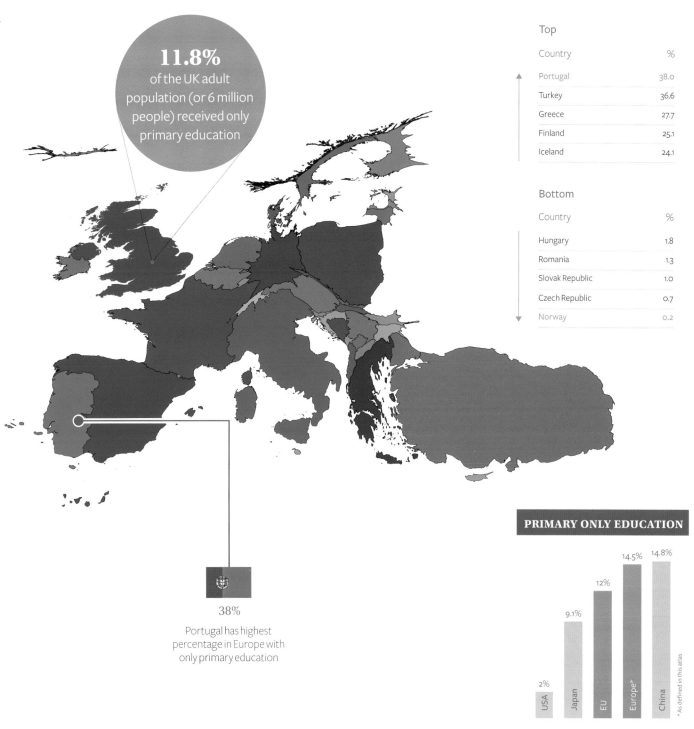

11.8% of the UK adult population (or 6 million people) received only primary education

38%
Portugal has highest percentage in Europe with only primary education

Top

Country	%
Portugal	38.0
Turkey	36.6
Greece	27.7
Finland	25.1
Iceland	24.1

Bottom

Country	%
Hungary	1.8
Romania	1.3
Slovak Republic	1.0
Czech Republic	0.7
Norway	0.2

PRIMARY ONLY EDUCATION

USA	Japan	EU	Europe*	China
2%	9.1%	12%	14.5%	14.8%

* As defined in this atlas

Secondary only education

2010

In 2010 Europe had an estimated 202 million people aged 15 and over who did not proceed beyond secondary education, and this map shows how they are spread.

Among older Europeans, completion of secondary education is the most common situation in Europe today. Of the 43 countries mapped in this atlas, there were 24 with a rate of over 40% of the population having completed, but not progressed beyond, secondary education. The UK is among these, with an estimated 47.3%.

Because access to education has been changing so quickly, this map is as much a map of older Europeans as it is a map that reveals which areas have provided less access to tertiary or vocational education in recent years.

In future a much higher proportion of Europeans will have gone to university than is depicted on this map. However, although most will have attended for free or at a very low tuition cost, a few will now owe very large debts to the state simply as a result of having gone on to tertiary education after secondary level.

Colour key, see Reference map A1, p 10

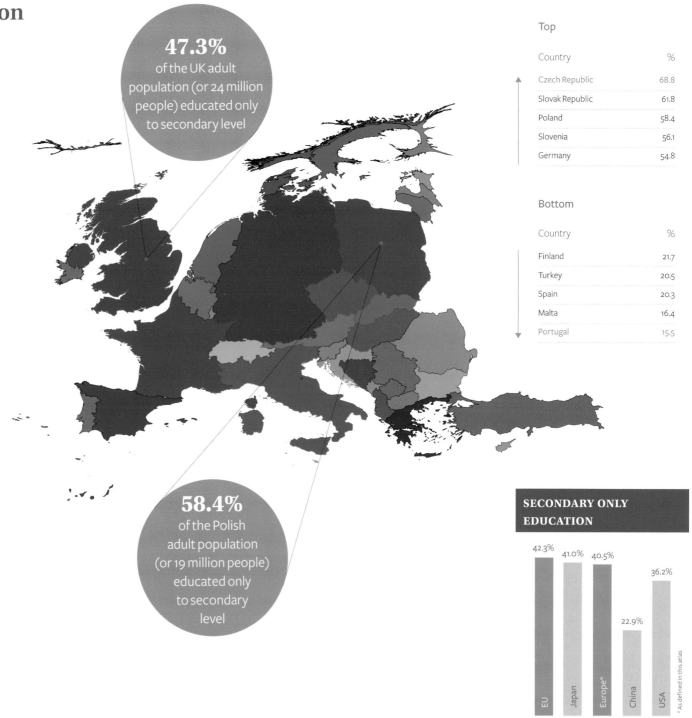

47.3% of the UK adult population (or 24 million people) educated only to secondary level

58.4% of the Polish adult population (or 19 million people) educated only to secondary level

Top	
Country	%
Czech Republic	68.8
Slovak Republic	61.8
Poland	58.4
Slovenia	56.1
Germany	54.8

Bottom	
Country	%
Finland	21.7
Turkey	20.5
Spain	20.3
Malta	16.4
Portugal	15.5

SECONDARY ONLY EDUCATION

42.3%	41.0%	40.5%	22.9%	36.2%
EU	Japan	Europe*	China	USA

* As defined in this atlas

Tertiary education

2010

This map shows the spread of all those holding a university degree or equivalent across Europe – 57 million had completed tertiary education by the first decade of the 21st century. This number is rising rapidly. This group currently represents 11.4% of all Europeans aged 15 and over, and very soon, possibly as you read this, it will exceed a fifth, as older people who are very unlikely to have attended university die.

Germany and the UK dominate the map. In relative terms, however, the highest rates are found in medium and small-sized countries, such as Ireland and Greece.

In 16 out of the 43 countries mapped in this atlas 15% or more of the adult population have completed tertiary education, which includes the UK, at 15.3%.

The highest rate in the world was recorded in the Republic of Korea at 30% and the lowest in Guatemala, near to 0%.

In future, by 2030 or 2040, it is almost certain that leaving university after completing tertiary education will be the normal point for the majority of young people across Europe to end their education. It is surprising that we find this hard to imagine given how much has changed in the past century.

Colour key, see Reference map A1, p 10

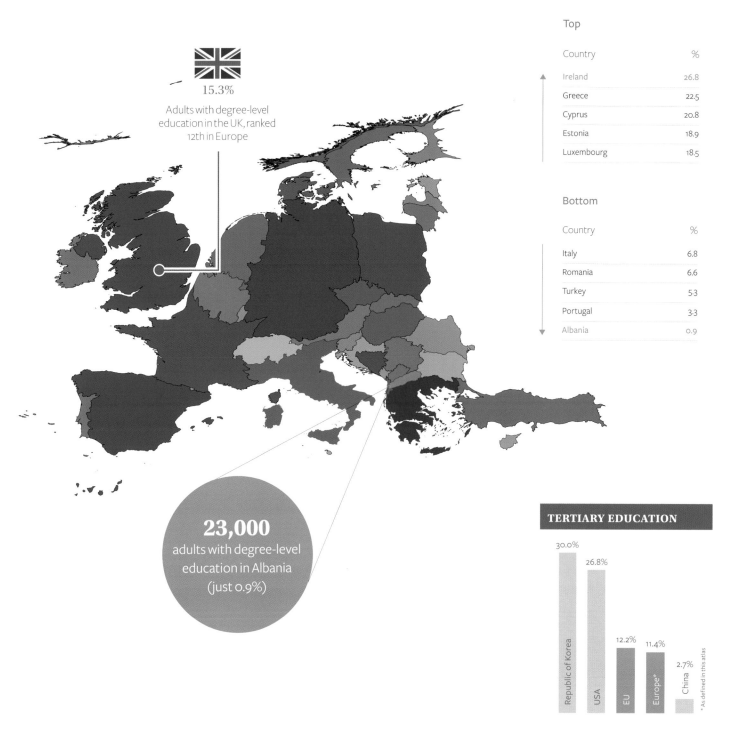

15.3%

Adults with degree-level education in the UK, ranked 12th in Europe

23,000 adults with degree-level education in Albania (just 0.9%)

Top

Country	%
Ireland	26.8
Greece	22.5
Cyprus	20.8
Estonia	18.9
Luxembourg	18.5

Bottom

Country	%
Italy	6.8
Romania	6.6
Turkey	5.3
Portugal	3.3
Albania	0.9

TERTIARY EDUCATION

- Republic of Korea 30.0%
- USA 26.8%
- EU 12.2%
- Europe* 11.4%
- China 2.7%

* As defined in this atlas

Graduates (aged 30–34)

REGIONAL MAP, 2014

31.6%

Lancashire is the UK region with fewest graduates aged 30–34

Graduates aged 30–34
(% of 30–34 population)

- <25
- 25–30
- 30–40
- 40–50
- >50
- no data

Population cartogram

Top

Region	%
Inner London (UK)	67.3
Oslo and Akershus (NO)	62.6
North Eastern Scotland (UK)	60.7
Midi-Pyrénées (FR)	60.6
Hovedstaden (DK)	58.7

Bottom

Region	%
Hatay, Kahramanmaraş, Osmaniye (TR)	14.5
Van, Muş, Bitlis, Hakkâri (TR)	10.4
Ağrı, Kars, Iğdır, Ardahan (TR)	10.2
Şanlıurfa, Diyarbakır (TR)	10.1
Mardin, Batman, Şırnak, Siirt (TR)	8.8

54.0%
of 30- to 34-year-olds with degree-level education in Madrid

45.7%
of 30- to 34-year-olds with degree-level education in Attica (Athens city region)

One of the key policy targets of the EU (as part of its Europe 2020 Strategy) is that by 2020 at least 40% of all 30- to 34-year-olds will have completed a qualification at tertiary or equivalent level. The estimated numbers having achieved this level (mostly with a university degree or equivalent) in 2014 are shown here as a percentage of the total population aged 30–34.

At EU level the estimated rate was 37.9%, not far off the 2020 target. Overall, the highest rates were mostly found in the UK (Inner London had by far the highest rate), the Scandinavian countries, France and Spain. The migration of graduates to the UK in recent years and especially to London made this possible.

Those regions with very high rates now include Cyprus and Lithuania, as well as the Slovak capital city region of Bratislava and the Polish capital city region of Warsaw (Mazovia).

Rates are very low where little tertiary education is offered, and in other places, particularly Southern and Eastern European regions, where large numbers of young adults who receive a higher education then decide to move away (the 'brain drain').

Raising graduate numbers

REGIONAL MAP, 2008–14

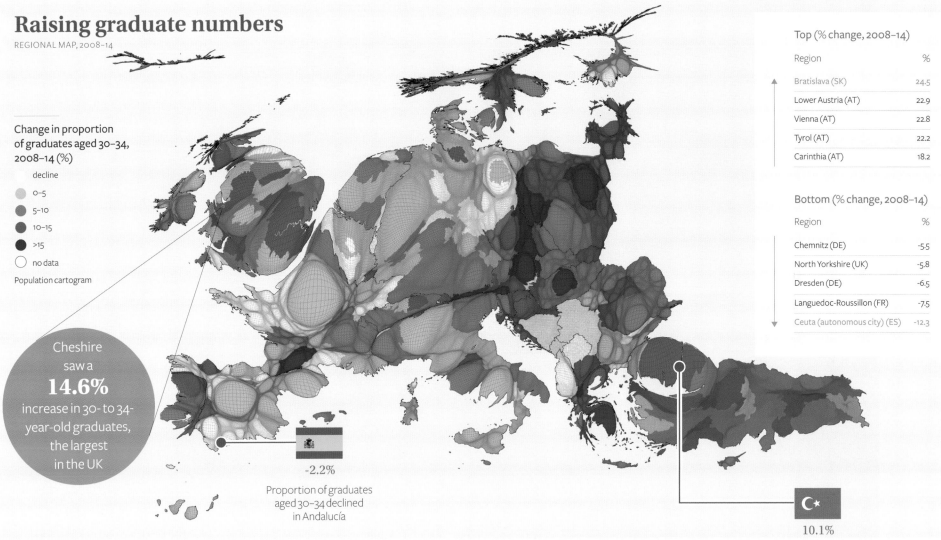

Change in proportion of graduates aged 30–34, 2008–14 (%)

- decline
- 0–5
- 5–10
- 10–15
- >15
- no data

Population cartogram

Cheshire saw a **14.6%** increase in 30- to 34-year-old graduates, the largest in the UK

-2.2%

Proportion of graduates aged 30–34 declined in Andalucía

10.1%

Increase in 30- to 34-year-old graduates in Istanbul

Top (% change, 2008–14)

Region	%
Bratislava (SK)	24.5
Lower Austria (AT)	22.9
Vienna (AT)	22.8
Tyrol (AT)	22.2
Carinthia (AT)	18.2

Bottom (% change, 2008–14)

Region	%
Chemnitz (DE)	-5.5
North Yorkshire (UK)	-5.8
Dresden (DE)	-6.5
Languedoc-Roussillon (FR)	-7.5
Ceuta (autonomous city) (ES)	-12.3

This map shows how the percentage of 30- to 34-year-olds with a university degree or equivalent changed between the years 2008 and 2014. The progress made by European regions towards the EU's policy target, set out in the Europe 2020 Strategy (for at least 40% of all 30- to 34-year-olds in Europe to have completed tertiary or equivalent education by 2020) is clear.

The regions with the highest increases are mostly found in Austria, the Czech Republic, Hungary, Poland, Slovak Republic, Greece, Turkey and the UK. Within the UK these areas now include Greater Manchester (+14.2%), Cheshire (+14.6%), Gloucestershire (+13.1%) and Cumbria (+12.9%).

On the other hand, there was a decline in 41 regions, mostly found in Spain, France and Germany (and in particular, the regions in the East of Germany).

However, four of the regions with a declining share of this age group having these qualifications were in the UK: North Yorkshire (–5.8%), Devon (–3.1%), Northumberland and Tyne and Wear (–2.4%) and East Yorkshire and Northern Lincolnshire (–1.2%).

Students

REGIONAL MAP, 2010

Students in tertiary education, as % of total population aged 20–24

- ⚪ <39.3
- ⚪ 39.3–47.4
- ⚫ 47.4–54.7
- ⚫ 54.7–69.3
- ⚫ >69.3
- ⚪ no data

Population cartogram

59.6%
students in London as % of resident population aged 20–24

36.6%
students in Yorkshire and the Humber as % of resident population aged 20–24

Top

Region	%
Bucharest (RO)	202.9
Prague (CZ)	197.2
Bratislava (SK)	185.8
Vienna (AT)	149.7
Brussels-Capital (BE)	130.3

Bottom

Region	%
Bolzano (IT)	9.6
Şanlıurfa (TR)	9.0
Central Bohemia (CZ)	5.2
North West Bulgaria (BG)	4.3
Mardin (TR)	3.5

The areas with the highest proportions of students tend to be those comprising Europe's large cities and city regions. London is an exception, as it no longer has as many undergraduate students studying there as other large European cities.

This is a map of students as a percentage of the total population aged 20–24. The reported share can often be higher than 100%, where there are more students who study and live in a city in term time than the numbers of 20- to 24-year-olds that the city officially houses. Also many students are counted who are aged 18, 19 or over 24.

The highest rates were mostly found in regions of Romania, Poland, Greece and the Scandinavian countries, but the Czech Republic, Slovak Republic, Austria, Belgium, Spain and Portugal also scored highly.

The areas with the lowest rates were mostly found in Turkey and Italy, but also in Austria.

Often areas with very high rates are surrounded by areas with very low rates from which young people move to study at university.

Vocational programmes

REGIONAL MAP, 2013

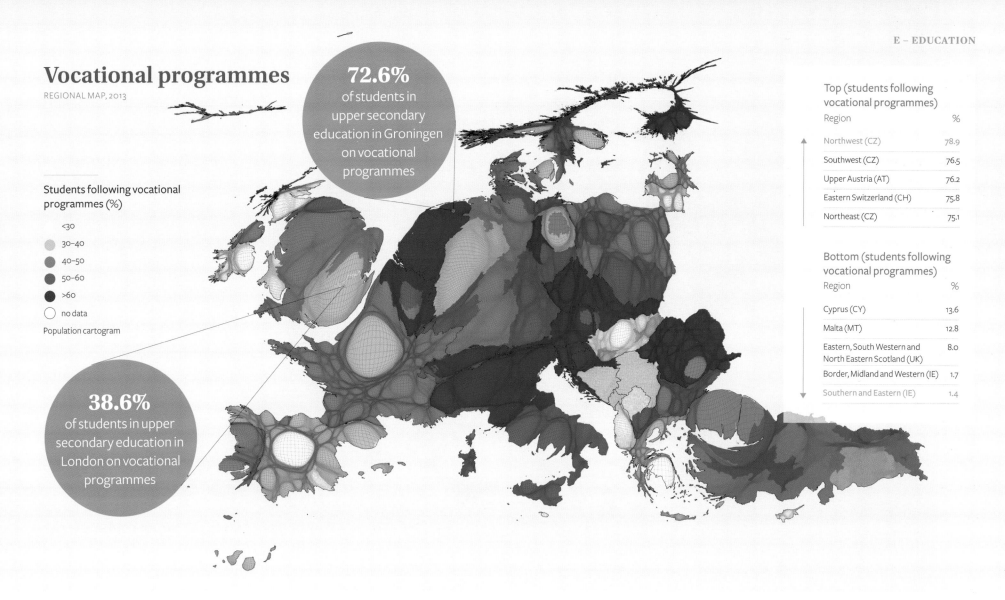

72.6% of students in upper secondary education in Groningen on vocational programmes

38.6% of students in upper secondary education in London on vocational programmes

Students following vocational programmes (%)

- <30
- 30–40
- 40–50
- 50–60
- >60
- no data

Population cartogram

Top (students following vocational programmes)

Region	%
Northwest (CZ)	78.9
Southwest (CZ)	76.5
Upper Austria (AT)	76.2
Eastern Switzerland (CH)	75.8
Northeast (CZ)	75.1

Bottom (students following vocational programmes)

Region	%
Cyprus (CY)	13.6
Malta (MT)	12.8
Eastern, South Western and North Eastern Scotland (UK)	8.0
Border, Midland and Western (IE)	1.7
Southern and Eastern (IE)	1.4

This map shows the number of young people undertaking vocational training as a percentage of all students in upper secondary education (typically, the last stage of secondary education, beginning at age 15/16).

Data was only available for larger regions in the UK and Germany, and for Croatia there was only national-level data. The EU rate is 48.9%. The areas with the highest rates are mostly found in the North of Italy and in Central and Eastern Europe, but also in Denmark, the Netherlands and Finland.

The lowest rates are mostly found in the Republic of Ireland, Scotland, Malta, Cyprus, but also in Greece, Hungary, Lithuania, and Wales.

Rates in Scotland may be especially low because Scottish schools tend to include a much higher proportion of children in academic study. Scotland continues to value academic education more highly than other parts of the UK, with free university tuition for students in Scotland (as is the case in most of the rest of Europe).

In a few regions of Europe, rates of vocational education exceed 60% of all young people. In almost all cases this is high-quality vocational education.

Early leavers from education and training

REGIONAL MAP, 2014

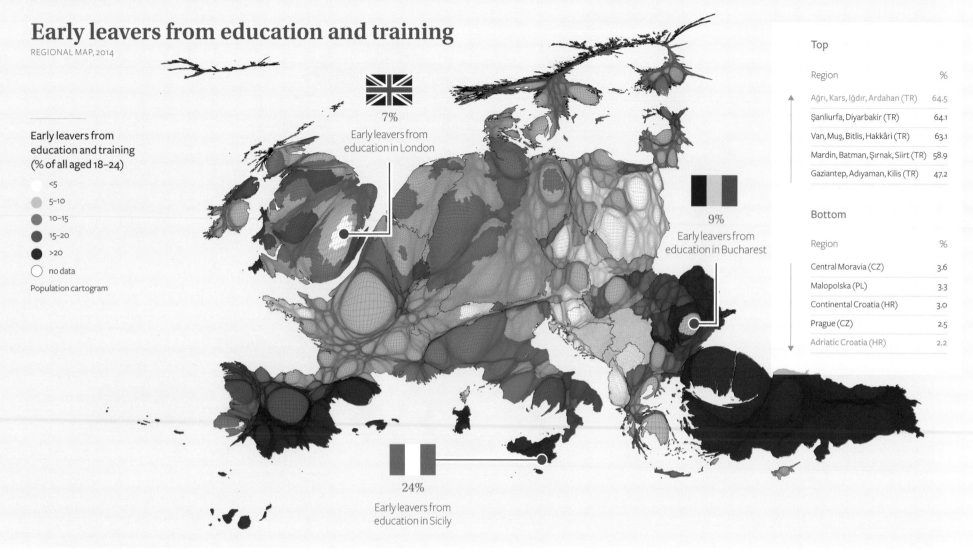

Early leavers from education and training (% of all aged 18–24)

- <5
- 5–10
- 10–15
- 15–20
- >20
- no data

Population cartogram

7%

Early leavers from education in London

9%

Early leavers from education in Bucharest

24%

Early leavers from education in Sicily

Top

Region	%
Ağrı, Kars, Iğdır, Ardahan (TR)	64.5
Şanlıurfa, Diyarbakir (TR)	64.1
Van, Muş, Bitlis, Hakkâri (TR)	63.1
Mardin, Batman, Şırnak, Siirt (TR)	58.9
Gaziantep, Adıyaman, Kilis (TR)	47.2

Bottom

Region	%
Central Moravia (CZ)	3.6
Malopolska (PL)	3.3
Continental Croatia (HR)	3.0
Prague (CZ)	2.5
Adriatic Croatia (HR)	2.2

On average, 11% of the EU's 18- to 24-year-olds leave education early, having attained at most a lower secondary education, without moving on to further education or training. This map shows where the highest and lowest concentrations of these early leavers are to be found.

All regions in Turkey have very high rates, all above 20%, and there are four regions in Eastern Turkey with rates of over 50%. Outside Turkey, there are areas with high rates in Eastern Europe (in particular, Romania and Bulgaria) and Spain, but also in Italy (the island region of Sicily), Portugal (the remote island region of the Azores), and the UK (Cornwall and the Isles of Scilly).

A desire to leave an area might be an incentive for young people to stay on in education, either leaving to attend or after finishing university, whereas growing up in regions where their labour is needed, or simply where it is nicer to stay, might encourage an earlier exit from formal education or training.

A more interesting education and more engaging and exciting schools should also encourage children to stay on and not leave as soon as they are able to.

Children in pre-school

REGIONAL MAP, 2013

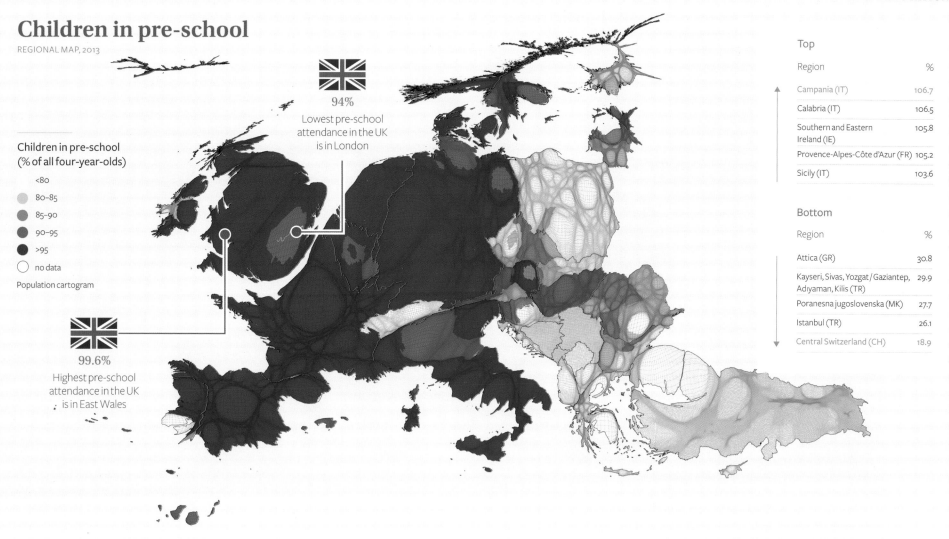

Children in pre-school
(% of all four-year-olds)

- <80
- 80–85
- 85–90
- 90–95
- >95
- no data

Population cartogram

94%
Lowest pre-school
attendance in the UK
is in London

99.6%
Highest pre-school
attendance in the UK
is in East Wales

Top

Region	%
Campania (IT)	106.7
Calabria (IT)	106.5
Southern and Eastern Ireland (IE)	105.8
Provence-Alpes-Côte d'Azur (FR)	105.2
Sicily (IT)	103.6

Bottom

Region	%
Attica (GR)	30.8
Kayseri, Sivas, Yozgat / Gaziantep, Adıyaman, Kilis (TR)	29.9
Poranesna jugoslovenska (MK)	27.7
Istanbul (TR)	26.1
Central Switzerland (CH)	18.9

The participation rates of children in pre-primary and primary education across European regions (as a percentage of all four-year-olds) are shown here.

At EU level, the rate is 91.8%. Almost all pre-school children attend some kind of kindergarten, nursery, playgroup or other form of early educational activity. The highest rates are generally observed in Central, Northern and Western Europe (with the exception of Switzerland, Western Ireland and Southern Portugal), whereas most of the regions with the lowest participation rates are found in Turkey and across South East and Eastern Europe.

There is an ongoing debate as to how beneficial formal primary and pre-primary education is for young children, and whether they are not better served by having more opportunities to play rather than learn. In Finland the age at which children start school is six, and the officially measured rate of pre-school education is low, but Finnish children rank among the best in the world for educational outcomes later on.

Areas with the highest pre-school attendance may be providing collective care for young children not so much for the educational benefits but so that both the parents can work.

CHILDREN AGED FOUR ENROLLED IN SOME FORM OF PRE-SCHOOL EDUCATION

5 million

IN EUROPE

Studying abroad: incoming students

2012

An estimated 743,100 European students were enrolled in tertiary education at a university in a different country from their country of origin in 2012. Over a quarter of these students were in the UK, and numbers continue to rise, despite high UK tuition fees.

Germany, Austria and France also host large numbers of incoming students, but their tuition fees are much lower (and in some cases zero). Overall, the pattern shown here is not surprising given that the official languages spoken in these countries are those most frequently taught and learned as a foreign language across Europe, and English is the most commonly used language of all. However, these patterns may change in the near future, given the result of the 2016 UK referendum on EU membership and the ensuing uncertainty.

There are relatively high numbers of incoming students to Austria, which may be attracting students from countries with strong linguistic and cultural links, possibly related to the imperial legacy of the Austrian-Hungarian empire.

Student mobility has increased greatly since the start of the EU Erasmus student exchange programme in 1987 (now Erasmus+). These young Europeans are often described as the 'emerging Erasmus generation', a group with an enhanced, collective European identity.

Colour key, see Reference map A1, p 10

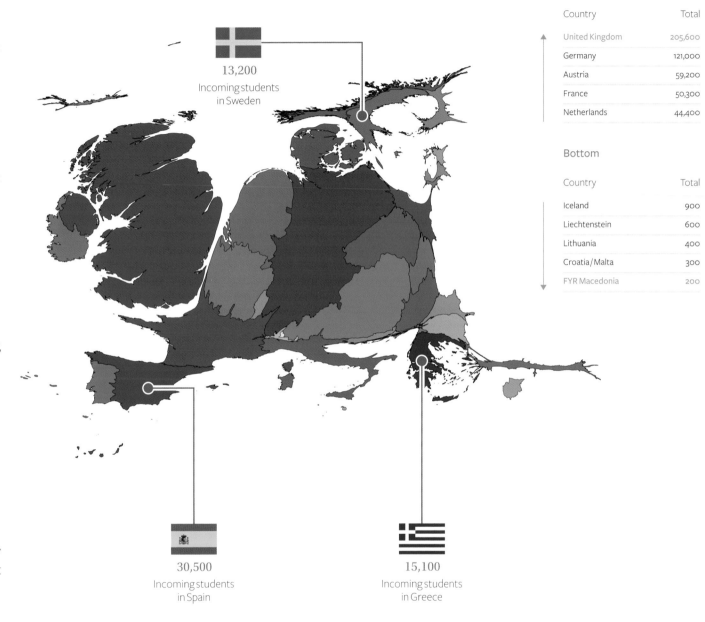

13,200
Incoming students
in Sweden

30,500
Incoming students
in Spain

15,100
Incoming students
in Greece

Studying abroad: outgoing students

2012

This map shows all European university students who were studying elsewhere in Europe in 2012 by country of origin.

Germany had the highest number of outgoing students, followed by Turkey and France. Cyprus, Greece and Portugal also have relatively large numbers of outgoing students, especially when their total population is considered.

A relatively small number of students go abroad to study from the UK, given its total population, although the UK is the most popular destination for students from overseas. This is especially interesting because the cost of higher education in the UK is currently far higher than in almost any other European country.

The cost of studying also varies within the UK. Students travelling from the rest of the EU to Scotland still benefit from 'normal' (near-free) education costs, but English, Welsh and Northern Irish students do not. They would have to travel outside of the UK to benefit from such low tuition fees. Perhaps language proficiency holds them back or perhaps they are simply not aware of the possibilities of studying abroad.

Even if free movement of students is lost after the UK leaves the EU, it may still be cheaper for UK students to study in many areas of mainland Europe as foreign students.

Colour key, see Reference map A1, p 10

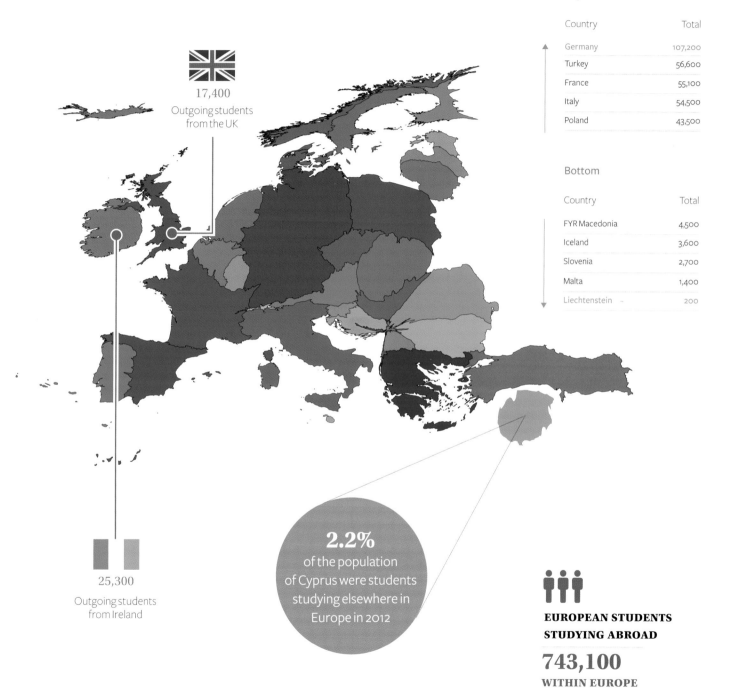

17,400
Outgoing students from the UK

25,300
Outgoing students from Ireland

2.2%
of the population of Cyprus were students studying elsewhere in Europe in 2012

Top	
Country	Total
Germany	107,200
Turkey	56,600
France	55,100
Italy	54,500
Poland	43,500

Bottom	
Country	Total
FYR Macedonia	4,500
Iceland	3,600
Slovenia	2,700
Malta	1,400
Liechtenstein	200

EUROPEAN STUDENTS STUDYING ABROAD

743,100
WITHIN EUROPE

F – Work

The goals of full employment and social progress were at the very centre of discussions that resulted in the founding treaties of the EU, and throughout the second half of the 20th century Europeans worked towards the goal of better workplaces for all. Following the economic crisis of 2007/08, however, some countries and regions of Europe have been sinking into a protracted period of mass unemployment, reminiscent of times before the Second World War.

- This chapter shows how much a few areas have suffered while others have seen little rise in **unemployment** at all since 2008. The unemployment rate in the EU rose from 7% in 2008 to 11% in 2013, with an estimated 32 million unemployed people, and of these, an estimated 7 million aged 15–24. The overall **youth unemployment** rate in the entire EU by 2013 was 25.8%, and there has been little sign of this improving recently.
- There are **huge variations** between countries and regions as well as within regions and cities, with the highest unemployment rates mostly found in austerity-stricken Greece, Italy and Spain.
- Even in the countries where unemployment was reduced, in some cases, this has been the result of punitive policies that involved imposing financial sanctions on the poorest. For example, in the UK over 1 million sanctions were applied to people claiming Jobseeker's Allowance in 2012 alone, encouraging people to take any job on offer or declare that they were self-employed.
- The themes explored in this chapter can be used to inform debates about these developments and the possible revival of the idea of **full employment**, better employment and **social progress** as a key European goal.
- Maps and infographics illustrate the detailed geography of employment by showing how many people work in different **occupations and industries** across Europe, and how much each industry contributes to local and regional economies.

Labour force

2013

The formal labour force of Europe consists of all people aged 15 upwards who are economically active, that is those who are working or who are unemployed and looking for work. This workforce consisted of an estimated total of 289 million people in 2013, representing approximately 56% of the total European population aged 15+. Just over half of this workforce was found in the combined countries of Germany, the UK, France, Turkey and Italy, which together dominate this map.

In relative terms, however, the highest labour force participation rates were mostly found in Northern European countries. The UK's share of economically active people as a proportion of the total population aged 15 and over was 62%. This is less than in the Nordic countries or Switzerland.

The highest rate in the world was recorded in Tanzania (89%) and the lowest in East Timor (38%).

The percentages are reduced where the proportion of retired older people increases, including as a result of lower retirement ages. It also falls where the informal (non-regulated) sector of the economy is larger, especially where childcare has not been made part of the formal labour market.

Colour key, see Reference map A1, p 10

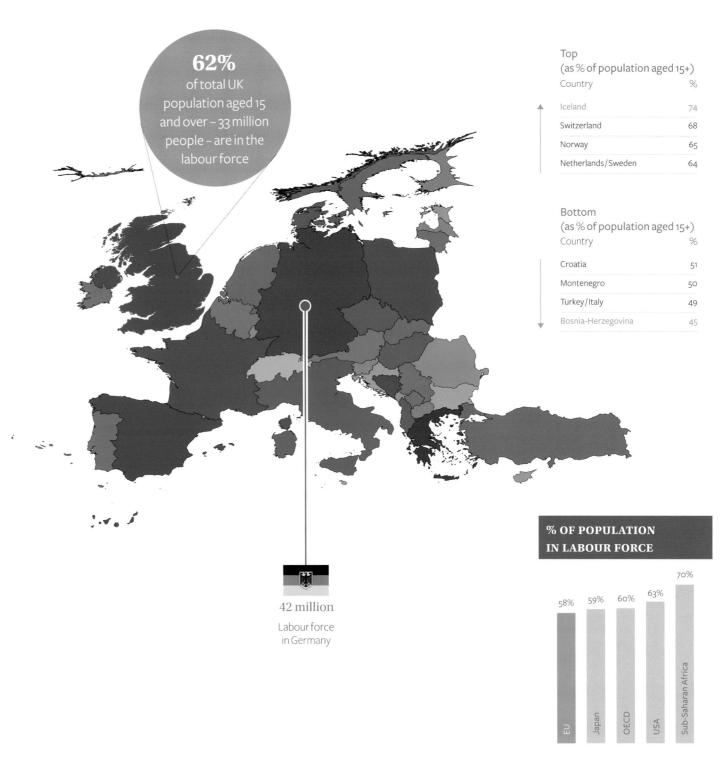

62%
of total UK population aged 15 and over – 33 million people – are in the labour force

42 million

Labour force in Germany

Top
(as % of population aged 15+)

Country	%
Iceland	74
Switzerland	68
Norway	65
Netherlands / Sweden	64

Bottom
(as % of population aged 15+)

Country	%
Croatia	51
Montenegro	50
Turkey / Italy	49
Bosnia-Herzegovina	45

% OF POPULATION IN LABOUR FORCE

EU	Japan	OECD	USA	Sub-Saharan Africa
58%	59%	60%	63%	70%

Women in labour force

2013

The total number of women aged 15 or over in work or looking for work throughout Europe in 2013 was 128 million (or 44% of the total European workforce). Just over half of this total (54%) is made up of women living and working in the five countries with the highest numbers that dominate the map: Germany, the UK, France, Italy and Spain.

In relative terms the largest proportions of women as a share of the total economically active population are mostly found in Northern Europe, although Cyprus in the South also has a relatively high rate (56%).

The lowest rates of female participation in the formal labour force are found in the South and South East of Europe.

Worldwide women work much longer hours than men, but much of that work is informal and unpaid. The highest formal female work rate recorded was in Tanzania (88%) and the lowest in Syria (14%).

Colour key, see Reference map A1, p 10

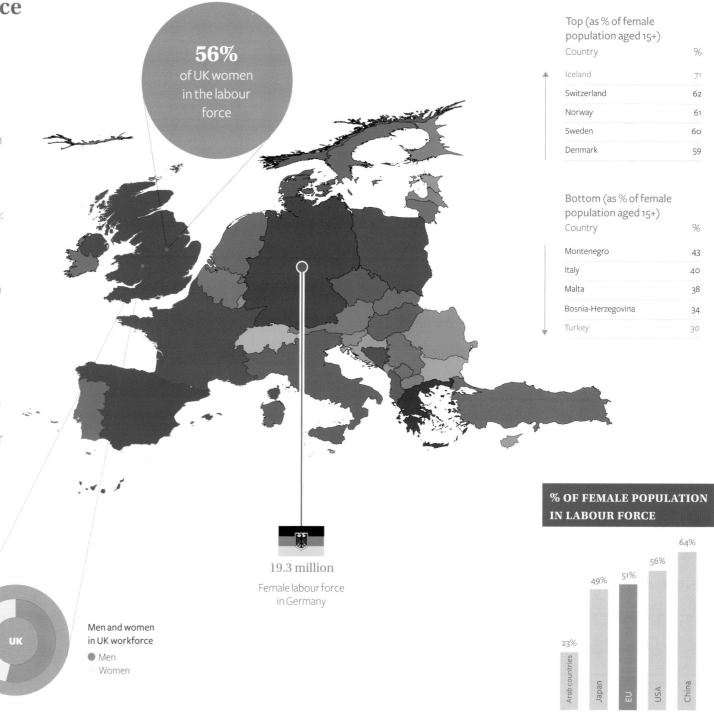

56%
of UK women in the labour force

Men and women in UK workforce
- Men
- Women

19.3 million
Female labour force in Germany

Top (as % of female population aged 15+)

Country	%
Iceland	71
Switzerland	62
Norway	61
Sweden	60
Denmark	59

Bottom (as % of female population aged 15+)

Country	%
Montenegro	43
Italy	40
Malta	38
Bosnia-Herzegovina	34
Turkey	30

% OF FEMALE POPULATION IN LABOUR FORCE

Arab countries	Japan	EU	USA	China
23%	49%	51%	56%	64%

Unemployment (national)

2013

There were an estimated 31.8 million people across Europe registered as out of work or looking for work in 2013, approximately 11% of the total European workforce, but there is huge variation between countries and regions.

Nearly one-fifth of all unemployed people in Europe lived in Spain, which had the greatest number of unemployed residents. In relative terms, Europe's highest unemployment rates are mostly found in the South of the continent and in the Balkans.

Employment is highest in Norway, Austria and Switzerland.

It is also interesting to compare European unemployment rates to those reported at the same time for other countries and regions around the world. In OECD member states as a whole the rate was higher, at 8.0%. The highest rate in the world was recorded in Mauritania (31%) and, technically, the lowest in Cambodia (0.3%), where in 2013 (and still in 2016) there were no national employment creation or unemployment compensation schemes and so nothing for which to register.

Colour key, see Reference map A1, p 10

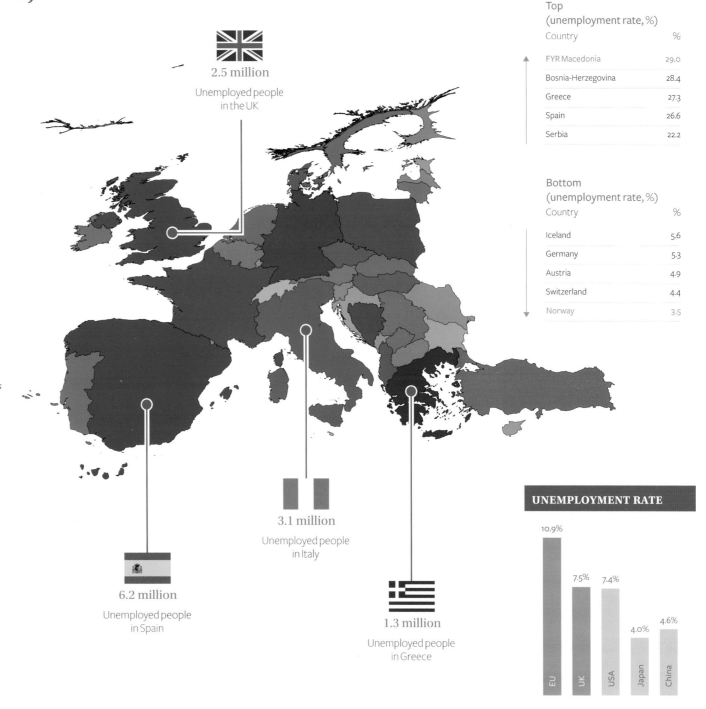

2.5 million

Unemployed people
in the UK

6.2 million

Unemployed people
in Spain

3.1 million

Unemployed people
in Italy

1.3 million

Unemployed people
in Greece

Top
(unemployment rate, %)

Country	%
FYR Macedonia	29.0
Bosnia-Herzegovina	28.4
Greece	27.3
Spain	26.6
Serbia	22.2

Bottom
(unemployment rate, %)

Country	%
Iceland	5.6
Germany	5.3
Austria	4.9
Switzerland	4.4
Norway	3.5

UNEMPLOYMENT RATE

10.9%	7.5%	7.4%	4.0%	4.6%
EU	UK	USA	Japan	China

Change in unemployment

2007–13

Unemployment in the EU rose from 7% in 2007 to 11% in 2013. This map shows the total increases between 2007 and 2013 in the numbers of people out of work and looking for work across Europe.

There are shocking national variations. The largest absolute increase is observed in Spain, where over 4 million more people were unemployed in 2013 than in 2007. Spain was also badly hit by the real estate crisis.

By contrast, Germany recorded one of its lowest rates of unemployment for two decades, as one of only four countries in Europe experiencing a fall during this period. Germany is often considered to have 'exported unemployment', as it benefited from the low value of the euro after the financial crisis. This meant that the price of goods Germany exported to other countries did not rise, and it could carry on selling as much as before. Germany's small initial advantage became much greater later on, as its export earnings meant many more jobs were created there, albeit often part time and less secure jobs than previously. Southern European countries might have fared better had their currencies been able to devalue, or had Europe had political as well as monetary union.

Colour key, see Reference map A1, p 10

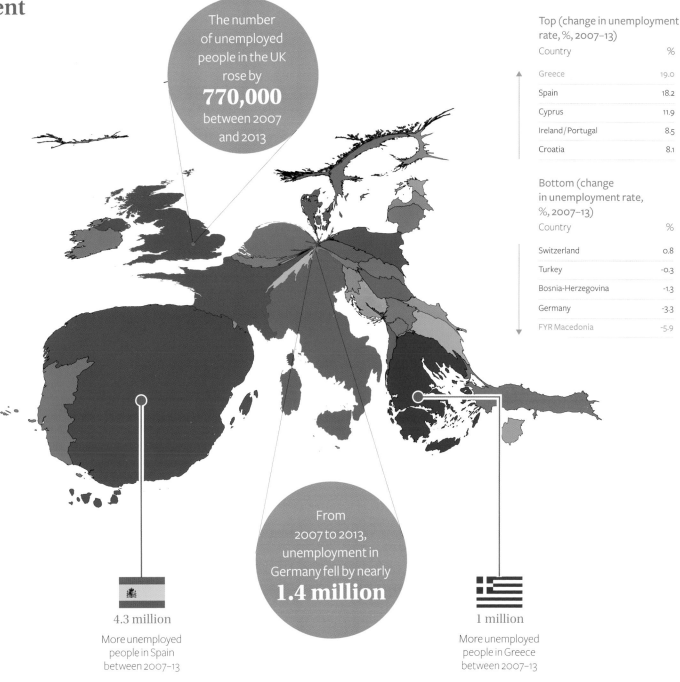

The number of unemployed people in the UK rose by **770,000** between 2007 and 2013

From 2007 to 2013, unemployment in Germany fell by nearly **1.4 million**

4.3 million
More unemployed people in Spain between 2007–13

1 million
More unemployed people in Greece between 2007–13

Top (change in unemployment rate, %, 2007–13)

Country	%
Greece	19.0
Spain	18.2
Cyprus	11.9
Ireland / Portugal	8.5
Croatia	8.1

Bottom (change in unemployment rate, %, 2007–13)

Country	%
Switzerland	0.8
Turkey	-0.3
Bosnia-Herzegovina	-1.3
Germany	-3.3
FYR Macedonia	-5.9

Youth unemployment

2013

About one-seventh of Europe's estimated 7 million unemployed 15- to 24-year-olds in 2013 lived in Turkey, with a similar number in the UK and Spain. France and Italy also had more than 500,000 young people unemployed.

The youth unemployment rate is the proportion of 15- to 24-year-olds registering as unemployed out of the total number who are economically active in that age group. In the EU-28, 57% of that group are classed as economically inactive, mainly students who have not 'signed on' or got any formal employment. The highest youth unemployment rates are mostly found in South East Europe and in Spain. Bosnia-Herzegovina, Greece and Spain had the highest recorded youth unemployment rates not just in Europe but in the world. The lowest rates were found in Central and Northern Europe.

The highest rate in the world outside Europe was recorded in South Africa (54%). The lowest was recorded in Cambodia and Rwanda (0.7%). There is no provision for unemployment benefit under Rwandan labour laws.

Recently Europe has been seeing historically low fertility rates, and so has never had so few young people entering the workforce, and yet there were still too few jobs for them to apply for and take up.

Colour key, see Reference map A1, p 10

Unemployed aged 15–24
Unemployed aged 25+

UK

Europe

Unemployed aged 15–24
Unemployed aged 25+

YOUNG UNEMPLOYED (% OF ECONOMICALLY ACTIVE AGED 15–24)

Japan	USA	OECD	UK	EU
7%	16%	17%	20%	26%

Change in youth unemployment

2007–13

This map shows where the biggest increases in youth unemployment between 2007 and 2013 could be found. This is the generation most acutely affected by the crash of 2008: most would not have started their working lives out of work had it not been for the crash and the way it was dealt with. If there had been a 'New Deal' across Europe, millions of them would have been employed in state-funded work to ensure that the long recession ended early.

Instead, extreme austerity meant that fewer young people than ever before were hired into new jobs, and this group then had less money to spend, particularly on local services, with more jobs lost as a result.

There were nine countries where youth unemployment fell, with notable considerable declines in some of the Balkan states, which might be due to out-migration of young, economically active people.

Germany had by far the largest decline, with 250,000 fewer young unemployed in 2013 than in 2007, but during 2015 the situation changed as hundreds of thousands of refugees arrived in Germany, moving towards the areas where work has been most plentiful. Although many will not yet be permitted to register as unemployed, this will happen eventually.

Colour key, see Reference map A1, p 10

420,000

More unemployed young people in Spain between 2007–13

Youth unemployment in Romania fell by **56,000** between 2007 and 2013

Top (change in youth unemployment rate, %, 2007–13)	
Country	%
Spain	38.2
Greece	35.5
Cyprus	27.3
Croatia	26.0
Portugal	21.2

Bottom (change in youth unemployment rate, %, 2007–13)	
Country	%
Austria	0.5
Malta	0.3
Turkey	-2.8
Germany	-3.8
FYR Macedonia	-5.9

Unemployment (regional)

REGIONAL MAP, 2014

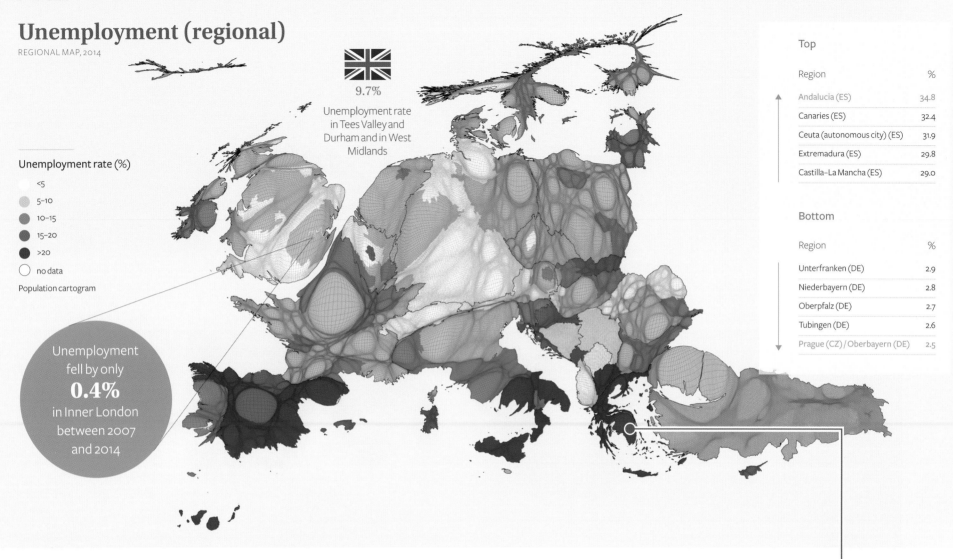

9.7%

Unemployment rate
in Tees Valley and
Durham and in West
Midlands

Unemployment rate (%)

- ⚪ <5
- ⚪ 5–10
- ⚪ 10–15
- ⚪ 15–20
- ⚫ >20
- ⚪ no data

Population cartogram

Unemployment
fell by only
0.4%
in Inner London
between 2007
and 2014

Top

Region	%
Andalucia (ES)	34.8
Canaries (ES)	32.4
Ceuta (autonomous city) (ES)	31.9
Extremadura (ES)	29.8
Castilla–La Mancha (ES)	29.0

Bottom

Region	%
Unterfranken (DE)	2.9
Niederbayern (DE)	2.8
Oberpfalz (DE)	2.7
Tubingen (DE)	2.6
Prague (CZ) / Oberbayern (DE)	2.5

20.6%

Attica saw
unemployment rise
by 20.6% between
2007 and 2014

This detailed map shows that the regions with the highest unemployment in 2014 (above 20%) were all found in four Southern European countries – Spain, Italy, Greece and FYR Macedonia, while the lowest rates (less than 5%) were mostly found in Central and Northern Europe, and in particular, Germany, Austria, Switzerland, and the Scandinavian countries.

Unemployment is often highest in areas where there are more men than women in the labour force, and also where the benefits system is less punitive.

Unemployment rates are lower in major cities than in the surrounding areas, both because there are more work opportunities and because the higher cost of living deters the precariously employed.

In 83 regions across Europe the unemployment rate in 2014 was lower than in 2007, mostly in Germany, but also in Eastern Europe and parts of the UK, where recently up to a million people a year have been 'sanctioned' if they do not meet rigorous searching-for-work criteria, and so accept unreasonable (including zero-hours) contracts, or opt out as 'self-employed' without realistic prospects.

People working in agriculture

2012

An estimated 18 million people were working in agriculture across Europe in 2012. Nearly a third were in Turkey, which dominates this map together with Eastern European countries.

Eastern European countries generally have the highest proportions of the workforce working in this sector, but rates are also high in Greece (13%) and Portugal (10%), whereas the lowest rates are mostly found in Northern and Western Europe.

Small family farms can employ many people, as can traditional fishing and forestry industries. However, all across Europe these are declining industries, partly as increased mechanisation leads to a smaller workforce.

It is worth noting that the highest rate in the world was recorded in Madagascar and Rwanda (75.3%), and the lowest in Macao, a special administrative region in China, where it was just 0.2%.

In 2006, for the first time in many years, the EU had an agricultural trade surplus of €4.5 billion but the trade balance reverted back to negative in 2007 (-€2.4 billion). Europe consumes more food than it produces, but there has been no fall in production as more and more food is consumed and wasted worldwide. (See also map of skilled agricultural, forestry and fishery workers below, p 120.)

Colour key, see Reference map A1, p 10

365,000 Agricultural workers in the UK

2 million Agricultural workers in Poland

6 million Agricultural workers in Turkey

Top (as % of total employment)

Country	%
Albania	41.5
Romania	29.0
Turkey	23.6
Serbia	21.0
Bosnia-Herzegovina	20.5

Bottom (as % of total employment)

Country	%
Germany	1.5
Luxembourg	1.3
Belgium/UK	1.2
Malta	1.0

AGRICULTURE AS % OF TOTAL EMPLOYMENT

USA 1.6% · Japan 3.7% · EU 5.1% · OECD 5.9% · India 47%

People working in industry (national)

2012

Europe still had an estimated industrial workforce of 64 million people in 2012, working in mining and quarrying, manufacturing, construction, and public utilities (electricity, gas and water). About 15% of that workforce was to be found in Germany, about 11% in Italy and another 11% in Turkey.

The countries with the highest percentages of the economically active population working in industry are found in Eastern Europe. Here industries tend to be labour-intensive, with work broken down into mundane and repetitive tasks that command low wages, allowing firms to be more competitive.

The rate in the Czech Republic, apart from being the highest in Europe, is also the second highest in the world. At the EU level taken as a whole, the respective rate was 25%. The country with the highest rate worldwide was Qatar (51.9%), and the lowest rate was recorded in Bhutan (8.6%).

In future as automation in manufacturing continues to increase we should expect most areas of Europe and much of the rest of the world to see fewer people working in these industries as a whole.

Colour key, see Reference map A1, p 10

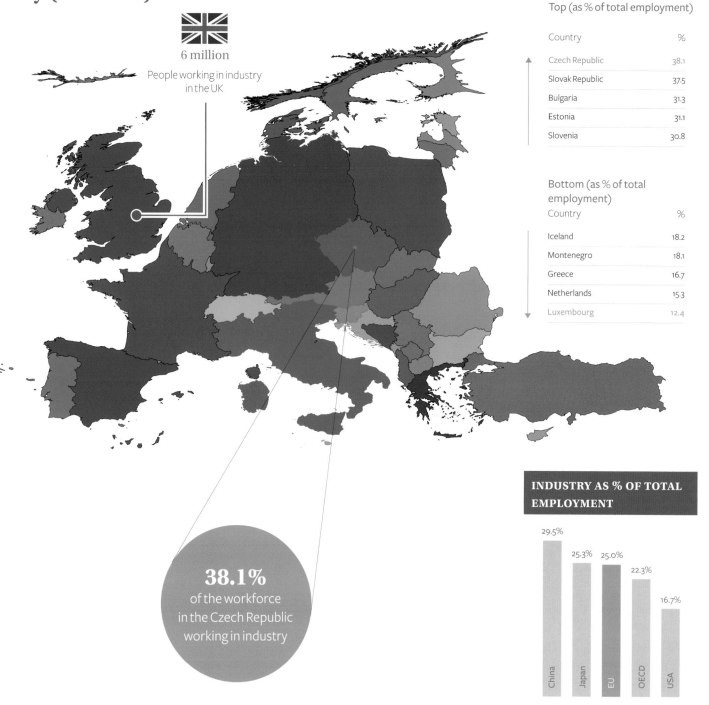

6 million
People working in industry in the UK

38.1%
of the workforce in the Czech Republic working in industry

Top (as % of total employment)

Country	%
Czech Republic	38.1
Slovak Republic	37.5
Bulgaria	31.3
Estonia	31.1
Slovenia	30.8

Bottom (as % of total employment)

Country	%
Iceland	18.2
Montenegro	18.1
Greece	16.7
Netherlands	15.3
Luxembourg	12.4

INDUSTRY AS % OF TOTAL EMPLOYMENT

China	Japan	EU	OECD	USA
29.5%	25.3%	25.0%	22.3%	16.7%

People working in services

2012

The European workforce is now overwhelmingly employed in the tertiary sector: that is, providing services, rather than producing raw materials (growing food, forestry, fishing or mining) or making goods.

An estimated 175 million people were working in the service sector across Europe in 2012, approximately 67% of the total economically active population, and about 100 million live in the top five countries that dominate this map: Germany, the UK, France, Italy and Spain.

In relative terms, the highest rates are found in Northern Europe. Luxembourg, with the highest rate in Europe, is ranked third globally, following Hong Kong (which has the highest rate globally, at 87.7%) and Puerto Rico (84.4%). The UK, ranked second in Europe, was fifth in the world.

The service sector covers many areas including education, health and social care, housing, government, all forms of trade, transport, defence, entertainment and hospitality; almost everyone you engage with outside your own employment, if not within it.

Just a century ago, services was the smallest sector, behind agriculture and industry, where many jobs have now been automated. The same could happen in services in future, with more mundane jobs (train drivers, coffee vendors) replaced by machines.

Colour key, see Reference map A1, p 10

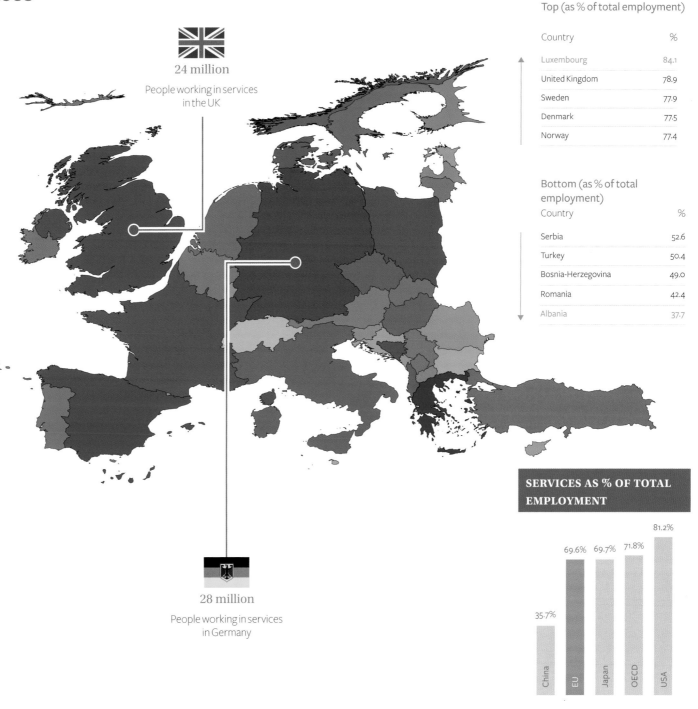

24 million
People working in services in the UK

28 million
People working in services in Germany

Top (as % of total employment)

Country	%
Luxembourg	84.1
United Kingdom	78.9
Sweden	77.9
Denmark	77.5
Norway	77.4

Bottom (as % of total employment)

Country	%
Serbia	52.6
Turkey	50.4
Bosnia-Herzegovina	49.0
Romania	42.4
Albania	37.7

SERVICES AS % OF TOTAL EMPLOYMENT

China	EU	Japan	OECD	USA
35.7%	69.6%	69.7%	71.8%	81.2%

People working in industry (regional)

REGIONAL MAP, 2012

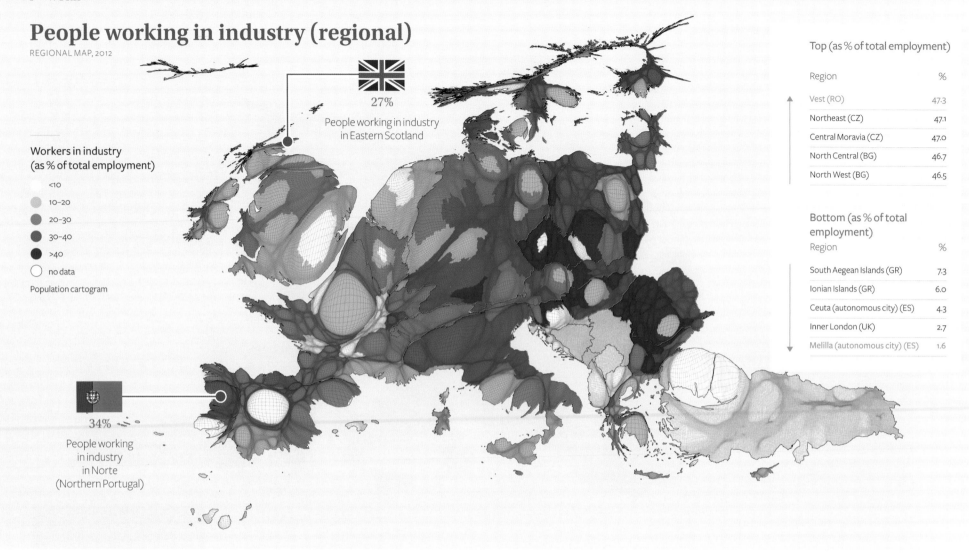

**Workers in industry
(as % of total employment)**

- ◯ <10
- ◯ 10–20
- ◯ 20–30
- ⬤ 30–40
- ⬤ >40
- ◯ no data

Population cartogram

27%

People working in industry
in Eastern Scotland

34%

People working
in industry
in Norte
(Northern Portugal)

Top (as % of total employment)

Region	%
Vest (RO)	47.3
Northeast (CZ)	47.1
Central Moravia (CZ)	47.0
North Central (BG)	46.7
North West (BG)	46.5

Bottom (as % of total employment)

Region	%
South Aegean Islands (GR)	7.3
Ionian Islands (GR)	6.0
Ceuta (autonomous city) (ES)	4.3
Inner London (UK)	2.7
Melilla (autonomous city) (ES)	1.6

This map shows where people working in the industrial sector across Europe's regions are most concentrated.

The highest levels of industrial employment (over 40%) tend to be found in Bulgaria, the Czech Republic, Hungary, Poland, Romania, Slovenia and the Slovak Republic. Tübingen in Germany is the only region outside Central and Eastern Europe to have such a high share.

The regions with the lowest levels (less than 10%) are found in Spain, Greece, Norway, France, the Netherlands, Belgium and the UK (in particular, in Inner and Outer London, Surrey, and East and West Sussex).

With an EU–28 average of 24.5%, this is a sector that could be expanded.

Europe needs more high-tech and medical service industries, and new green industries involved in making solar panels and wind turbines, for example.

However, even as employment in some of these industries is expanded, routine and production-line work in other industries is likely to contract at a faster rate in the near future.

People working in construction

REGIONAL MAP, 2012

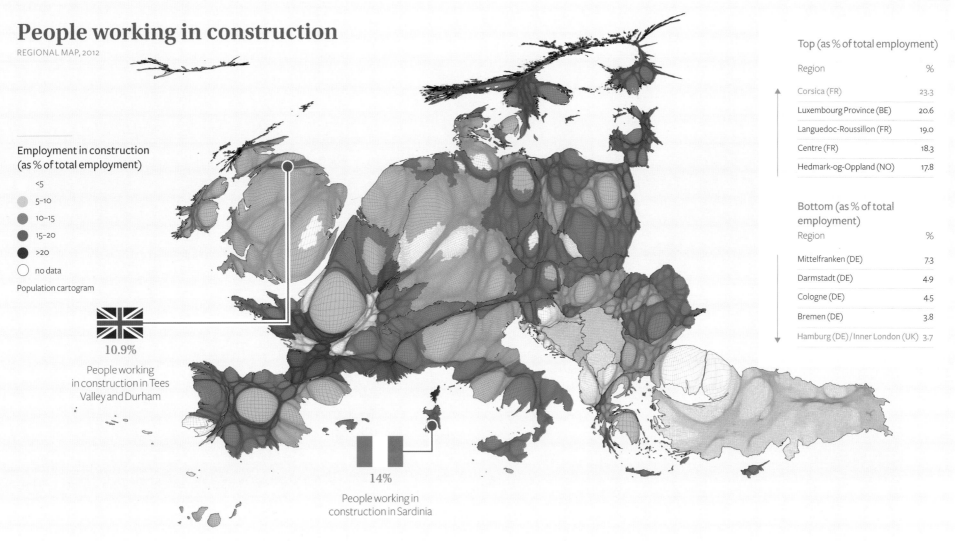

Employment in construction
(as % of total employment)

- <5
- 5–10
- 10–15
- 15–20
- >20
- no data

Population cartogram

10.9%

People working
in construction in Tees
Valley and Durham

14%

People working in
construction in Sardinia

Top (as % of total employment)

Region	%
Corsica (FR)	23.3
Luxembourg Province (BE)	20.6
Languedoc-Roussillon (FR)	19.0
Centre (FR)	18.3
Hedmark-og-Oppland (NO)	17.8

Bottom (as % of total employment)

Region	%
Mittelfranken (DE)	7.3
Darmstadt (DE)	4.9
Cologne (DE)	4.5
Bremen (DE)	3.8
Hamburg (DE) / Inner London (UK)	3.7

Construction workers make up an average of 9.4% of all employed people in the EU, about 24 million people.

The regions with the largest shares are mostly found in France, Belgium, Luxembourg, Norway, Italy and Austria; the smallest in Germany and the UK.

The geographical pattern shown here has been changing considerably as a result of the 2008 financial crash.

Before the crash there were a number of regions in Southern Europe – especially in Spain, Portugal, Southern Italy, Greece and Cyprus – where construction played a major role in the local economy.

Rates tend to be higher in countries and regions within them experiencing population growth and requiring more housing, more shops and more schools.

Particular construction projects in progress at the time the statistics were collected can have an effect. In 2012 there were big infrastructure projects under way in Eastern Europe and Spain, for example, and also the final preparations for the London Olympics. However, this might affect the economic contribution of construction, rather than employment, as a lot of money can be spent without employing that many people if prices are set high.

People working in the service sector

REGIONAL MAP, 2012

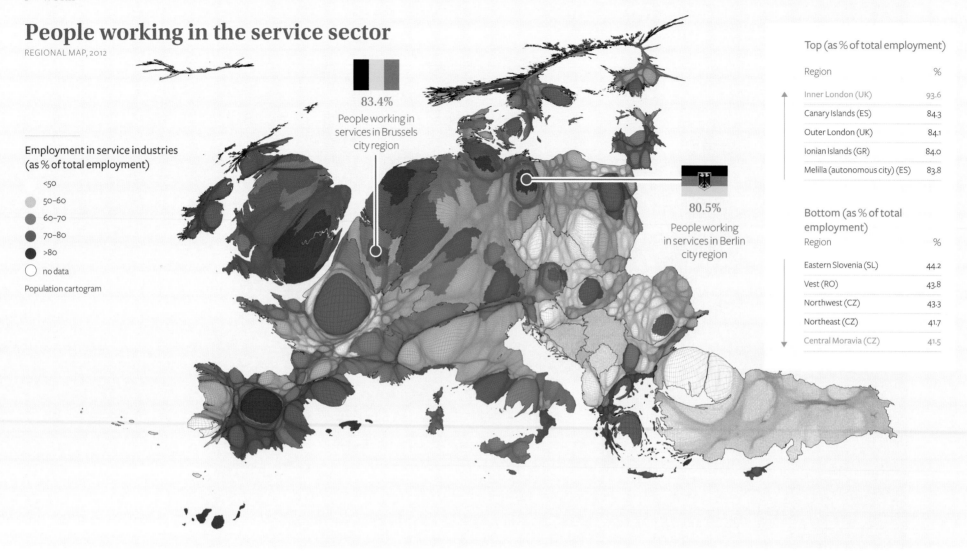

83.4%
People working in
services in Brussels
city region

80.5%
People working
in services in Berlin
city region

**Employment in service industries
(as % of total employment)**

- <50
- 50–60
- 60–70
- 70–80
- \>80
- no data

Population cartogram

Services tend to be concentrated in large city regions and especially in capital city regions, such as Inner London, Luxembourg and Paris.

Almost two-thirds of all European workers work in services (also known as the tertiary sector). This sector will account for an even higher proportion of economic output because of the way in which standard accounting is carried out. Because the salaries of workers in service industries tend, on average, to be higher than those of people working in agriculture or industry, it is claimed that services as a whole are more productive. (In future it is likely that our current accounting practices will be regarded with some amusement.)

There is an extremely wide level of variation in salaries within the service sector, but the highest paid (particularly financiers) are not generally the most productive compared to the lowest paid (who may empty their bins). Financiers can destroy value. Advertisers can encourage people to buy things they do not need and increase pollution as a result. Lawyers can always justify a need for their services. Thus, just because a job is said to be 'most productive' because it commands a high salary, that does not mean that the work done is actually productive according to the normal meaning of the word.

People working in high-tech sectors

REGIONAL MAP, 2014

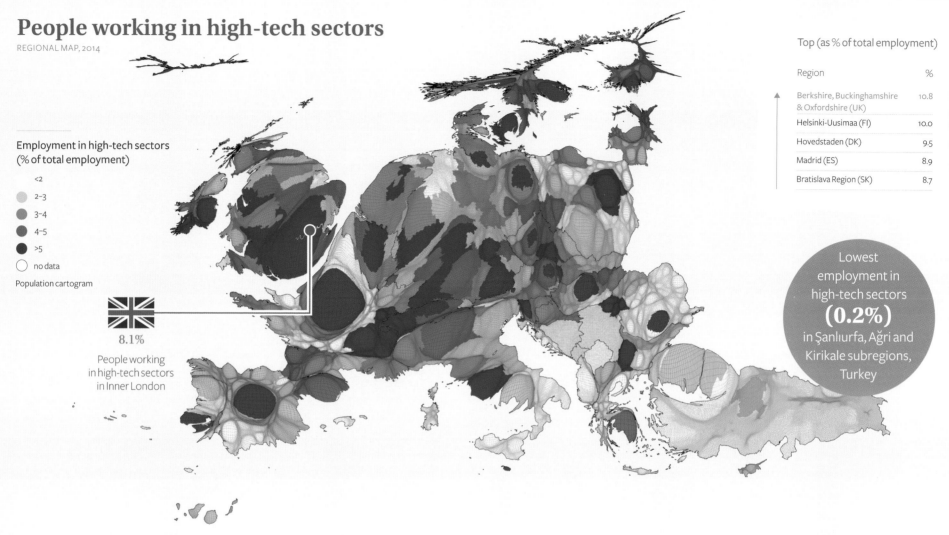

Employment in high-tech sectors
(% of total employment)

- <2
- 2–3
- 3–4
- 4–5
- >5
- ○ no data

Population cartogram

8.1%

People working
in high-tech sectors
in Inner London

Top (as % of total employment)

Region	%
Berkshire, Buckinghamshire & Oxfordshire (UK)	10.8
Helsinki-Uusimaa (FI)	10.0
Hovedstaden (DK)	9.5
Madrid (ES)	8.9
Bratislava Region (SK)	8.7

Lowest
employment in
high-tech sectors
(0.2%)
in Şanlıurfa, Ağri and
Kirikale subregions,
Turkey

Within almost every country on this map showing high-tech employment as a proportion of total employment there is at least one region where there appear to be clusters of high-tech opportunities.

Europe does not appear to have developed any agglomeration as large as Silicon Valley, the densest high-tech US agglomeration located in California – but it does have dozens of little silicon valleys, with the highest rates found in the UK, Denmark, Spain, the Czech Republic, Austria, Belgium, Hungary, France, Sweden and Switzerland.

The lowest rates are generally found in rural areas, but especially in the more rural and peripheral regions of countries in Eastern and South Eastern Europe, Turkey, and in the South of Italy and Spain.

With the distributed nature of work on the internet, high-tech firms do not need to be concentrated in any one part of the continent. Europe has many interesting and exciting places in which to live and work, both historic cities and vibrant towns, and this may be part of the reason for the pattern shown here. Also, each country in Europe may be trying to encourage its own high-tech industries within its own borders, and crossing state boundaries is still a bigger barrier for people in Europe than it is for the virtually monolingual United States.

Occupational categories

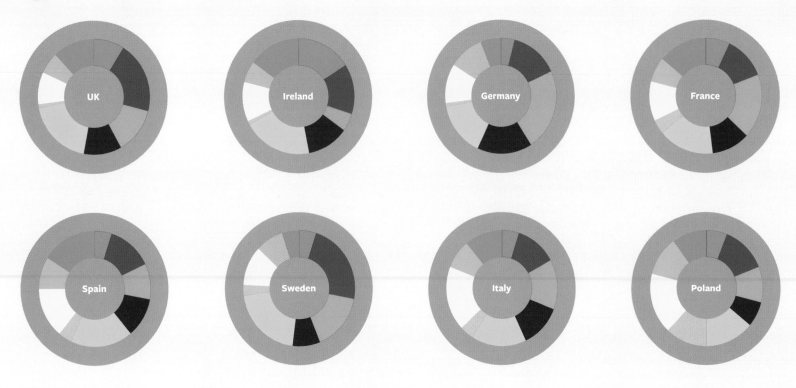

Occupational categories

- Managers
- Professionals
- Technicians and associate professionals
- Clerical support workers
- Service and sales workers

- Skilled agricultural, forestry and fishery workers
- Craft and related trades workers
- Plant and machine operators, and assemblers
- Elementary occupations

In the following nine maps, the size of every country is drawn in proportion to its total population, and the shading shows how common it is for people to be employed in each occupational category (highest rates in darkest colours). Occupations are classified using the International Standard Classification of Occupations.

Managers

2011

Managers
(% of workforce)

- <4.7
- 4.7–5.3
- 5.3–6.8
- 6.8–7.7
- >7.7
- no data

Top			Bottom	
Country	%		Country	%
Ireland	16.3		Germany	4.3
Switzerland	9.4		Czech Republic	4.2
United Kingdom	9.2		Hungary	4.0
Estonia	8.2		Romania	2.2
Greece	8.1		Cyprus	2.0

The proportion of 'managers' in the workforce appears to vary widely across Europe, although note that the word 'manager' may mean different degrees of leadership or management in different jurisdictions.

7.2%

Managers in France

Professionals

2011

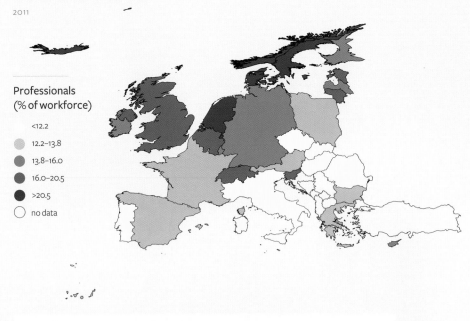

**Professionals
(% of workforce)**

- <12.2
- 12.2–13.8
- 13.8–16.0
- 16.0–20.5
- >20.5
- no data

Top		Bottom	
Country	%	Country	%
Norway	24.1	Hungary	12.2
Sweden	23.5	Romania	12.1
Netherlands	23.0	Italy	11.8
Denmark	21.8	Malta / Slovak Republic	11.4
Iceland	21.6	Portugal	10.4

Again, what is meant by 'professional' may differ between jurisdictions, but a job may be made more professional if the individual undertaking that work is given a greater degree of autonomy, if higher qualifications and more training are required to undertake it, and if higher competency and responsibility is expected.

14.1%

Professionals
in Germany

Technicians and associate professionals

2011

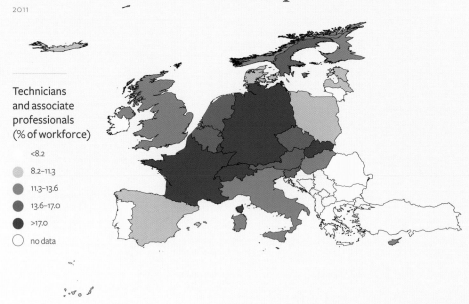

**Technicians
and associate
professionals
(% of workforce)**

- <8.2
- 8.2–11.3
- 11.3–13.6
- 13.6–17.0
- >17.0
- no data

Top		Bottom	
Country	%	Country	%
Germany	22.4	Portugal	8.2
Slovak Republic	20.3	Greece	7.3
Luxembourg	19.9	Lithuania / Romania	7.2
Switzerland	18.7	Bulgaria	6.6
France	17.7	Ireland	5.4

Officially the term is 'associate professionals'. This map should be considered in conjunction with that for 'managers'. Although Ireland claims by far the highest proportion of managers to be found anywhere in Europe, it is possible that many are supervisors or working in lower levels of management, or that many jobs and forms of work that would be labelled as 'technical or associated professional' elsewhere in Europe might be called 'management' in Ireland (and to a lesser extent in the UK). This category includes jobs such as computer assistants, medical equipment operators, air traffic controllers, health and safety inspectors and quality inspectors.

Clerical support workers

2011

Clerical support
workers
(% of workforce)

- <7.0
- 7.0–8.4
- 8.4–10.7
- 10.7–11.9
- >11.9
- no data

Top		Bottom	
Country	%	Country	%
Germany	15.8	Latvia	6.5
Belgium	14.7	Bulgaria	6.3
Greece	13.5	Estonia	5.8
Cyprus	13.0	Romania	4.6
Ireland	12.0	Lithuania	4.1

At a time when bank clerks were rare and few people could perform the arithmetic required well, clerical jobs were once ranked among the highest-paid occupations, and the posts were mostly filled by middle-class men. As the work became more automated and feminised in many areas of Europe, clerking became a lower-ranking occupation, classified as clerical support. The job of 'secretary' similarly once had higher status (as in 'secretary to the board'), but over time has changed its meaning. However, it will still be defined differently in different parts of the world.

Service and sales workers

2011

Service and sales
workers
(% of workforce)

- <13.9
- 13.9–14.7
- 14.7–17.5
- 17.5–19.7
- >19.7
- no data

Top		Bottom	
Country	%	Country	%
Norway	23.7	Slovenia	13.6
Iceland	23.3	Estonia	13.3
Denmark	22.3	Belgium	13.1
Sweden	21.2	Lithuania	11.7
Ireland	20.3	Romania	11.5

As the proportion of people working in sales has increased, sales workers are now often separated out from the general area of services. In the UK roughly 80% of the workforce work in the service sector at all occupational levels and a tenth of those are employed in retail sales.

Apart from salespersons, this group includes hotel housekeeping and restaurant services workers (such as cooks, waiters and bartenders), personal care and related workers (such as child-care workers and home-based personal care workers), hairdressers, and also public protection services workers such as fire fighters and police officers.

Skilled agricultural, forestry and fishery workers

2011

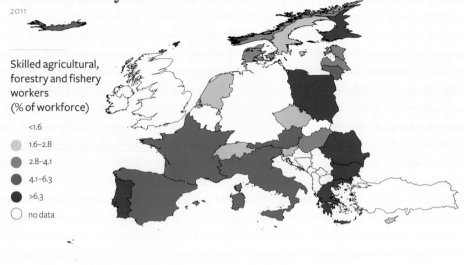

Skilled agricultural, forestry and fishery workers (% of workforce)

- <1.6
- 1.6–2.8
- 2.8–4.1
- 4.1–6.3
- >6.3
- no data

Top		Bottom	
Country	%	Country	%
Romania	19.3	Belgium / Malta	1.6
Greece	14.2	Germany	1.3
Poland	12.0	Slovak Republic	1.2
Portugal	8.5	United Kingdom	1.1
Bulgaria	6.6	Ireland	0.6

In financial terms, the EU has become a net exporter of agricultural products, increasing the trade balance from €3 billion in 2011 to €18 billion in 2013. The larger sizes of farms and the higher degree of mechanisation partly account for the lower numbers in much of the North of Europe, and fishing for the higher rates in Norway and Iceland.

Terminology is interesting. For centuries the most common occupation in Europe was 'peasant'. We now see the term 'skilled' diplomatically placed in front of these occupational groups.

Craft and related trades workers

2011

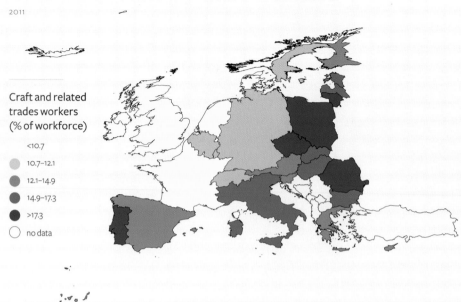

Craft and related trades workers (% of workforce)

- <10.7
- 10.7–12.1
- 12.1–14.9
- 14.9–17.3
- >17.3
- no data

Top		Bottom	
Country	%	Country	%
Romania	20.2	France	10.5
Portugal	19.6	Iceland	10.1
Czech Republic	18.1	Netherlands	10.0
Lithuania	17.7	Norway	9.9
Poland	17.4	United Kingdom	8.9

There is a clear geographic pattern to be seen again here – rates of employment in these occupations are higher the further East and South you travel in Europe. Again it is very likely that this partly reflects nuances of language and tradition – occupations that are regarded as craft in one country may be classed as manufacturing in another.

It is hard to tell how much of this pattern reflects differences in actual work performed, or in how the same types of work are described in different places.

Plant and machine operators and assemblers

2011

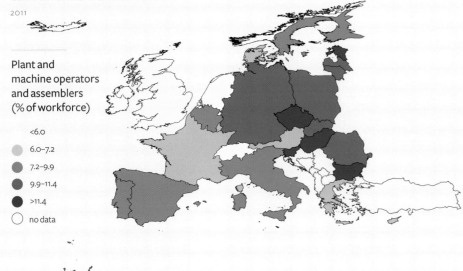

Plant and machine operators and assemblers (% of workforce)

- <6.0
- 6.0–7.2
- 7.2–9.9
- 9.9–11.4
- >11.4
- ○ no data

Top			Bottom	
Country	%		Country	%
Malta	13.8		Austria/Greece	6.5
Hungary	13.4		United Kingdom	6.0
Czech Republic/Estonia	13.3		Norway	5.6
Bulgaria	12.8		Ireland	5.4
			Iceland/Netherlands/Switzerland	4.3

Here the split is more East–West than North–South. This may better reflect actual work done rather than the same work being named differently in different places as assembly line work is harder to mistake. However, if a product is produced by workers each doing a complex series of processes, that might be described as 'craft work', whereas the very same goods made by people each working on narrower aspects of the manufacture would be called 'assembly work'.

Elementary occupations

2011

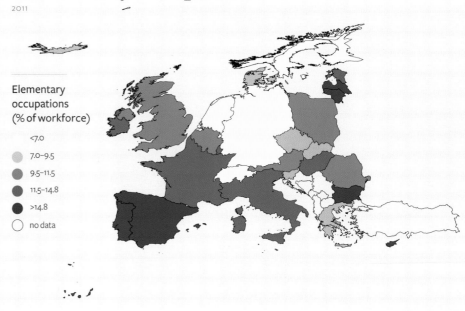

Elementary occupations (% of workforce)

- <7.0
- 7.0–9.5
- 9.5–11.5
- 11.5–14.8
- >14.8
- ○ no data

Top			Bottom	
Country	%		Country	%
Cyprus	18.5		Netherlands	6.1
Latvia	17.0		Germany	6.0
Spain	16.6		Sweden/Switzerland	4.8
Lithuania	16.2		Norway	3.9
Portugal	15.3			

The temptation is to think that this category refers to 'unskilled workers'. In reality a much better term would be 'very poorly paid occupations'. Caring for elderly people is a very difficult job that requires many skills, but because it is usually poorly paid, it is often characterised as 'elementary'. There are clear patterns, with Central Northern Europe and the Scandinavian countries being least likely to label jobs and people in this way and having the fewest people working in demeaningly labelled jobs.

11.5%

Workers in elementary occupations in the UK

G – Environment

Growth in green energy, protecting nature and biodiversity and improving the quality of the environment have long been key issues in EU policy debates. Since the late 1990s European law has required that all activities and decisions taken by governments must fully consider environmental concerns and possible impacts on the environment. This chapter presents just a small fraction of data that holds European governments to account.

- **Greenhouse gas emissions** are routinely monitored and reported to support the compliance of Europe's international obligations regarding efforts to address climate change and to help the EU achieve its 20% emissions reduction target by 2020. We look at the particular vulnerability of certain European countries to climate change.
- There has been an increased focus on investment in **green energy sources**, and a further 2020 EU goal is to obtain 20% of its energy from renewables, including wind, solar, hydroelectric and tidal power, as well as geothermal energy and biomass.
- Widespread **environmental awareness** initiatives have been supported, encouraging **behaviours that reduce the ecological footprint**, from using public transport, walking and cycling, through to improving and extending the railway infrastructure across much of Europe.
- The European Commission also aims to **protect land and marine habitats**; for example, the Natura 2000 programme is the largest coordinated network of protected areas in the world, aimed at ensuring the long-term survival of Europe's most valuable and threatened species and habitats, covering 18% of the EU's land area and 6% of its marine territory.

Carbon dioxide emissions

2011

Carbon dioxide (CO_2) accounts for about 79% of greenhouse gas emissions in all countries mapped in this atlas. Estimated CO_2 emissions produced by burning fossil fuels and manufacturing cement totalled just over 4 gigatons.

Nearly a fifth of this was produced by Germany, followed by the UK (10.9%) and Italy (9.75%). Luxembourg had by far the highest level per person, whereas countries in Eastern Europe dominated the bottom five rankings.

Throughout the EU, CO_2 emissions were estimated at 7.1 metric tons per person, compared with a worldwide average of 4.9.

Pollution resulting from aircraft flights or generated elsewhere to manufacture goods brought into each country is not included in these figures.

The lowest levels of pollution are found where there are alternative sources of power, little highly polluting industry, and where individual levels of material consumption are lower.

There is now an aim to reduce CO_2 pollution across all of Europe, with the so-called 2020 Climate and Energy package of binding legislation aiming to achieve a set of key targets by 2020, in particular reducing greenhouse gas emissions by 20% (from 1990 levels), ensuring that at least 20% of all EU energy comes from renewables and improving energy efficiency.

Colour key, see Reference map A1, p 10

The UK produced
7.1 metric tons
CO_2 per person

Top (CO_2 emissions, per person)

Country	Metric tons
Luxembourg	20.9
Estonia	14.0
Czech Republic	10.4
Finland	10.2
Netherlands	10.1

Bottom (CO_2 emissions, per person)

Country	Metric tons
Romania	4.2
Montenegro	4.1
Latvia	3.8
Albania	1.6
Liechtenstein	1.4

Top
(total CO_2 emissions, megatons)

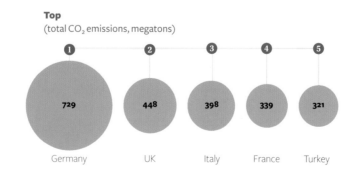

1	2	3	4	5
729	448	398	339	321
Germany	UK	Italy	France	Turkey

CO_2 EMISSIONS (METRIC TONS PER PERSON)

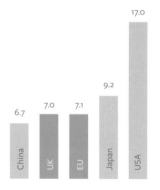

China	UK	EU	Japan	USA
6.7	7.0	7.1	9.2	17.0

Nitrous oxide emissions

2010

The greenhouse gas effect of releasing 1 kg of nitrous oxide (N_2O) into the atmosphere is equivalent to releasing almost 300 kg of CO_2. Estimated emissions from agriculture (from fertilisers and animal manure), fossil fuel combustion, industrial processes and the burning of live and dead vegetation produced 6% of Europe's greenhouse gas emissions, equivalent to 330 megatons of CO_2.

Germany has the largest volume of nitrous oxide emissions (13% of the European total), followed by France, Turkey, Poland and the UK, which together emit another 40% of the total volume.

Estimated world total emissions in 2010 were equivalent to 2.8 gigatons of CO_2. This means that the total volume produced by all the countries mapped in this atlas was approximately 11% of the world total.

Very small countries and countries with little agriculture or more sustainable agricultural practices pollute less in total.

Colour key, see Reference map A1, p 10

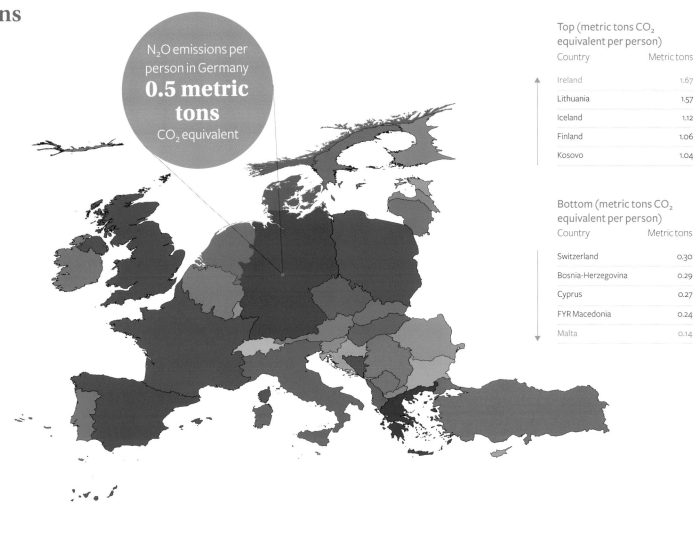

N_2O emissions per person in Germany
0.5 metric tons
CO_2 equivalent

Top (metric tons CO_2 equivalent per person)

Country	Metric tons
Ireland	1.67
Lithuania	1.57
Iceland	1.12
Finland	1.06
Kosovo	1.04

Bottom (metric tons CO_2 equivalent per person)

Country	Metric tons
Switzerland	0.30
Bosnia-Herzegovina	0.29
Cyprus	0.27
FYR Macedonia	0.24
Malta	0.14

Worldwide
N_2O emissions

- Europe
- USA
- China
- Rest of world

Methane emissions

2010

Methane has 25 times the greenhouse gas effect of CO_2 per kilogram. Globally and in Europe it constitutes about 12% of all greenhouse gas emissions. The methane emissions from human activities such as livestock farming, landfills, and the production and use of fossil fuels shown here are the equivalent of 640 megatons of CO_2.

France has the highest volume (with 13% of the total), followed by Turkey (12%), Poland (10%), the UK (10%) and Germany (9%).

The global total in 2010 was equivalent to about 7.5 gigatons of CO_2 emissions, the countries mapped in this atlas accounting for approximately 8% of that total.

What these figures don't include are estimates of methane generated in other countries to produce meat products that are then consumed in Europe. Figures showing how much European consumption was contributing to greenhouse gases produced both in Europe and in the world to satisfy such demands would be very telling.

Colour key, see Reference map A1, p 10

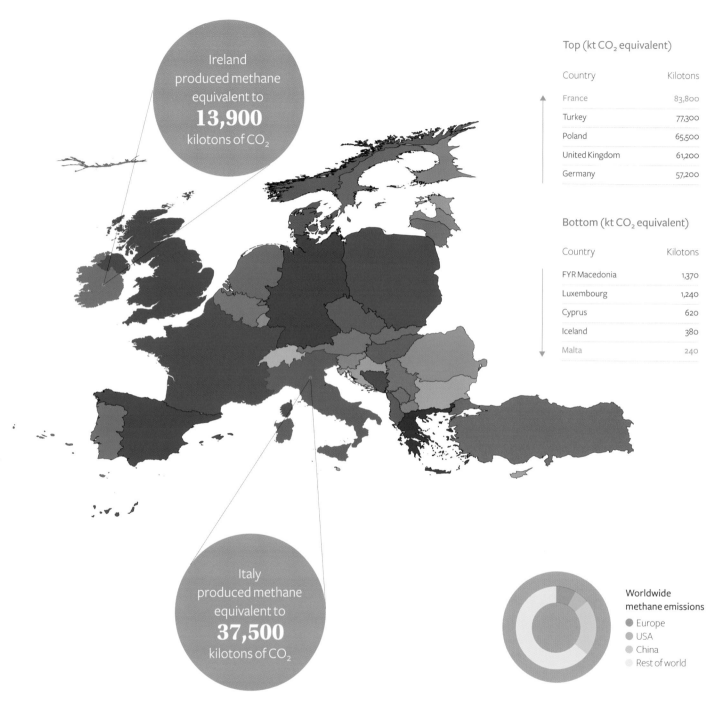

Ireland produced methane equivalent to
13,900
kilotons of CO_2

Italy produced methane equivalent to
37,500
kilotons of CO_2

Top (kt CO_2 equivalent)

Country	Kilotons
France	83,800
Turkey	77,300
Poland	65,500
United Kingdom	61,200
Germany	57,200

Bottom (kt CO_2 equivalent)

Country	Kilotons
FYR Macedonia	1,370
Luxembourg	1,240
Cyprus	620
Iceland	380
Malta	240

Worldwide methane emissions
- Europe
- USA
- China
- Rest of world

Other greenhouse gas emissions

2010

Other greenhouse gases include HFCs (hydrofluorocarbons – used in refrigeration and foam production), PFCs (perfluorocarbons – used in semiconductor manufacture) and SF_6 (sulfur hexafluoride, which insulates high-voltage electrical equipment).

Combined, these gases produced less than 3% of Europe's greenhouse gas emissions, equivalent to 146 megatons of CO_2, with Germany, France, Italy, the UK and Spain producing approximately 60% of the European total. The estimated world total was equivalent to approximately 1 gigaton of CO_2, which means that Europe (as defined in this atlas) accounts for approximately 15% of the global total.

The rise in the use of air conditioning, which uses refrigeration to cool the air, has contributed to recent increases in emissions from Southern Europe.

Germany has by far the highest emissions of SF_6 (45% of the European total), although as insulating material reduces power loss, greenhouse emissions may actually be reduced as less fossil fuel is burnt to generate electricity that is then wasted. However, if more energy was generated at low voltage locally from more renewable sources, there would be less need for many of these materials. Spain and Norway produce the highest volume of PFCs (16% of the European total each).

Colour key, see Reference map A1, p 10

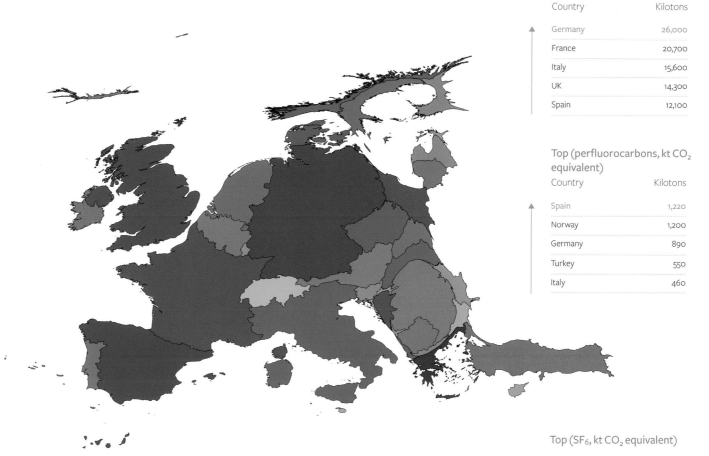

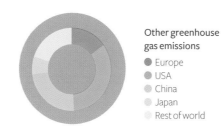

Other greenhouse gas emissions

● Europe
● USA
● China
● Japan
● Rest of world

Top (all other greenhouse gases, kt CO_2 equivalent)

Country	Kilotons
Germany	26,000
France	20,700
Italy	15,600
UK	14,300
Spain	12,100

Top (perfluorocarbons, kt CO_2 equivalent)

Country	Kilotons
Spain	1,220
Norway	1,200
Germany	890
Turkey	550
Italy	460

Top (SF_6, kt CO_2 equivalent)

Country	Kilotons
Germany	6,470
Turkey	1,900
France	1,790
Italy	990
Spain	890

Motor vehicles

2012

One of the greatest contributors to pollution in Europe is exhaust fumes from all kinds of road-going passenger and freight transport, and in 2012 there were an estimated 300 million vehicles on the roads, some 258 million of which were cars.

The largest numbers of vehicles were found in Germany (15.6% of all vehicles in Europe), followed by Italy (13.8%), France (12.6%), the UK (10.9%) and Spain (9%).

However, some of the smallest European countries have the highest numbers of vehicles per population. In San Marino, even if everyone was able to drive (including all children), at least a seventh of all cars could not be driven at any one time.

In practice it is the richest European countries that have the most households where there are more cars than adults to drive them, and those countries will also contribute far more per person to European pollution levels. Pollution is often highest in rural commuting areas around major cities that are not well served by public transport.

These national figures can mask important local variations. For example in the UK the Home Counties around London record the highest rates of carbon emissions per person due to heavy reliance on a car culture.

Colour key, see Reference map A1, p 10

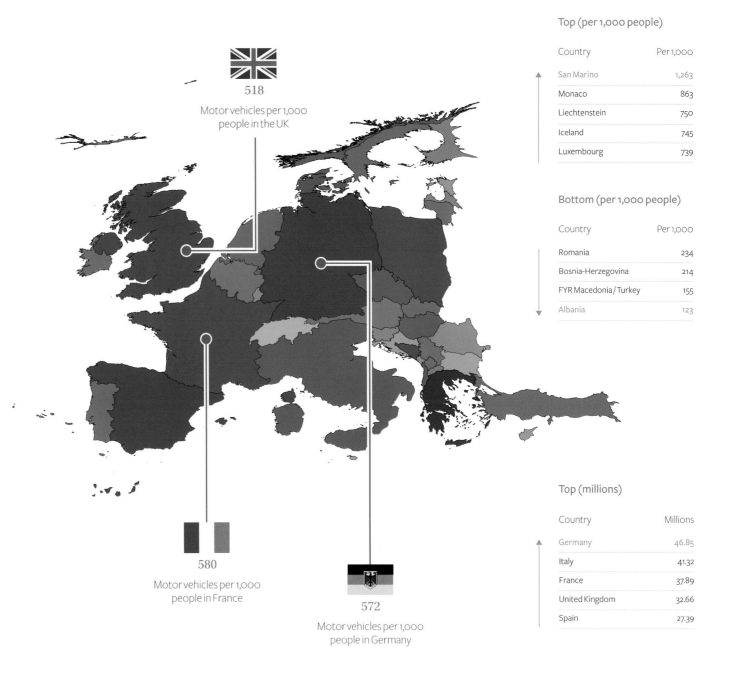

518
Motor vehicles per 1,000 people in the UK

580
Motor vehicles per 1,000 people in France

572
Motor vehicles per 1,000 people in Germany

Top (per 1,000 people)

Country	Per 1,000
San Marino	1,263
Monaco	863
Liechtenstein	750
Iceland	745
Luxembourg	739

Bottom (per 1,000 people)

Country	Per 1,000
Romania	234
Bosnia-Herzegovina	214
FYR Macedonia / Turkey	155
Albania	123

Top (millions)

Country	Millions
Germany	46.85
Italy	41.32
France	37.89
United Kingdom	32.66
Spain	27.39

Railway lines

2012

This map gives an example of the capacity of countries around Europe to offer alternative modes of transport to motor vehicles. The total length of railtrack available for train services in all countries mapped in this atlas amounted to approximately 260,000 km.

Germany has the longest available railway network, closely followed by France.

In relation to population, however, Scandinavian and Eastern and Central European countries dominate, with some countries in South East Europe plus the Netherlands at the other end of the league table.

The following states have no rail lines at all (or extremely limited rail services) – Andorra, Cyprus, Iceland, Kosovo, Liechtenstein, Malta, Montenegro, San Marino and the Vatican – although you do not have to travel far from some of these countries, by taxi in many instances, to get to a railway station in a neighbouring or surrounding country!

Colour key, see Reference map A1, p 10

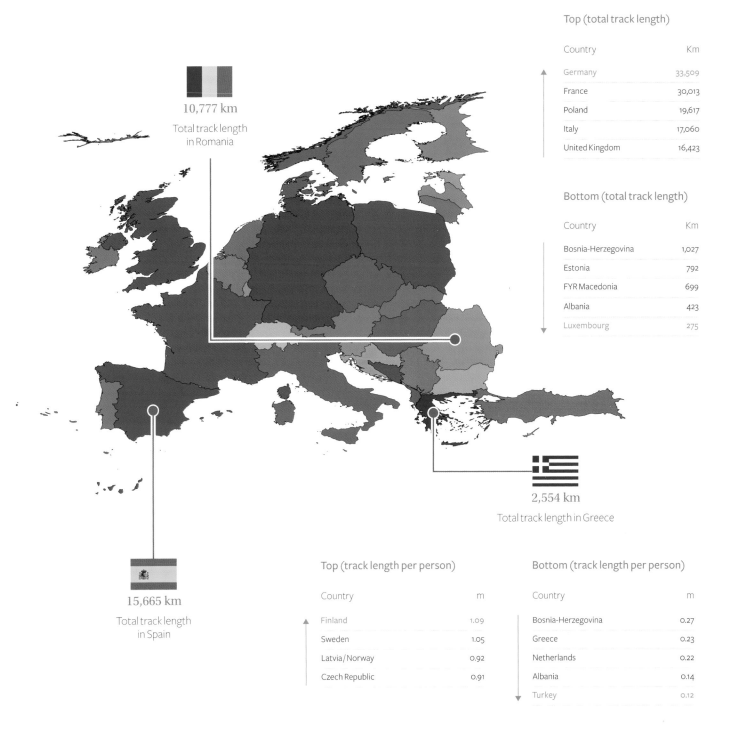

10,777 km
Total track length in Romania

15,665 km
Total track length in Spain

2,554 km
Total track length in Greece

Top (total track length)

Country	Km
Germany	33,509
France	30,013
Poland	19,617
Italy	17,060
United Kingdom	16,423

Bottom (total track length)

Country	Km
Bosnia-Herzegovina	1,027
Estonia	792
FYR Macedonia	699
Albania	423
Luxembourg	275

Top (track length per person)

Country	m
Finland	1.09
Sweden	1.05
Latvia/Norway	0.92
Czech Republic	0.91

Bottom (track length per person)

Country	m
Bosnia-Herzegovina	0.27
Greece	0.23
Netherlands	0.22
Albania	0.14
Turkey	0.12

Vulnerability of European regions to climate change

REGIONAL MAP, 2010

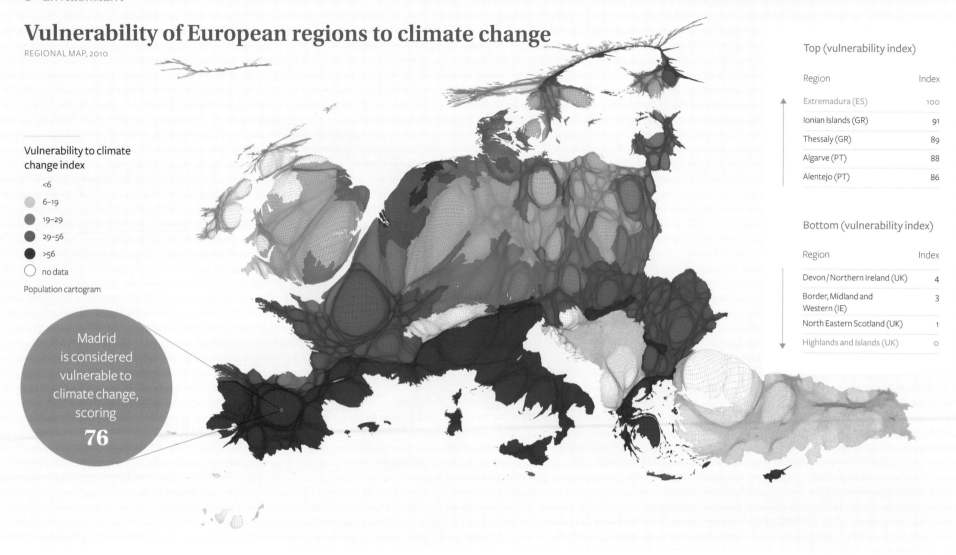

Vulnerability to climate change index

- <6
- 6–19
- 19–29
- 29–56
- >56
- no data

Population cartogram

Madrid is considered vulnerable to climate change, scoring **76**

Top (vulnerability index)

Region	Index
Extremadura (ES)	100
Ionian Islands (GR)	91
Thessaly (GR)	89
Algarve (PT)	88
Alentejo (PT)	86

Bottom (vulnerability index)

Region	Index
Devon / Northern Ireland (UK)	4
Border, Midland and Western (IE)	3
North Eastern Scotland (UK)	1
Highlands and Islands (UK)	0

The European Commission has produced an index expressing how vulnerable each European region is projected to be to climate change from an environmental as well as a socioeconomic point of view. The regions with the highest composite index are mostly found in South and East Europe. The most vulnerable region is Extremadura in Western Spain, where the index takes its maximum possible value of 100.

The lowest value, 0, is observed in the Highlands and Islands in the UK, with the second lowest index recorded in North East Scotland. The UK is currently thought to be one of the areas of the world that may be less vulnerable to climate change, due to the Gulf Stream and its northern extension towards Europe, the North Atlantic Drift. However, if the latter is affected then this may change and the patterns shown in this map would need to be updated accordingly.

Energy production

2010

Europe's energy sources produced the equivalent of 1.1 gigatons of oil (Gtoe) in 2010.

The largest producer of energy was Norway, where nearly a fifth of the European total is produced. Norway, the UK, France, Germany and the Netherlands produce approximately 60% of all energy in Europe, with far more energy produced in Northern Europe compared to in the South.

With solar power and wind power increasingly being used (particularly in Denmark), the shape of this map will change. There is also scope for more efficient use of existing energy sources, and less waste of energy. Better home insulation, better public transport systems and measures to encourage cycling, planning for homes to be built nearer to workplaces, less production of energy-intensive goods – all of this could have a very significant effect on reducing the amount of energy we need to produce.

Colour key, see Reference map A1, p 10

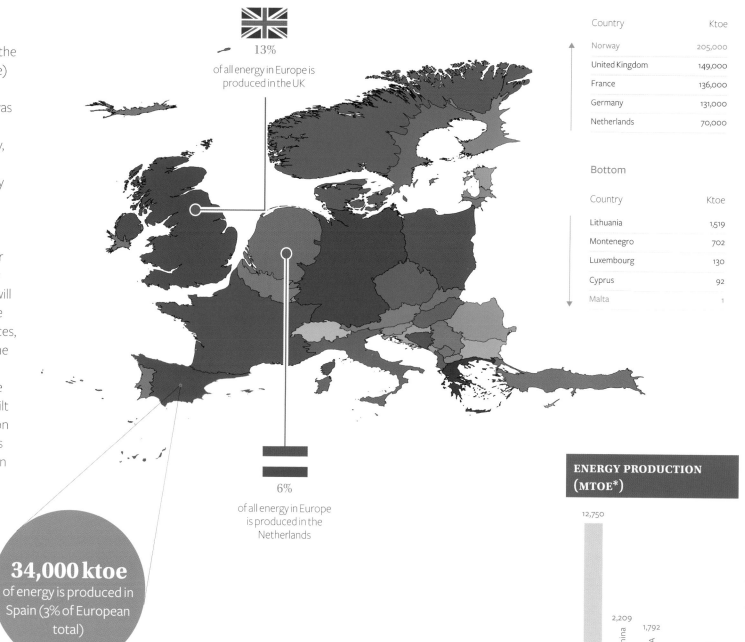

13%
of all energy in Europe is produced in the UK

6%
of all energy in Europe is produced in the Netherlands

34,000 ktoe
of energy is produced in Spain (3% of European total)

Top

Country	Ktoe
Norway	205,000
United Kingdom	149,000
France	136,000
Germany	131,000
Netherlands	70,000

Bottom

Country	Ktoe
Lithuania	1,519
Montenegro	702
Luxembourg	130
Cyprus	92
Malta	1

ENERGY PRODUCTION (MTOE*)

	Value
World	12,750
China	2,209
USA	1,792
EU	839
Japan	97

* Mtoe = Million tonnes oil equivalent

Energy use

2010

Europe's estimated total energy use was equivalent to approximately 1.9 gigatons of oil (Gtoe) in 2010.

Germany, France, the UK, Italy and Spain account for more than half (57%) of that total.

The energy shown here is not primarily that used by households, but by industry, thus it is aluminium smelting that propels Iceland to the top of the league table for energy use per head. Those countries that produce the most energy often use more, and because Iceland has access to geothermal sources and hydropower, it is largely the oil equivalent of these two renewable sources that is shown here for that country.

In France, much more of the energy is nuclear, in the UK more comes from gas, and in Norway more is from oil.

There are huge variations both within Europe and in comparison with otherwise similarly affluent countries worldwide in their main sources and use of energy.

Colour key, see Reference map A1, p 10

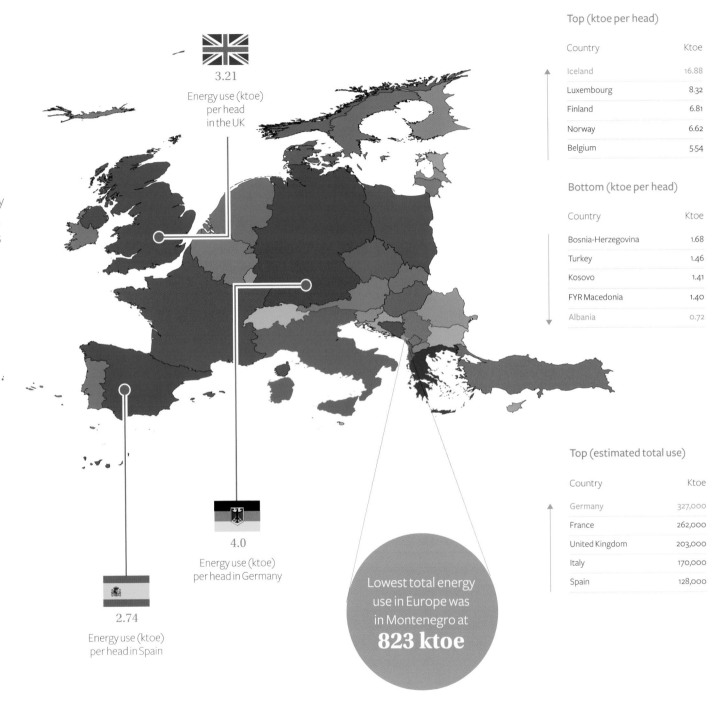

3.21

Energy use (ktoe) per head in the UK

4.0

Energy use (ktoe) per head in Germany

2.74

Energy use (ktoe) per head in Spain

Lowest total energy use in Europe was in Montenegro at **823 ktoe**

Top (ktoe per head)

Country	Ktoe
Iceland	16.88
Luxembourg	8.32
Finland	6.81
Norway	6.62
Belgium	5.54

Bottom (ktoe per head)

Country	Ktoe
Bosnia-Herzegovina	1.68
Turkey	1.46
Kosovo	1.41
FYR Macedonia	1.40
Albania	0.72

Top (estimated total use)

Country	Ktoe
Germany	327,000
France	262,000
United Kingdom	203,000
Italy	170,000
Spain	128,000

Energy use: fossil fuels

2010

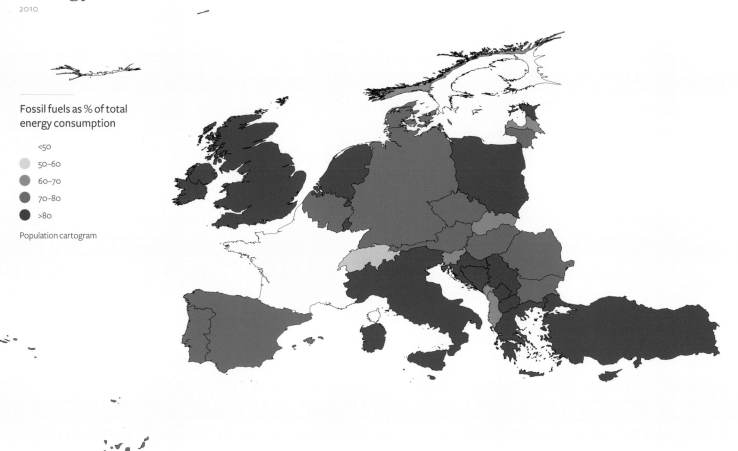

Fossil fuels as % of total energy consumption

- <50
- 50–60
- 60–70
- 70–80
- >80

Population cartogram

Country	Ktoe
Germany	256,000
United Kingdom	179,000
Italy	147,000
France	131,000
Spain	97,000

Bottom

Country	Ktoe
Kosovo	2,150
Albania	1,300
Iceland	940
Malta	840
Montenegro	550

Top (fossil fuels as % of total energy consumption)

Country	%
Malta	99.9
Cyprus	95.3
Netherlands	93.8
Poland	92.2
Bosnia-Herzegovina	91.5

Bottom (fossil fuels as % of total energy consumption)

Country	%
Switzerland	51.5
France	50.0
Finland	49.0
Sweden	34.1
Iceland	17.5

The fossil fuel energy consumption of Germany, the UK, Italy, France and Spain is approximately 55% of the European total, but as a percentage of the total energy consumption in each country, Malta has the highest figure, at 99.9%. Malta is the most densely populated state in Europe and so has less space (per person) to use to generate energy than other areas (although it could arguably use more solar power).

Cyprus, the Netherlands, Poland, Bosnia-Herzegovina and Greece also rely on fossil fuels for more than 90% of their energy requirements.

However, if we look at total extraction of fossils fuels in each country since extraction began worldwide several centuries ago and calculate the total resulting carbon pollution, then the UK has been historically the most polluting country worldwide, having extracted and burnt more tons of fossil fuels than any other country.

Energy use: combustible renewables and waste

2010

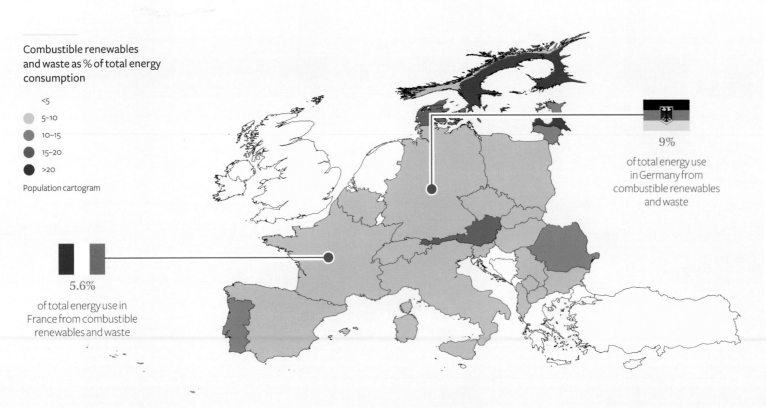

Combustible renewables and waste as % of total energy consumption

- <5
- 5–10
- 10–15
- 15–20
- >20

Population cartogram

9%

of total energy use in Germany from combustible renewables and waste

5.6%

of total energy use in France from combustible renewables and waste

Top (combustible renewables and waste as % of total energy consumption)

Country	%
Latvia	29.3
Sweden	23.2
Finland	22.6
Denmark	18.6
Austria	17.8

Bottom (combustible renewables and waste as % of total energy consumption)

Country	%
Montenegro	3.1
UK / Bosnia-Herzegovina	2.9
Ireland	2.6
Cyprus	1.8
Iceland / Malta	0.0

The highest rates of combustible renewables and waste used for energy are found in Northern Europe, in particular in the Scandinavian countries and Baltic States, but also in Austria, Poland and Portugal.

The smallest rates are found in South East Europe, but also the UK, Ireland and Iceland. The highest rate in the world was recorded in Ethiopia (94.1%).

Much of what is being burnt is wood, which is renewable – planting more trees for firewood absorbs carbon from the air before it is released again, when that wood is burnt.

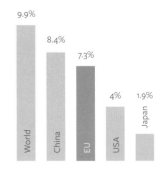

COMBUSTIBLE RENEWABLES AND WASTE AS % OF TOTAL ENERGY CONSUMPTION

- World 9.9%
- China 8.4%
- EU 7.3%
- USA 4%
- Japan 1.9%

Freshwater withdrawals

2013

In 2013 there were an estimated 292 billion cubic metres of freshwater withdrawals from all the countries mapped in this atlas for agricultural, industrial and domestic use.

The European total represents approximately 7.5% of the worldwide total in 2013. Freshwater withdrawals in the US were estimated at 478 billion m³ (third highest in the world), representing 12% of the total, while withdrawals in Japan represented 2%. In India and China, which withdrew the largest volumes in the world in absolute terms, the figures were 19% and 14% respectively. Total freshwater withdrawals by all OECD members were just over a quarter of the world total, at 26%.

Whether the level of freshwater withdrawal in a country is problematic depends very much on how much rainfall that country is receiving. Using up sources stored underground often creates problems not only for future supplies but also sometimes causing saltwater intrusion.

Colour key, see Reference map A1, p 10

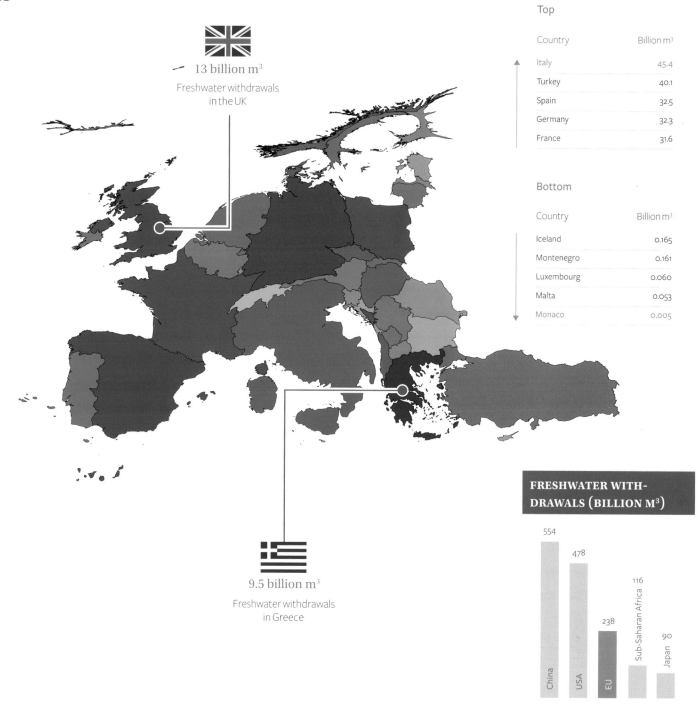

13 billion m³

Freshwater withdrawals in the UK

9.5 billion m³

Freshwater withdrawals in Greece

Top

Country	Billion m³
Italy	45.4
Turkey	40.1
Spain	32.5
Germany	32.3
France	31.6

Bottom

Country	Billion m³
Iceland	0.165
Montenegro	0.161
Luxembourg	0.060
Malta	0.053
Monaco	0.005

FRESHWATER WITHDRAWALS (BILLION M³)

554 China
478 USA
238 EU
116 Sub-Saharan Africa
90 Japan

Renewable freshwater resources

2013

There was an estimated 2,402 billion m³ of renewable internal freshwater resources (such as internal river flows and groundwater from rainfall) in the countries mapped in this atlas.

Norway has the largest share (16% of the total), followed by Turkey, France, Italy and Sweden. When taking population size into account, Iceland has by far the largest volume per head – the highest in Europe, and also in the world.

A country such as Italy that is relatively small on this map, but where extraction is above average (see previous map), will potentially have more problems with water access in future.

Countries have to interact when it comes to freshwater resources. Switzerland has huge freshwater resources, but the rivers flow to neighbouring countries. Within the UK Wales has abundant freshwater, some of which is harnessed to provide the North West of England with water. With water increasingly becoming a scarce resource in many regions around the world it risks becoming just another exploitable commodity rather than, in moderation, a universal human right.

Colour key, see Reference map A1, p 10

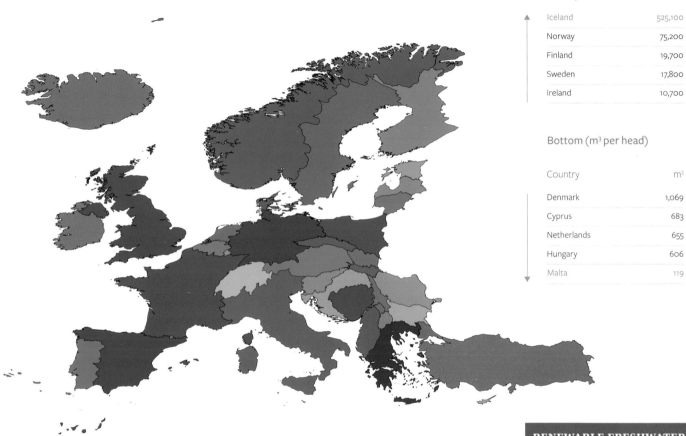

Top (m³ per head)

Country	m³
Iceland	525,100
Norway	75,200
Finland	19,700
Sweden	17,800
Ireland	10,700

Bottom (m³ per head)

Country	m³
Denmark	1,069
Cyprus	683
Netherlands	655
Hungary	606
Malta	119

Top
(total, billion m³)

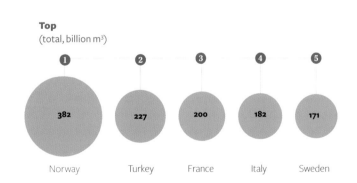

❶	❷	❸	❹	❺
382	227	200	182	171
Norway	Turkey	France	Italy	Sweden

RENEWABLE FRESHWATER RESOURCES (M³ PER HEAD)

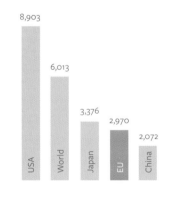

USA	World	Japan	EU	China
8,903	6,013	3,376	2,970	2,072

Terrestrial and marine protected areas

2010

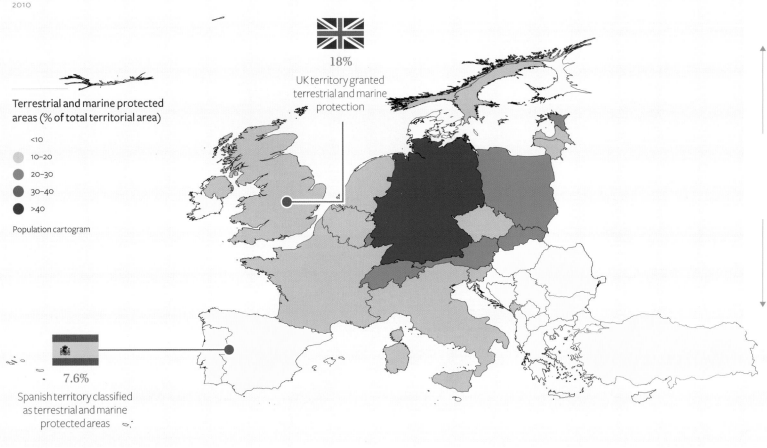

Terrestrial and marine protected areas (% of total territorial area)

- <10
- 10–20
- 20–30
- 30–40
- >40

Population cartogram

18%
UK territory granted terrestrial and marine protection

7.6%
Spanish territory classified as terrestrial and marine protected areas

Monaco has 98% of its territory classified as a terrestrial and marine protected area, by far the highest percentage in Europe and also worldwide, although Germany has the largest absolute area. Bosnia-Herzegovina has the least of any country as a proportion of its total land area.

Attempts to harmonise the protection of highly sensitive areas across Europe are ongoing, both within the continent and by agencies working worldwide. The very high degree of variation illustrated by this map shows how much further work is needed, with the East of Europe currently protecting more of its land than the West.

It is becoming increasingly realised how commercial activities can damage marine habitats. People everywhere need the right to roam in unspoilt open countryside near to where they live. This is likely to be increasingly recognised and planned for, not just left to chance. The same is also true of the right to visit unspoilt marine habitats, and for those habitats to be protected for the wider benefit of the environment and for us, in ways that may not be immediately obvious to us.

Forest area

2012

Forests play an extremely important role in the mitigation of climate change absorbing carbon dioxide from the atmosphere. They provide a habitat for animals, including many rare and endangered species, and a source of wood as well as jobs and livelihoods. Healthy forests have a vital role in moderating water movement, preventing soil erosion and helping to reduce flooding in the built-up environment.

More than 1.9 million km² of the European countries mapped in this atlas was under forest in 2012, approximately 5% of the world's total forest area. This excludes trees in agricultural production systems and in urban parks and gardens, so most of this forest is 'natural' and could be long-lasting.

About a quarter of all European forest area is found in Sweden (15%) and Finland (12%).

In relative terms, five countries, all in the North of Europe, have more than 50% of their total land area classified as forest. In contrast, the islands and small city states with almost no forest are in the South of Europe.

Worldwide an estimated 30% of all land area is classed as 'forest'.

Colour key, see Reference map A1, p 10

12%

total land area in the UK classed as forest

Top (km² forest per head)

Country	Km²
Sweden	282,000
Finland	221,600
Spain	185,300
France	160,500
Turkey	115,700

Bottom (km² forest per head)

Country	Km²
Iceland	317
Andorra	160
Liechtenstein	69
Malta	3
Monaco / San Marino	0

Top (% of all land)

Country	%
Finland	72.9
Sweden	69.2
Slovenia	62.4
Latvia	54.3
Estonia	51.8

Bottom (% of all land)

Country	%
Ireland	11.0
Netherlands	10.8
Malta	0.9
Iceland	0.3
Monaco / San Marino	0

FOREST AS % OF TOTAL LAND AREA

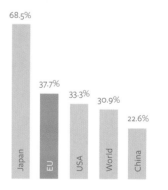

Japan	EU	USA	World	China
68.5%	37.7%	33.3%	30.9%	22.6%

Lonely Europe

2011

This map highlights the most sparsely populated and the most remote parts of the continent, areas that have remained mostly unacknowledged in this atlas so far. In effect, the map makes visible a rarely seen image of a 'Lonely Europe', of the remotest and most untouched spaces. Here areas are drawn larger when they are further away from the urban centres that tend to characterise European civilisation in the 21st century: the larger an area appears in this map, the longer it takes you to travel overland from there to the nearest city with a population of at least 50,000.

This is a map of where to go within Europe if you are looking for tranquillity and solitude. It relates clearly to key current debates about sustainable and green growth, and the need to preserve pristine spaces and areas of natural beauty and biodiversity.

As Europe continues to urbanise, the patterns on this map are slowly changing, with younger people more frequently moving to the larger cities in search of work or to study, and older people not moving far from those cities because they need access to the services located there.

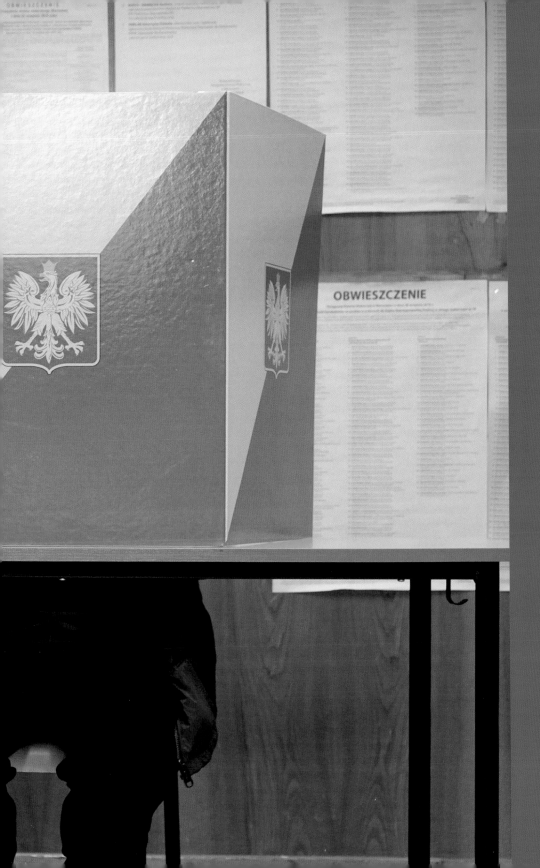

H – Politics

Europe is the birthplace of democracy, and the European Union has long been a strong driver for democratic change. According to the EU's founding Treaty, any country may apply for membership as long as it respects the democratic values of the EU, and is committed to promoting them.

- The maps in this section look at the importance of politics in people's lives, including **trust in government** and **voter engagement**. Data here is taken from the last 9-yearly European Values Study, conducted between 2008 and 2010. Many of the patterns of **social and political attitudes** presented here tend to change very slowly.
- Particularly topical regarding the more recent joiners to the EU is whether people value democracy as the best **system of government**, or favour other alternatives, including army rule.
- With concerns about violations of democratic rights and freedom of expression (and especially more recently the freedom of the press), it is also interesting to look at **how people protest**, from lawful demonstrations and belonging to peace movements, to strike action and occupying buildings.
- Other **inequalities in politics** are explored here, such as the number of women in parliament. We also consider the relative popularity of left, right and centrist parties.

There are currently lively debates regarding governance, democratic accountability and social cohesion, and the need to move forward and further enhance democracy in Europe, all building on the remarkable achievements of the past seven decades. It is often through awareness of appearing not to fit in, and concern about being extreme, that European states slowly move away from authoritarianism.

How important is politics?

2008

This map shows the estimated numbers of people who regard politics as 'very important' in their lives, according to 2008 data from the European Values Survey.

Turkey and Sweden dominate the map, and both have been expanded to a size greater here than that which would be expected given their relative populations.

In relative terms, Sweden has the largest estimated proportion of its population considering politics to be 'very important' in their lives, and stands out not just in relation to the rest of Europe, but also compared to its other Scandinavian neighbours.

The answers here may be influenced by language, and how much the word *'politics'* is seen to encompass. However, a bigger factor is likely to be when the question is asked. Is there an impending referendum or election, and if so does it risk changing everything, or is it unlikely to change anything much? Two of the Baltic States and countries involved in or situated near the war in the former Yugoslavia are among those where people appear to be least likely to say that politics is very important.

Colour key, see Reference map A1, p 10

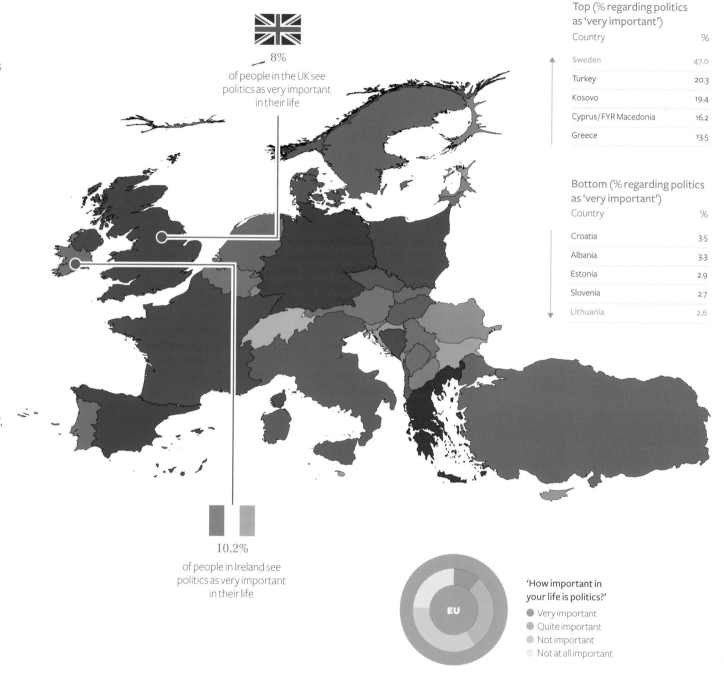

8%

of people in the UK see politics as very important in their life

10.2%

of people in Ireland see politics as very important in their life

Top (% regarding politics as 'very important')

Country	%
Sweden	47.0
Turkey	20.3
Kosovo	19.4
Cyprus / FYR Macedonia	16.2
Greece	13.5

Bottom (% regarding politics as 'very important')

Country	%
Croatia	3.5
Albania	3.3
Estonia	2.9
Slovenia	2.7
Lithuania	2.6

EU

'How important in your life is politics?'

● Very important
● Quite important
● Not important
○ Not at all important

Is democracy the best political system?

2008

Only a small fraction of European Values Survey respondents in 2008 said they 'disagreed strongly' when asked if democracy is the best political system. This relatively small number of people are mapped here.

People disagreeing strongly with this statement may believe that democratic systems are too indecisive, poor at maintaining order and not efficient at running the economy. Alternatively, they may think that what is called a 'democratic' system may, in fact, be easily manipulated by a few people with special interests, who are usually those with the most access to money, the media and politicians. Those not favouring democracy may include people who are harking back to a less democratic 'Golden Age' when they think their country was better run than it is today. However, despite their political troubles, Italy and Greece in 2008, very few people were strongly opposed to democracy.

Voting for far right-parties was lower in Greece in 2015 than in 2012, and also fell in Belgium, Finland, Hungary, Italy and the Netherlands recently. Spain and Portugal have no significant far-right parties.

Colour key, see Reference map A1, p 10

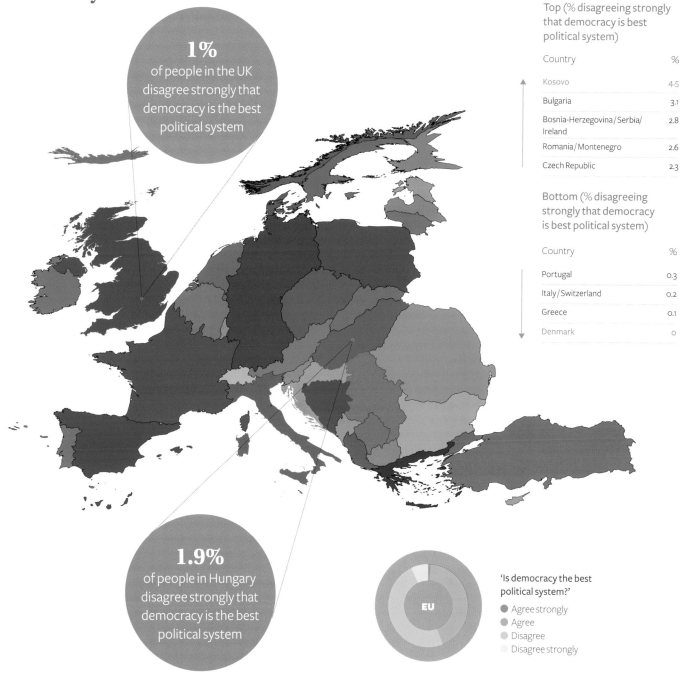

1% of people in the UK disagree strongly that democracy is the best political system

1.9% of people in Hungary disagree strongly that democracy is the best political system

Top (% disagreeing strongly that democracy is best political system)

Country	%
Kosovo	4.5
Bulgaria	3.1
Bosnia-Herzegovina / Serbia / Ireland	2.8
Romania / Montenegro	2.6
Czech Republic	2.3

Bottom (% disagreeing strongly that democracy is best political system)

Country	%
Portugal	0.3
Italy / Switzerland	0.2
Greece	0.1
Denmark	0

EU

'Is democracy the best political system?'
- ● Agree strongly
- ● Agree
- ● Disagree
- ● Disagree strongly

Is army rule a very good political system?

2008

An estimated 2% of all Europeans in 2008 believed army rule would be a very good political system. Nearly half were in Turkey, where 10.5% agreed with this statement. Turkey also has the highest figure in relative terms, closely followed by Kosovo (10.2%) and Serbia (9.7%).

What might be the thinking behind such attitudes? People may be saying that, given all the other alternatives they can think of working practically where they live, they believe that having the army in charge is the safest option, and for them, 'safest' means having a 'very good' political system.

In various parts of Europe in recent decades the army has been in charge either officially or unofficially. This often includes areas that have experienced recent wars or war-like situations, such as Northern Ireland or Turkey.

Colour key, see Reference map A1, p 10

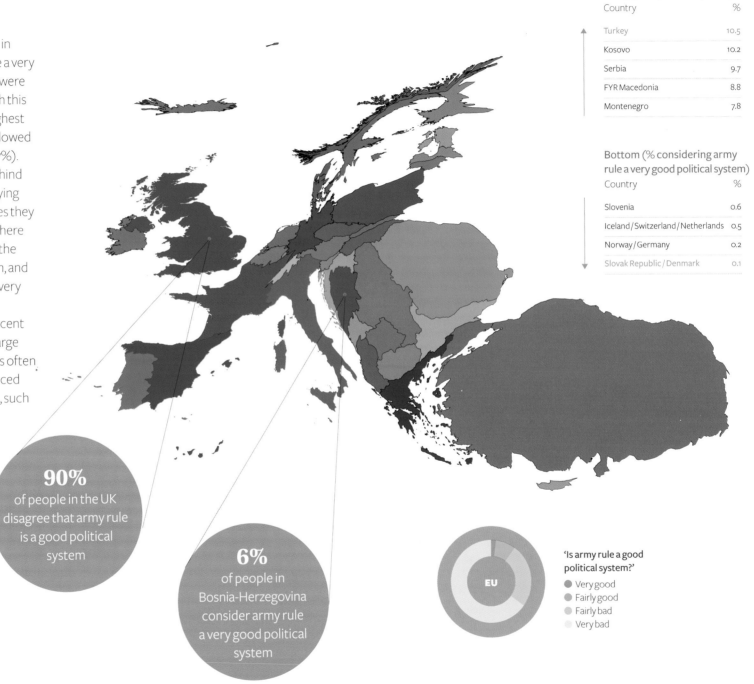

90% of people in the UK disagree that army rule is a good political system

6% of people in Bosnia-Herzegovina consider army rule a very good political system

'Is army rule a good political system?'
- Very good
- Fairly good
- Fairly bad
- Very bad

EU

Top (% considering army rule a very good political system)

Country	%
Turkey	10.5
Kosovo	10.2
Serbia	9.7
FYR Macedonia	8.8
Montenegro	7.8

Bottom (% considering army rule a very good political system)

Country	%
Slovenia	0.6
Iceland / Switzerland / Netherlands	0.5
Norway / Germany	0.2
Slovak Republic / Denmark	0.1

How much interest in politics?

2008

According to 2008 data from the European Values Survey, 23% of all Europeans said they were 'not at all interested' in politics.

The country with the highest absolute number with no interest in politics was Turkey, followed by the UK, Spain and Italy. Did their lack of interest contribute to subsequent events? In relative terms the highest proportion of all those aged 15 and over declaring a lack of interest was found in Albania, closely followed by Montenegro.

It would be interesting to know now whether the 22,000 Icelanders who said they were not at all interested in politics in 2008 still have the same view. This is a tiny proportion of Iceland's population, less than 9% of all those living there, but given the major economic and political crisis following the default of all major banks in Iceland and the upheaval and events that occurred there subsequently, it is likely that many of these people became more interested in politics, although at the same time others perhaps became more disillusioned.

Colour key, see Reference map A1, p 10

Top (% not at all interested in politics)

Country	%
Albania	36.9
Montenegro	36.6
Andorra/Spain	33.5
Croatia	32.1

Bottom (% not at all interested in politics)

Country	%
Latvia	11.1
Germany	9.3
Iceland	8.7
Norway	7.2
Denmark	6.7

'How interested are you in politics?'

- Very interested
- Somewhat interested
- Not very interested
- Not at all interested

Voting preferences – left, right or centre?

2008

In 2008, the left was strongest in countries in the East of Europe, but in the West it had most support in some of Europe's most economically equitable countries: Norway, Switzerland and Finland. The left was weakest in Luxembourg, Sweden and the UK at this time.

Overall, right-wing parties were most popular in Greece in 2008, followed in the West of Europe by Norway and Iceland, and in the East by Cyprus, Albania, Serbia and Poland. The right had the support of only 6.3% of voters in Hungary in 2008.

Inevitably 'left' and 'right' mean different things in different countries. What is perhaps most interesting here is the number of countries where the most popular political parties at the time tried to present themselves as centrist and not 'extremists'. Any political parties in power in 2008 during the global financial crisis tended to become unpopular whichever side of politics they stood on.

In the UK in 2008, 92% of the population supported 'moderate' parties. The Labour Party had been 'intensely relaxed about people getting filthy rich', and the Conservatives talked about 'compassionate Conservatism'. When the latter gained power, many argued that their policies were neither compassionate nor traditionally Conservative.

'Which political party would you vote for on left/right scale?' Left   Centre   Right

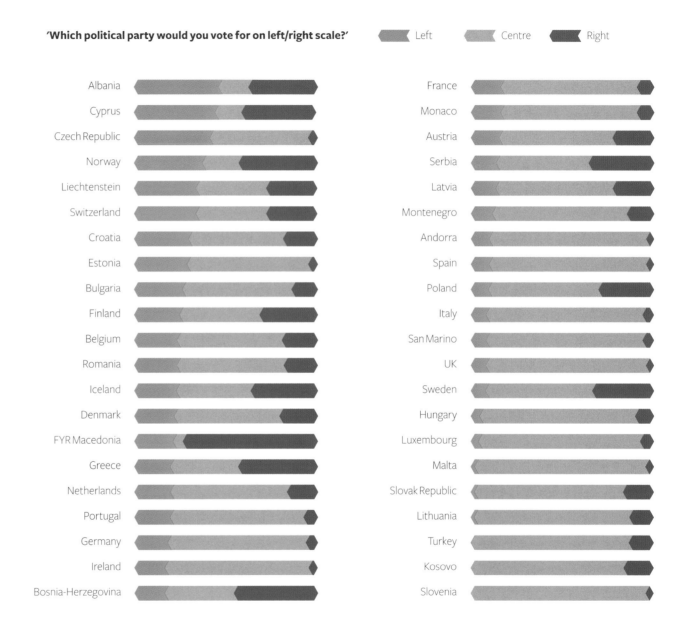

Attending lawful demonstrations

2008

In 2008, 23% of all survey respondents had attended lawful demonstrations. This was before the mass protests in Europe against austerity began.

Nearly three-quarters of the total are in the top five countries, with about a fifth in France. France is also far ahead in relative terms, with an estimated 45.6% of its population aged 15 and over having ever taken part in demonstrations.

In contrast, the smallest percentages are mostly found in Eastern European countries, but also in Turkey. The Slovak Republic, Estonia, Turkey, Bosnia-Herzegovina, Romania, Lithuania, Poland, Bulgaria and Croatia all have percentages of less than 10%.

The lowest figure of all, 3.9% in Hungary, may well relate to the fateful consequences of the 1956 Hungarian Uprising, suppressed by Soviet tanks: 2,500 Hungarians and 700 Soviet troops killed, mass arrests and imprisonment, numerous executions and 200,000 Hungarians fleeing as refugees. But not protesting has consequences. In 2016 Hungary was the only country in Europe to be governed by a far-right party.

Colour key, see Reference map A1, p 10

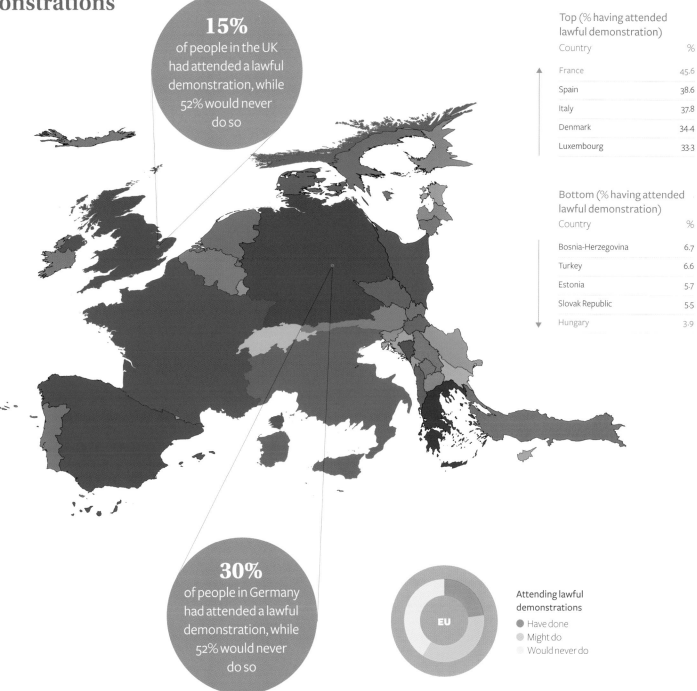

15% of people in the UK had attended a lawful demonstration, while 52% would never do so

30% of people in Germany had attended a lawful demonstration, while 52% would never do so

Attending lawful demonstrations
- Have done
- Might do
- Would never do

Top (% having attended lawful demonstration)

Country	%
France	45.6
Spain	38.6
Italy	37.8
Denmark	34.4
Luxembourg	33.3

Bottom (% having attended lawful demonstration)

Country	%
Bosnia-Herzegovina	6.7
Turkey	6.6
Estonia	5.7
Slovak Republic	5.5
Hungary	3.9

Joining unofficial strikes

2008

Unofficial strikes are those that have not been lawfully called by a trade union, and where workers' rights are thus not protected.

According to the 2008 European Values Survey, around 5% of all Europeans aged 15 and over had previously joined unofficial strikes, and the map is dominated by the top five countries, which between them include approximately 70% of the total unofficial strikers, with France standing out (having just over a fifth, 22% of the total). In relative terms, however, France is ranked second, after Denmark.

The lowest rates are found in Eastern Europe, with Hungary, Cyprus, Estonia and the Slovak Republic having the lowest percentages (all below 1%). Unofficial strikes appear much more common in Western Europe. Under communist rule in the East before 1989 it was almost impossible to take part in an unofficial strike. When those in power paint themselves as the workers' representatives, they tend to have very little tolerance of workers behaving in unorganised ways – but this is what happened when the Solidarity movement in Poland grew. Poland is larger on the map than any other country in the former Eastern bloc.

Colour key, see Reference map A1, p 10

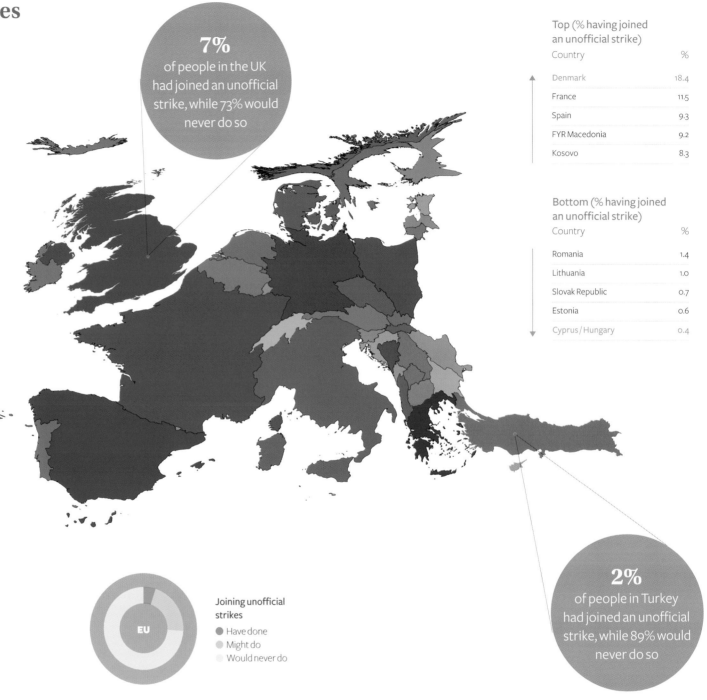

7% of people in the UK had joined an unofficial strike, while 73% would never do so

2% of people in Turkey had joined an unofficial strike, while 89% would never do so

Joining unofficial strikes

- Have done
- Might do
- Would never do

EU

Top (% having joined an unofficial strike)

Country	%
Denmark	18.4
France	11.5
Spain	9.3
FYR Macedonia	9.2
Kosovo	8.3

Bottom (% having joined an unofficial strike)

Country	%
Romania	1.4
Lithuania	1.0
Slovak Republic	0.7
Estonia	0.6
Cyprus / Hungary	0.4

Belonging to welfare organisations

2008

The 2008 European Values Survey asked a number of questions regarding membership of voluntary organisations and groups. Five per cent of all respondents said that they belonged to a 'social welfare organisation'.

This is about 'social capital': the networks of relationships between people who live and work in a particular society, enabling that society to function effectively. These networks are marked by trust, cooperation and include substantial voluntary and unpaid work. Here we look at such work in local community initiatives and charitable organisations benefiting, for example, elderly, handicapped or deprived people.

Northern and Western European countries dominate the map, but it is also worth noting that Portugal has a relatively prominent place here.

The rates are lowest in Hungary, which may well have been one of the most individualistic countries in Europe at this time, and which elected a far-right government two years later in 2010.

Colour key, see Reference map A1, p 10

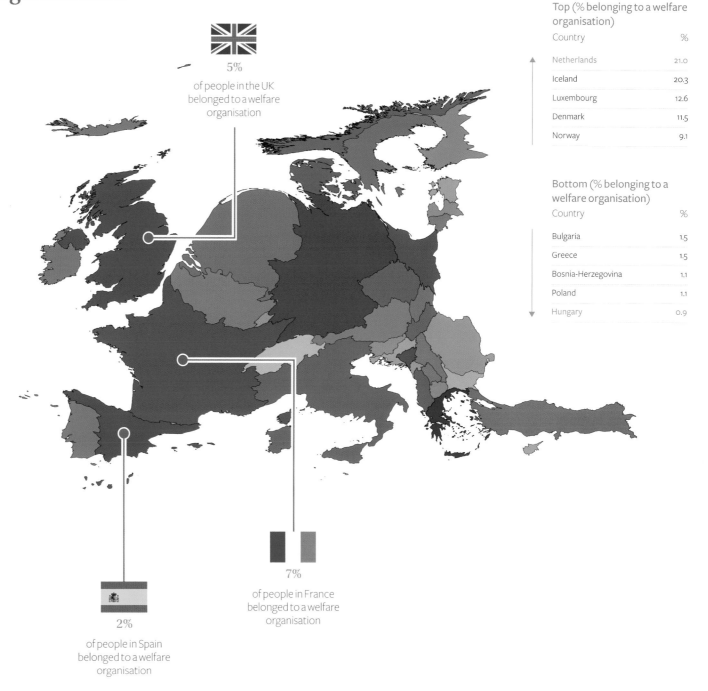

5%
of people in the UK belonged to a welfare organisation

2%
of people in Spain belonged to a welfare organisation

7%
of people in France belonged to a welfare organisation

Top (% belonging to a welfare organisation)

Country	%
Netherlands	21.0
Iceland	20.3
Luxembourg	12.6
Denmark	11.5
Norway	9.1

Bottom (% belonging to a welfare organisation)

Country	%
Bulgaria	1.5
Greece	1.5
Bosnia-Herzegovina	1.1
Poland	1.1
Hungary	0.9

Belonging to peace movements

2008

One per cent of all European Values Survey respondents in 2008 mentioned that they had belonged to some form of peace movement. Peace movements in Europe began to grow in number in the aftermath of the slaughter of the First World War. They saw a revival again following the Second World War, and then grew greatly during the Cold War, when Europe was divided in two between East and West.

As war within Europe becomes more and more of a distant memory for most Europeans, membership of peace movements also diminishes. In relative terms, the countries with the highest rates of membership of peace movements have also most recently experienced war and tensions. New wars, supposedly declared 'on terror' or other abstract concepts, may lead more young people to take part in organisations that protect liberty over peace.

It is in those countries from within Europe that take part in bombing people in countries on the edge of Europe where we should expect opposition to the use of force to grow. This opposition includes campaigns against the sale of arms, which is a big business within many European countries.

Colour key, see Reference map A1, p 10

1%
of people in the UK had belonged to a peace movement

1%
of people in Cyprus had belonged to a peace movement

Top (% ever belonging to a peace movement)

Country	%
Kosovo	6.2
Albania	4.8
Netherlands	3.1
Luxembourg	2.2
Iceland	1.9

Bottom (% ever belonging to a peace movement)

Country	%
Poland/Greece	0.4
Bulgaria/France/Lithuania	0.3
Malta	0.2
Hungary	0.1

Occupying buildings/factories

2008

Four per cent of all Europeans aged 16 and over had taken part in the occupation of buildings or factories, according to the European Values Survey 2008. The map is clearly dominated by Italy and France, but Greece is also relatively prominent. These occupations could include school buildings or university buildings being occupied by protesting students.

No time limit was put on the length of the occupation to count as an occupier. Note also how many people cannot envisage any circumstances in which they might feel they need to occupy a building in protest.

Politics in the recent past has been very differently practised across this small continent. Contrast France and the UK in this map to see how different the political experiences of so many people in these two neighbouring large countries are.

This is not just about the numbers taking part, but also about how much such activity is considered by the community to be a valid form of protest, the immediate risks involved if non-peaceful methods are used to try to stop it, and the possible legal consequences for those engaged in protest.

Colour key, see Reference map A1, p 10

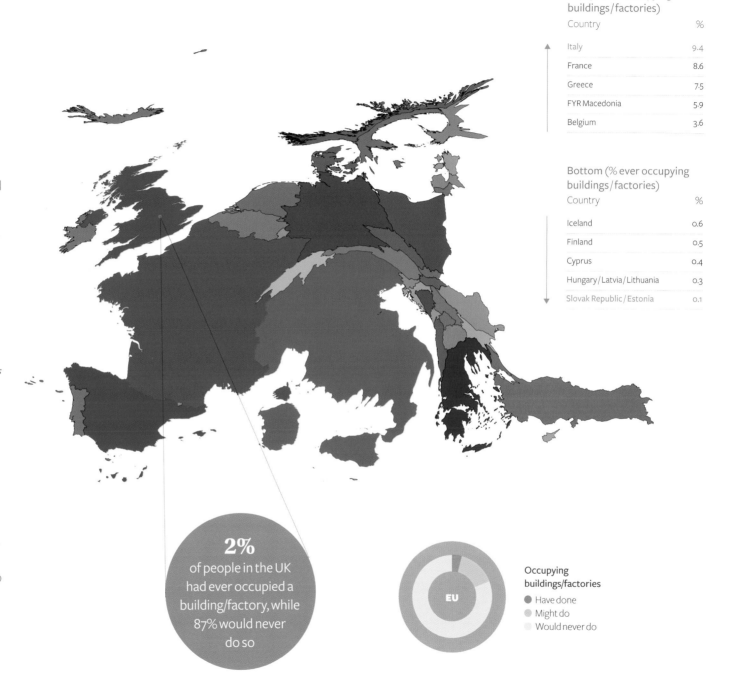

Top (% ever occupying buildings/factories)

Country	%
Italy	9.4
France	8.6
Greece	7.5
FYR Macedonia	5.9
Belgium	3.6

Bottom (% ever occupying buildings/factories)

Country	%
Iceland	0.6
Finland	0.5
Cyprus	0.4
Hungary/Latvia/Lithuania	0.3
Slovak Republic/Estonia	0.1

2%
of people in the UK had ever occupied a building/factory, while 87% would never do so

EU

Occupying buildings/factories
- Have done
- Might do
- Would never do

Trust in national government

VARIOUS YEARS, 2007–12

This map, which shows estimated numbers of people who trust their national governments, is dominated by five of the largest countries – Germany, Turkey, France, the UK and Italy – which together account for just over 60% of all Europeans expressing trust in their national government. In relative terms, however, the top five includes three Scandinavian countries as well as Luxembourg, Serbia and Switzerland. Trust does not appear to be reduced where the major political parties do not seek the centre ground.

The bottom five is dominated by Eastern Europe and the Baltic States.

The country with the lowest rate of trust in government is Greece (which also had the lowest percentage of trust in the world for the countries for which data were available), which had been going through a severe economic crisis, at the time these surveys were conducted, resulting in a massive and rapid increase in its unemployment rate.

In the UK the percentage of people who were estimated to trust their government at that time was 42%, whereas the world average was 48%. In the US it was 35% and in Japan it was 17%. Trust can rise or fall quickly in reaction to events.

Colour key, see Reference map A1, p 10

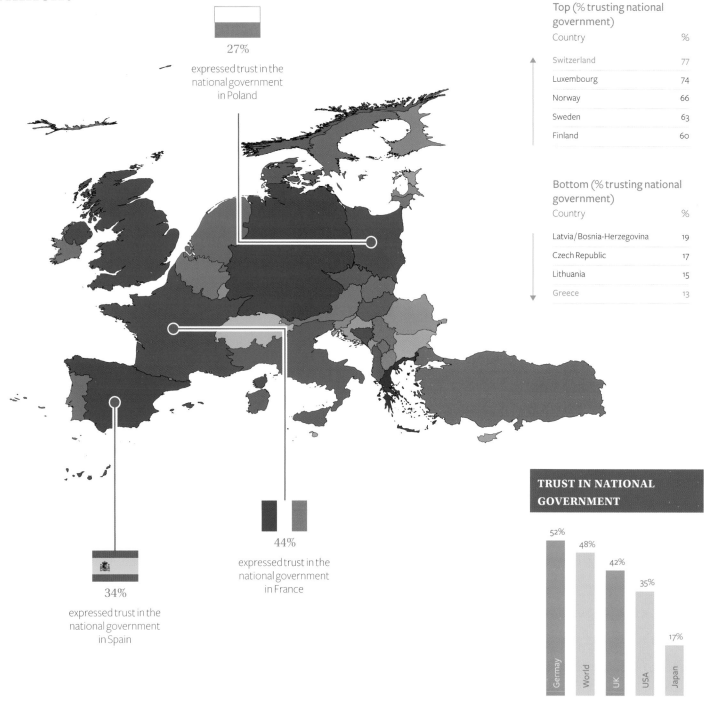

27%
expressed trust in the
national government
in Poland

44%
expressed trust in the
national government
in France

34%
expressed trust in the
national government
in Spain

Top (% trusting national government)

Country	%
Switzerland	77
Luxembourg	74
Norway	66
Sweden	63
Finland	60

Bottom (% trusting national government)

Country	%
Latvia/Bosnia-Herzegovina	19
Czech Republic	17
Lithuania	15
Greece	13

TRUST IN NATIONAL GOVERNMENT

Germany	World	UK	USA	Japan
52%	48%	42%	35%	17%

Women in parliament

2013

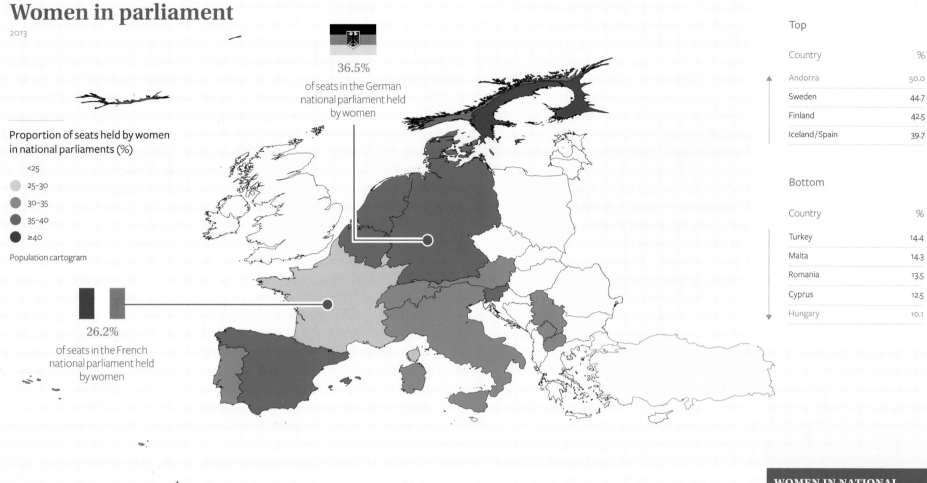

Proportion of seats held by women in national parliaments (%)

- <25
- 25–30
- 30–35
- 35–40
- ≥40

Population cartogram

36.5%
of seats in the German national parliament held by women

26.2%
of seats in the French national parliament held by women

Top

Country	%
Andorra	50.0
Sweden	44.7
Finland	42.5
Iceland / Spain	39.7

Bottom

Country	%
Turkey	14.4
Malta	14.3
Romania	13.5
Cyprus	12.5
Hungary	10.1

This map shows the proportions of seats held by women in national parliaments across Europe in 2013.

Andorra had the highest rate in Europe, and the second highest in the world (after Rwanda, with a rate of 51.9%). Overall, the highest rates are observed in the Scandinavian countries, but also in Central Europe, some countries of the Western Balkans and in Spain. The UK is ranked 25th out of the 43 European states, with 22.6% of the seats in its parliament in 2013 held by women.

In the US the rate was 18.2% and in Japan 10.8%, whereas the world average was 21.1%. The lowest rates worldwide were recorded in Qatar, Micronesia and Vanuatu (0.1%).

What this map does not show is how much power women had within each of the parliaments of their respective countries, whether they were in executive positions, and how often (if ever) a woman had been a head of state.

At the start of 2017, in two of Europe's largest countries, Germany and the UK, a woman held the position of head of state.

WOMEN IN NATIONAL PARLIAMENTS (BY UN HDI* SCORES)

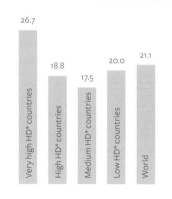

*Human Development Index

Quality of government

REGIONAL MAP, 2013

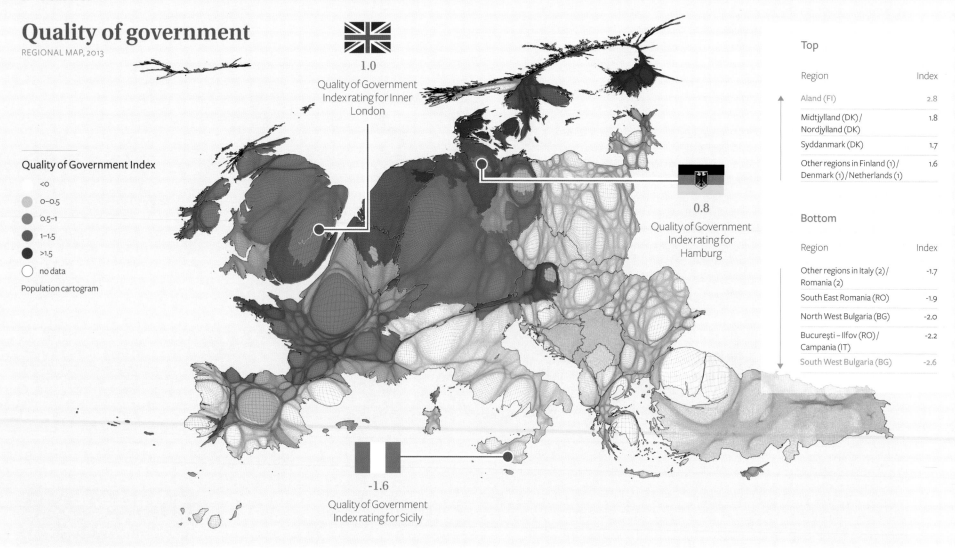

Quality of Government Index

○	<0
○	0–0.5
●	0.5–1
●	1–1.5
●	>1.5
○	no data

Population cartogram

1.0
Quality of Government
Index rating for Inner
London

0.8
Quality of Government
Index rating for
Hamburg

-1.6
Quality of Government
Index rating for Sicily

Top

Region	Index
Aland (FI)	2.8
Midtjylland (DK) / Nordjylland (DK)	1.8
Syddanmark (DK)	1.7
Other regions in Finland (1) / Denmark (1) / Netherlands (1)	1.6

Bottom

Region	Index
Other regions in Italy (2) / Romania (2)	-1.7
South East Romania (RO)	-1.9
North West Bulgaria (BG)	-2.0
Bucureşti – Ilfov (RO) / Campania (IT)	-2.2
South West Bulgaria (BG)	-2.6

This map is based on the European Quality of Government Index, which measures perceptions and experiences of public sector corruption, and rates public sector services in terms of quality and the fair allocation of resources to the general public, calculated from survey data. Results are converted to a standard score with 0 being the mean score and 1 and -1 being one standard deviation above or below that.

There is a clear East–West and to some extent also a North–South divide in Europe, but there are also considerable regional variations within some countries, and especially within the UK, France, Spain and Germany. For instance, in the UK the Index values range from a minimum of 0.4 in West Wales and the Valleys and in East Wales to a maximum of 1.1 in Berkshire, Buckinghamshire and Oxfordshire, Surrey East and West Sussex, Hampshire and the Isle of Wight, and Kent.

One possible reason for the regional variations seen in this map is that those areas where there was more support for the current government in power at the time of the survey might well contain more people who also think that what government is doing is fair. However, in much of the poorer periphery of Europe only a minority of people believe that any government is working in their interests.

I – Identity and Culture

"Europe is a thought that needs to become a feeling. When Americans talk about their United States, they get all misty eyed, they get emotional. Hell, when the Irish talk about the United States, we get misty eyed. Do we think that way about Europe? And if not, why not?"
(Bono, addressing delegates at the European People's Party Congress in Dublin, 7 March 2014)

Many things about Europe can provoke its citizens to become passionate and emotional.

- This chapter includes broad-ranging themes that relate to **European identity** and **culture**, such as views on the death penalty, religion, work, friends and family, and the extent to which people feel they belong to Europe. (Although a number of the maps derive from the European Values Survey of 2008, views on many of the subjects canvassed will change only slowly.)
- Other themes include **life satisfaction** and **happiness**, whether people feel that **competition** is good, **trust** in other people and finally, the results of a 'special' music festival that brings many Europeans together every year – the **Eurovision** Song Contest.

For Europeans to get 'misty eyed' when talking about Europe, for them to feel 'united not just by bonds of interest, but by bonds of affection', this will take more change and greater understanding than we have now.

General happiness

2008

When asked the subjective 'general happiness' question – 'Taking all things together, how happy are you?' – and given four answers to choose from ('very happy', 'quite happy', 'not very happy', 'not at all happy'), 26% of the 2008 European Values Survey respondents answered 'very happy'. This map shows the geographical distribution of these apparently 'very happy' Europeans.

There are two countries (the Netherlands and Iceland) where the estimated numbers of 'very happy' people make up more than half of the population aged 16 and over, whereas the three Baltic States all have a percentage of less than 10%. Caution is needed, however, when looking at the geography of happiness, as there may be cultural as well as perhaps linguistic issues affecting responses to happiness questions in surveys.

Overall, Europe appears to be quite a happy place, where 84% were at least 'quite happy' when this survey was taken. International comparisons often label South America as the happiest continent.

Colour key, see Reference map A1, p 10

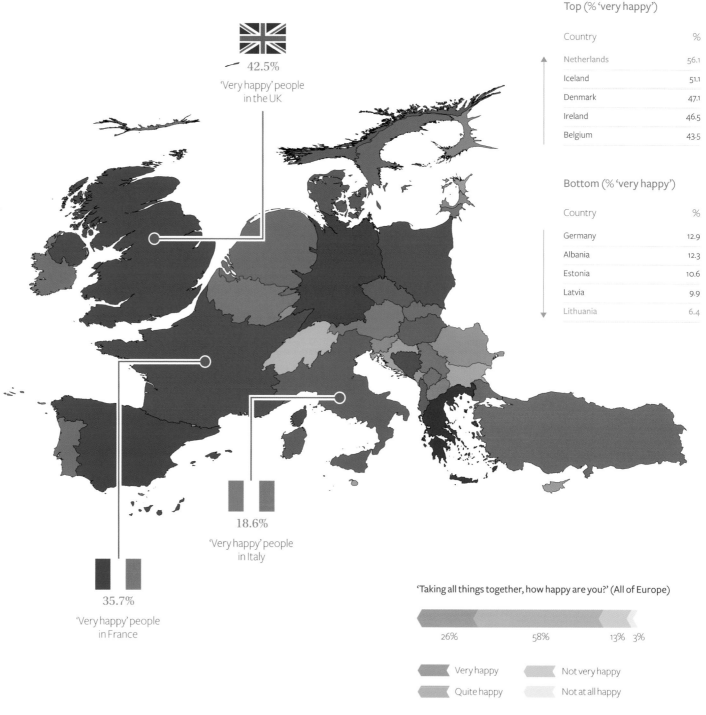

42.5%
'Very happy' people
in the UK

35.7%
'Very happy' people
in France

18.6%
'Very happy' people
in Italy

Top (% 'very happy')

Country	%
Netherlands	56.1
Iceland	51.1
Denmark	47.1
Ireland	46.5
Belgium	43.5

Bottom (% 'very happy')

Country	%
Germany	12.9
Albania	12.3
Estonia	10.6
Latvia	9.9
Lithuania	6.4

'Taking all things together, how happy are you?' (All of Europe)

26%   58%   13% 3%

Very happy   Not very happy
Quite happy   Not at all happy

Life satisfaction

VARIOUS YEARS 2007–12

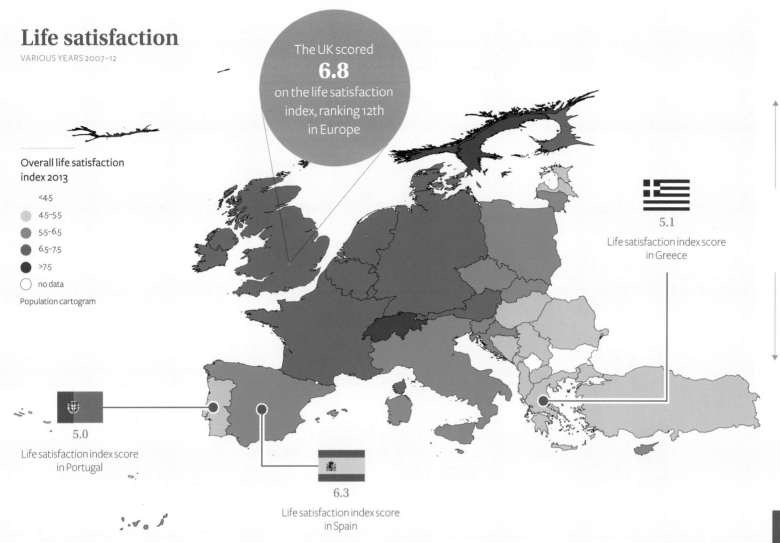

The UK scored
6.8
on the life satisfaction
index, ranking 12th
in Europe

Overall life satisfaction index 2013

- <4.5
- 4.5–5.5
- 5.5–6.5
- 6.5–7.5
- >7.5
- no data

Population cartogram

5.1
Life satisfaction index score
in Greece

5.0
Life satisfaction index score
in Portugal

6.3
Life satisfaction index score
in Spain

Top (life satisfaction index)

Country	Index
Switzerland	7.8
Norway	7.7
Iceland/Sweden	7.6
Denmark/Netherlands	7.5
Austria/Finland	7.4

Bottom (life satisfaction index)

Country	Index
Portugal	5.0
Bosnia-Herzegovina	4.8
Hungary	4.7
FYR Macedonia	4.6
Bulgaria	4.2

Here we look at overall life satisfaction scores across Europe based on responses to a Gallup World Poll questionnaire.

There is an apparent East–West and to some extent a North–South divide, but it is interesting to note Cyprus having a relatively higher average index score than its neighbours. The top six countries in Europe were also the top six worldwide,

with Canada, ranked joint seventh, as the first non-European country in the world league. The lowest average value recorded worldwide was in Togo (2.9), whereas the world average was 5.3.

Countries with a relatively high index score tend to have lower levels of inequality, and well-established and developed welfare systems. Index levels dropped between 2007 and 2012 in

countries where people faced extreme austerity measures (e.g. Greece, Spain and Ireland).

GLOBAL LIFE SATISFACTION SCORES

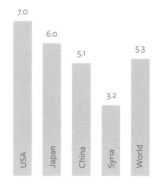

USA 7.0 · Japan 6.0 · China 5.1 · Syria 3.2 · World 5.3

Feeling 'European'

2008

The 2008 European Values Survey included a question asking, 'To which geographic group do you feel you belong most?', with the following possible answers: 'Locality or town', 'Region/country', 'Country as a whole', 'Europe' and 'World as a whole'. This map shows the survey-based estimates of total numbers answering 'Europe' – just 3% of the total European population, a small but very interesting group, who could be considered to be most European in terms of their identity.

In some of the countries with the highest proportions identifying most strongly with Europe, many people have moved from one country to another within Europe and so may identify more with the continent as a whole than with the place where they are currently living or their country of origin.

Many of the countries with the lowest proportions of people who consider themselves foremost as European now have (or have always had) very few residents who were born abroad. It is also interesting to note that twice as many people, 6%, identify most closely with the world as a whole as those who identify with Europe.

Colour key, see Reference map A1, p 10

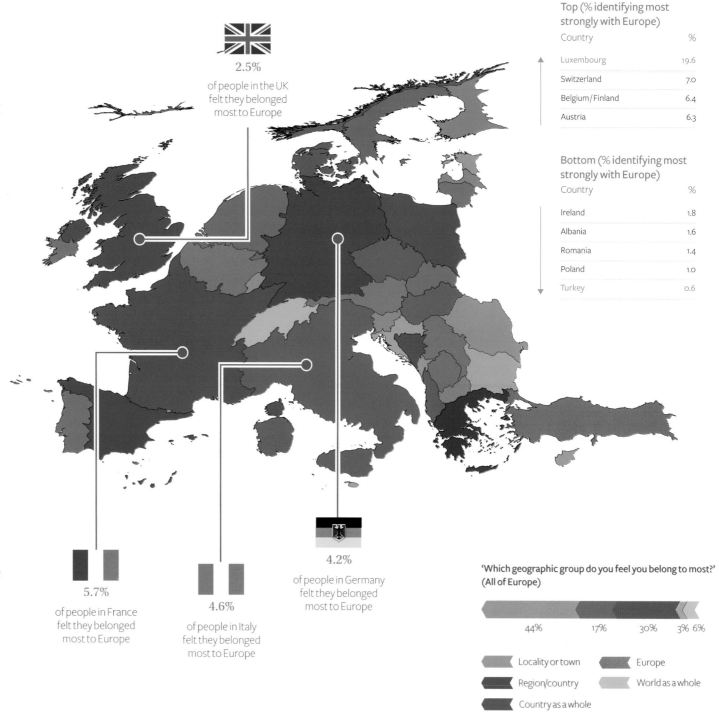

2.5% of people in the UK felt they belonged most to Europe

5.7% of people in France felt they belonged most to Europe

4.6% of people in Italy felt they belonged most to Europe

4.2% of people in Germany felt they belonged most to Europe

Top (% identifying most strongly with Europe)

Country	%
Luxembourg	19.6
Switzerland	7.0
Belgium/Finland	6.4
Austria	6.3

Bottom (% identifying most strongly with Europe)

Country	%
Ireland	1.8
Albania	1.6
Romania	1.4
Poland	1.0
Turkey	0.6

'Which geographic group do you feel you belong to most?' (All of Europe)

44% 17% 30% 3% 6%

Locality or town — Europe
Region/country — World as a whole
Country as a whole

Fear of losing national identity

2008

The 2008 European Values Survey asked a number of questions regarding 'fears' associated with the EU. One of these explored such fears in relation to loss of national identity and culture, and there was a 10-point answer scale (from 1 = very much afraid to 10 = not afraid at all). This map shows the spread of those 19% of Europeans who answered that they were 'very much afraid' of losing their national identity.

Fear of losing national identity is a question that results in one of the widest range of answers being recorded. The geographical patterns here are relevant to recent events and developments in the summer of 2016 in countries with very high percentages, such as the Brexit result in the UK referendum on EU membership and the attempted coup in Turkey and the subsequent instability and increased uncertainty over this country's status as a candidate member of the EU.

Interestingly, it is countries that are located a little further towards the periphery of Europe that appear to think they have the most to fear. Those located more centrally within the continent appear to be less fearful that their national identity is somehow threatened.

Colour key, see Reference map A1, p 10

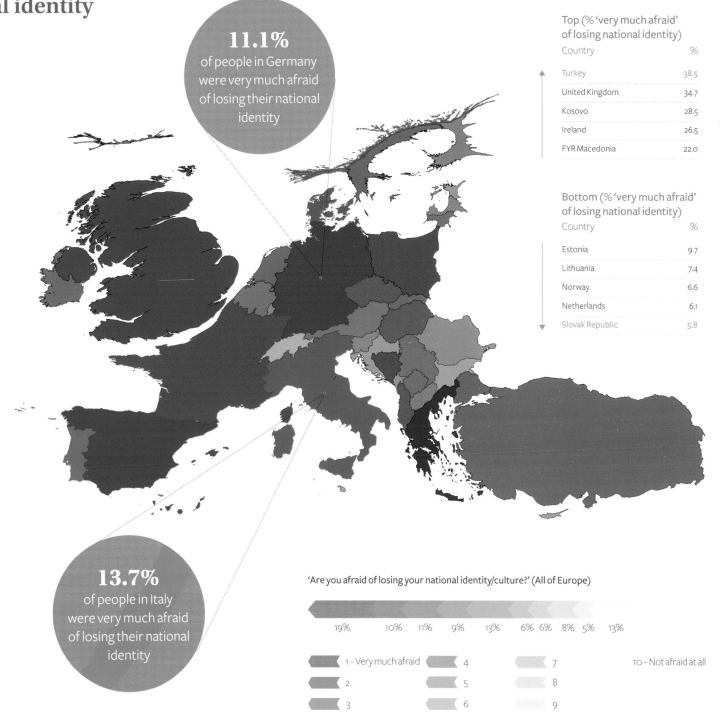

11.1% of people in Germany were very much afraid of losing their national identity

13.7% of people in Italy were very much afraid of losing their national identity

Top (% 'very much afraid' of losing national identity)

Country	%
Turkey	38.5
United Kingdom	34.7
Kosovo	28.5
Ireland	26.5
FYR Macedonia	22.0

Bottom (% 'very much afraid' of losing national identity)

Country	%
Estonia	9.7
Lithuania	7.4
Norway	6.6
Netherlands	6.1
Slovak Republic	5.8

'Are you afraid of losing your national identity/culture?' (All of Europe)

| 19% | 10% | 11% | 9% | 13% | 6% | 6% | 8% | 5% | 13% |

1 – Very much afraid	4	7	10 – Not afraid at all
2	5	8	
3	6	9	

How important is leisure time?

2008

The estimated numbers of people who believe that leisure is 'very important' in their lives are shown here, according to 2008 data from the European Values Survey.

As with other questions on values, the precise translation of the word 'leisure' may well influence the results. Where the translated word more strongly implies 'partying', fewer may agree. Where it implies relaxing or 'having a rest', more may agree.

With no common language used across Europe, and different Europeans having different conceptions of words such as 'leisure', it is difficult to be sure that this map is not just as much about different interpretations of the word 'leisure', rather than a reflection of the actual time people might get to enjoy undertaking some activity they count as leisure. Some leisure activities can, of course, also be quite arduous, sport being an obvious example. Overall, a large majority of Europeans, 86%, see leisure as at least quite important.

Colour key, see Reference map A1, p 10

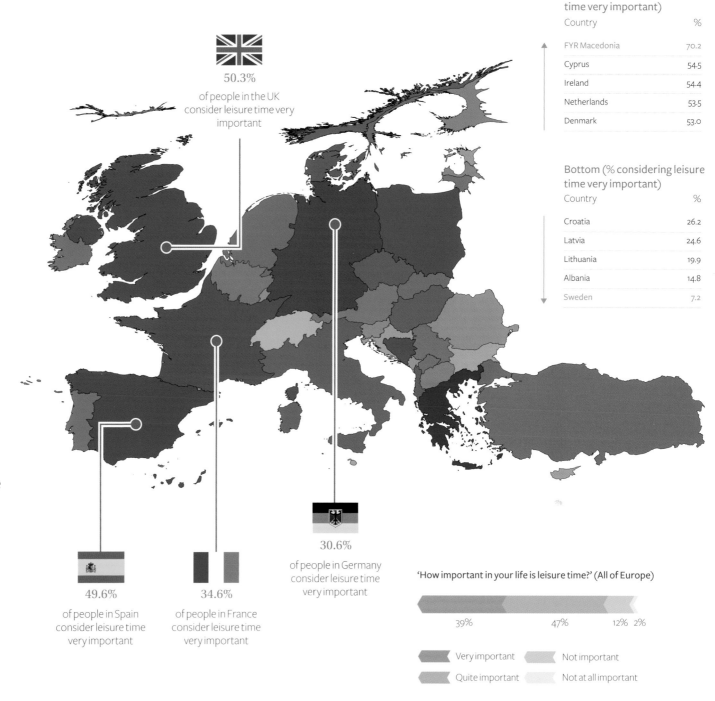

50.3%
of people in the UK consider leisure time very important

49.6%
of people in Spain consider leisure time very important

34.6%
of people in France consider leisure time very important

30.6%
of people in Germany consider leisure time very important

Top (% considering leisure time very important)

Country	%
FYR Macedonia	70.2
Cyprus	54.5
Ireland	54.4
Netherlands	53.5
Denmark	53.0

Bottom (% considering leisure time very important)

Country	%
Croatia	26.2
Latvia	24.6
Lithuania	19.9
Albania	14.8
Sweden	7.2

'How important in your life is leisure time?' (All of Europe)

39%   47%   12% 2%

Very important   Not important

Quite important   Not at all important

How important is work?

2008

When asked to rate the importance of work in their lives on a 4-point scale (ranging from 'not at all important' to 'very important'), 60% of respondents in the European Values Survey said that it was 'very important'.

It is interesting that two neighbouring countries, Sweden and Finland, should be at the opposite ends of this spectrum. Although they are very similar in many ways, their languages come from very different origins, making it more likely that translated words have differing implications.

Work can be seen as 'very important' if the issue is whether you have work or not and need earnings from work to survive. It can also be seen as 'very important' if it is believed that work brings some kind of discipline to life, or that without people being obliged to work society could not function.

It can be seen as far less important if many things that are essential in life, such as childcare, are not counted as work, or if much paid employment brings no obvious benefits to society.

Colour key, see Reference map A1, p 10

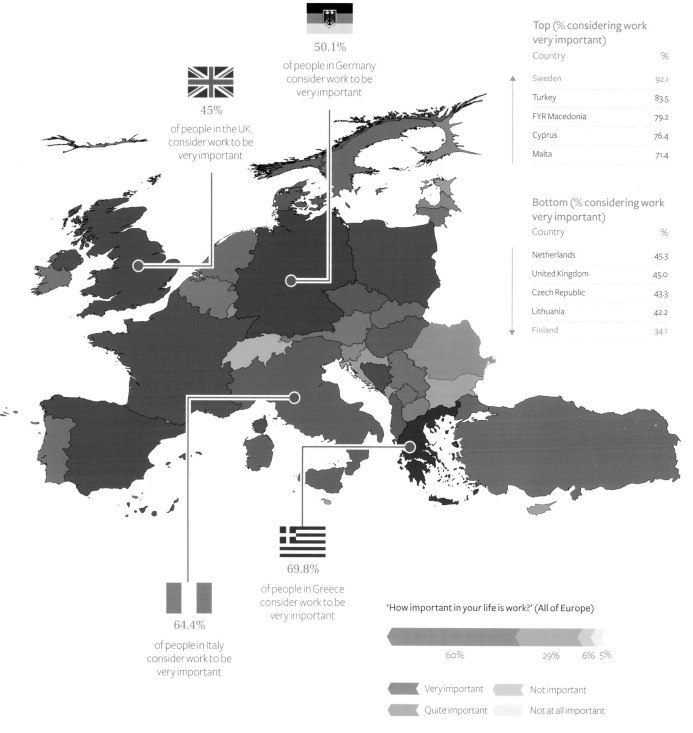

50.1%
of people in Germany consider work to be very important

45%
of people in the UK consider work to be very important

69.8%
of people in Greece consider work to be very important

64.4%
of people in Italy consider work to be very important

Top (% considering work very important)

Country	%
Sweden	92.1
Turkey	83.5
FYR Macedonia	79.2
Cyprus	76.4
Malta	71.4

Bottom (% considering work very important)

Country	%
Netherlands	45.3
United Kingdom	45.0
Czech Republic	43.3
Lithuania	42.2
Finland	34.1

'How important in your life is work?' (All of Europe)

60%   29%   6%   5%

Very important	Not important
Quite important	Not at all important

How important is family?

2008

When asked about the importance of family in their lives in the 2008 European Values Survey, 86% of all respondents answered that they considered family to be 'very important'.

The highest percentages in Europe are observed in those countries at the geographical extremities of Europe, in Turkey and Iceland, at 96%, followed by FYR Macedonia, Cyprus, Malta, Montenegro, Italy, Hungary, Luxembourg and the Slovak Republic (all with more than 90% agreeing that family is 'very important' in their lives).

At the other extreme, the smallest percentage is observed in Sweden, which is also where the highest numbers of people are known to live alone.

Overall, some 98% of people in Europe agree that family is at least 'quite important'.

Colour key, see Reference map A1, p 10

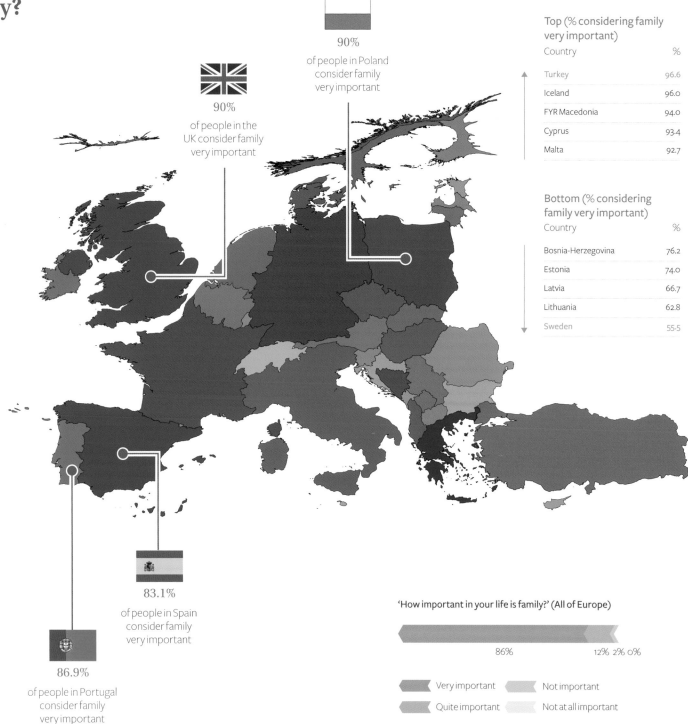

90%

of people in Poland consider family very important

90%

of people in the UK consider family very important

83.1%

of people in Spain consider family very important

86.9%

of people in Portugal consider family very important

Top (% considering family very important)

Country	%
Turkey	96.6
Iceland	96.0
FYR Macedonia	94.0
Cyprus	93.4
Malta	92.7

Bottom (% considering family very important)

Country	%
Bosnia-Herzegovina	76.2
Estonia	74.0
Latvia	66.7
Lithuania	62.8
Sweden	55.5

'How important in your life is family?' (All of Europe)

86%   12% 2% 0%

| Very important | Not important |
| Quite important | Not at all important |

How important are friends?

2008

The estimated numbers of people who believe that friends are 'very important' in their lives are shown here, according to data from the 2008 European Values Survey.

A total of 50% of all Europeans consider friends and acquaintances as 'very important' in their lives.

In many cases, countries where more people say family is important also have high proportions considering friends to be important. Perhaps people value sociability more in some places, whether it be with family or friends, whereas in other parts of Europe they are able to occupy themselves alone more easily?

There are interesting exceptions. The Baltic States and Albania are even smaller on this map than on the previous one showing the importance of family, but Switzerland is significantly larger, friends counting there for a lot, but still not as much as family.

Colour key, see Reference map A1, p 10

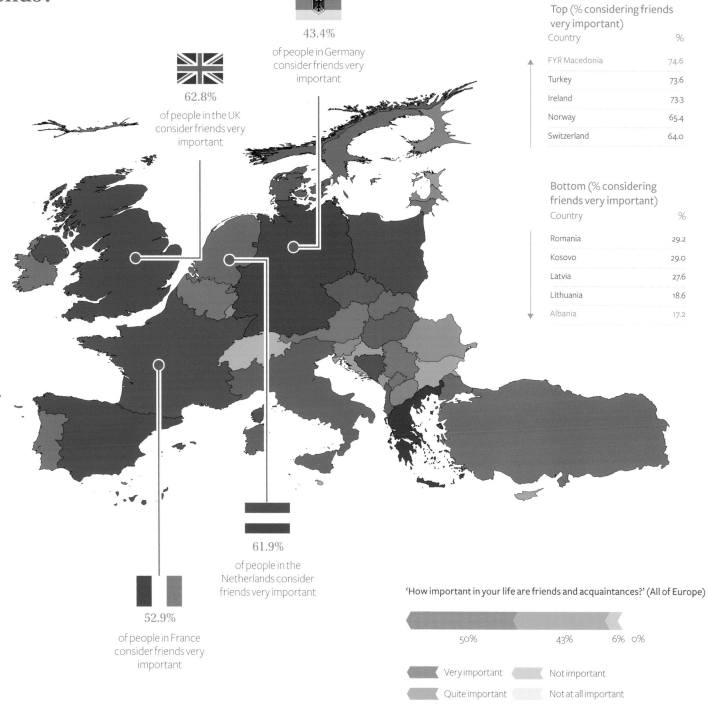

43.4%
of people in Germany consider friends very important

62.8%
of people in the UK consider friends very important

52.9%
of people in France consider friends very important

61.9%
of people in the Netherlands consider friends very important

Top (% considering friends very important)

Country	%
FYR Macedonia	74.6
Turkey	73.6
Ireland	73.3
Norway	65.4
Switzerland	64.0

Bottom (% considering friends very important)

Country	%
Romania	29.2
Kosovo	29.0
Latvia	27.6
Lithuania	18.6
Albania	17.2

'How important in your life are friends and acquaintances?' (All of Europe)

50%   43%   6% 0%

Very important   Not important

Quite important   Not at all important

Attitude to competition

2008

When asked to rate on a scale from 1 to 10 whether competition was 'good' (1) or 'harmful' (10) for people, 16% of the 2008 European Values Survey respondents chose the highest value, 10.

In relative terms, the largest support for competition is mostly found in Eastern European countries. Competition tends to be seen more favourably in former Soviet bloc countries, and is less popular in those countries that were part of the original free trade area that has experienced more open competition for the longest time.

Support for competition here was being measured just at the start of the great recession. However, as this recession didn't affect the East as much as the West, it is hard to tell where support for competition over cooperation will have strengthened or weakened in more recent years. Support for competition may also be due to people disliking corruption and nepotism.

Colour key, see Reference map A1, p 10

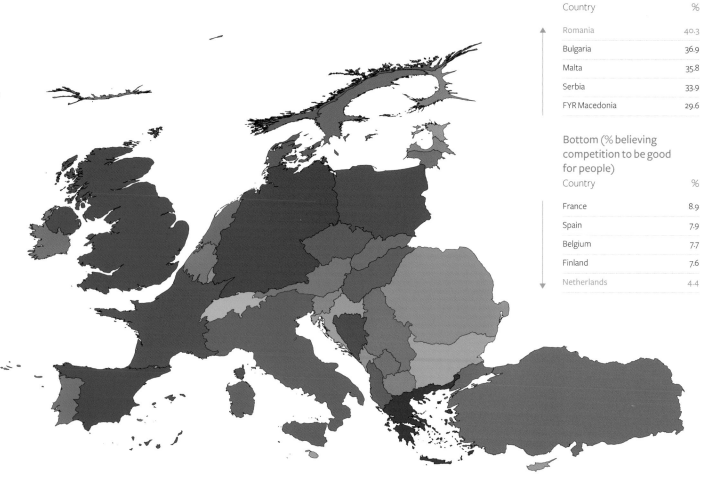

Top (% believing competition to be good for people)	
Country	%
Romania	40.3
Bulgaria	36.9
Malta	35.8
Serbia	33.9
FYR Macedonia	29.6

Bottom (% believing competition to be good for people)	
Country	%
France	8.9
Spain	7.9
Belgium	7.7
Finland	7.6
Netherlands	4.4

'Is competition good for people?' (All of Europe)

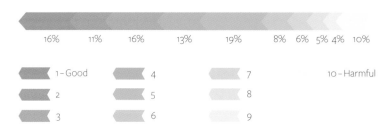

16% 11% 16% 13% 19% 8% 6% 5% 4% 10%

1 – Good	4	7
2	5	8
3	6	9

10 – Harmful

Trust in other people

VARIOUS YEARS 2009–11

A Gallup World Poll question asked: 'Generally speaking, would you say that most people can be trusted or that you have to be careful in dealing with people?' This map shows those who answered that most people 'can be trusted'.

Northern and Western European countries dominate the map. In relative terms, Denmark had the highest recorded percentage in Europe, and also in the world.

On the other hand, Albania had the lowest percentage in Europe, and also the lowest in the world (together with Lebanon).

The world average (for the countries for which there was available data) was 30%. The number of people who answered that they would trust others as a proportion of the total population in the US was 37%, in Canada 42%, in Japan 33%, in China 57%, in India 20% and in Brazil 15%.

Comparing this map to the previous one, it can be seen that frequently where there are high levels of trust, more people believe there to be less need for competition.

Colour key, see Reference map A1, p 10

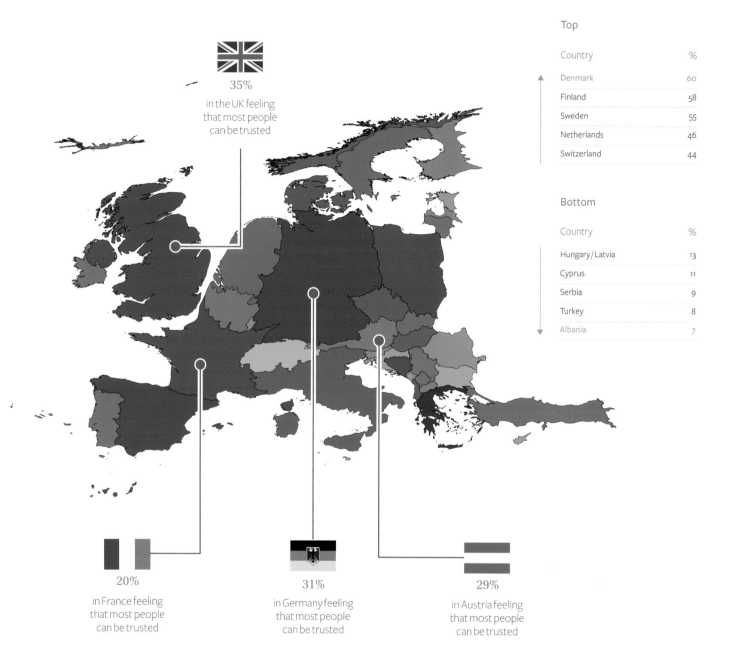

35%
in the UK feeling that most people can be trusted

20%
in France feeling that most people can be trusted

31%
in Germany feeling that most people can be trusted

29%
in Austria feeling that most people can be trusted

Top

Country	%
Denmark	60
Finland	58
Sweden	55
Netherlands	46
Switzerland	44

Bottom

Country	%
Hungary/Latvia	13
Cyprus	11
Serbia	9
Turkey	8
Albania	7

The importance of religion

2008

There have long been debates about the importance of religion in shaping European identity, and in particular, of Christianity, Islam and Judaism (and their various denominations), which are often described as the 'great religions of the West'. But how important is religion in the life of Europeans today? This map shows the estimated numbers of people who believe that religion is 'very important'.

According to 2008 data from the European Values Survey, 27% of all Europeans consider religion to be 'very important', and another 27% as 'quite important', whereas for 22%, it is 'not at all important'.

Colour key, see Reference map A1, p 10

Colour key, see Reference map A1, p 10

16.5%
of people in the UK
consider religion
very important

28.1%
of people in Ireland
consider religion
very important

12.6%
of people in France
consider religion
very important

Top (% considering religion very important)

Country	%
Turkey	79.9
Cyprus	59.5
Malta	58.8
Romania	55.1
Kosovo	48.0

Bottom (% considering religion very important)

Country	%
Denmark	8.6
Sweden	8.3
Germany	7.9
Czech Republic	6.3
Estonia	5.1

'How important in your life is religion?' (All of Europe)

27%	27%	24%	22%

Very important   Not important

Quite important   Not at all important

Belonging to religious organisations

2008

According to the 2008 European Values Survey, some 8% of all respondents across Europe mentioned that they belong to a religious organisation. This map shows how they are distributed geographically.

The map is dominated by the United Kingdom, Germany and Italy, which have the largest absolute numbers. In relative terms, however, the highest percentages are found in Iceland and Denmark, followed by the Netherlands and the Republic of Ireland.

Note that this category is not about people being members of a church or having a particular religious belief or affiliation. If it were, then the percentages would be far higher in many countries, including the countries in the bottom five list.

Here what is being measured is a commitment above what is normally expected of members of their particular religion. This may partly reflect how much the laity are able to get involved in the activities of specifically religious organisations (explaining the low proportions in Greece and Turkey).

Colour key, see Reference map A1, p 10

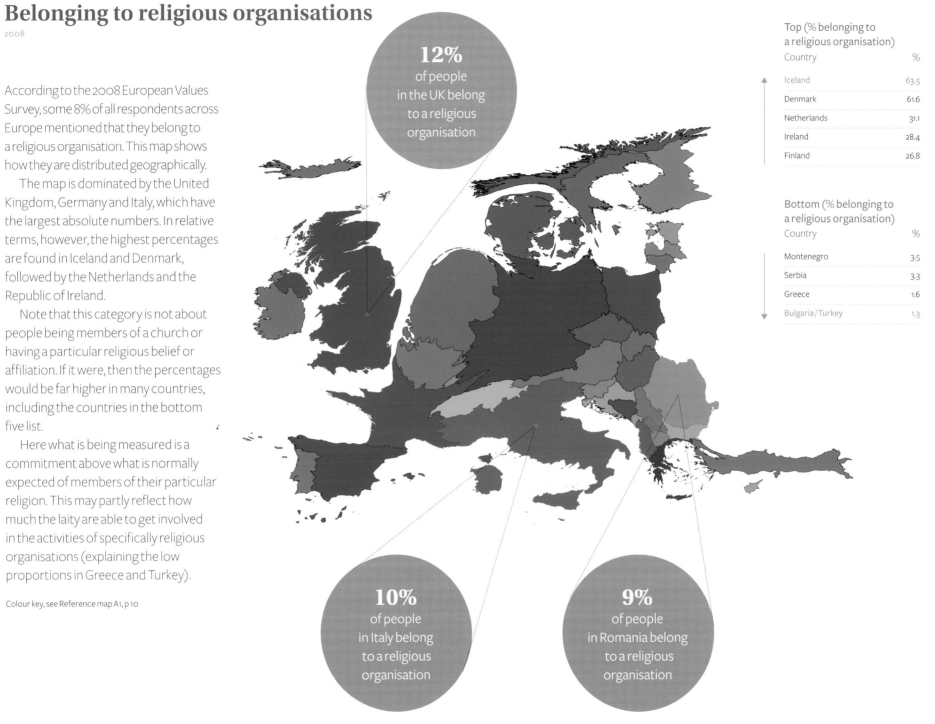

12% of people in the UK belong to a religious organisation

10% of people in Italy belong to a religious organisation

9% of people in Romania belong to a religious organisation

Top (% belonging to a religious organisation)

Country	%
Iceland	63.5
Denmark	61.6
Netherlands	31.1
Ireland	28.4
Finland	26.8

Bottom (% belonging to a religious organisation)

Country	%
Montenegro	3.5
Serbia	3.3
Greece	1.6
Bulgaria / Turkey	1.3

Can the death penalty be justified?

2008

Protecting human rights and most importantly, the right not to be executed, is recognised as a key European value. Indeed, the abolition of the death penalty is one of the essential 'Copenhagen criteria' that must be met before an application from any country to join the EU is even considered. This map shows the spread of Europeans who stated they would 'never' accept the death penalty.

According to 2008 data from the European Values Survey, on a scale of 1 ('never') to 10 ('always'), 45% of all Europeans answered 'never' when asked if they could justify the death penalty, whereas a small percentage of 8% answered 'always'. '5' was chosen by those who were most unsure.

Perhaps not surprisingly, where the memory of executions is most recent, opposition to the death penalty ever being reintroduced appears to be strongest.

Colour key, see Reference map A1, p 10

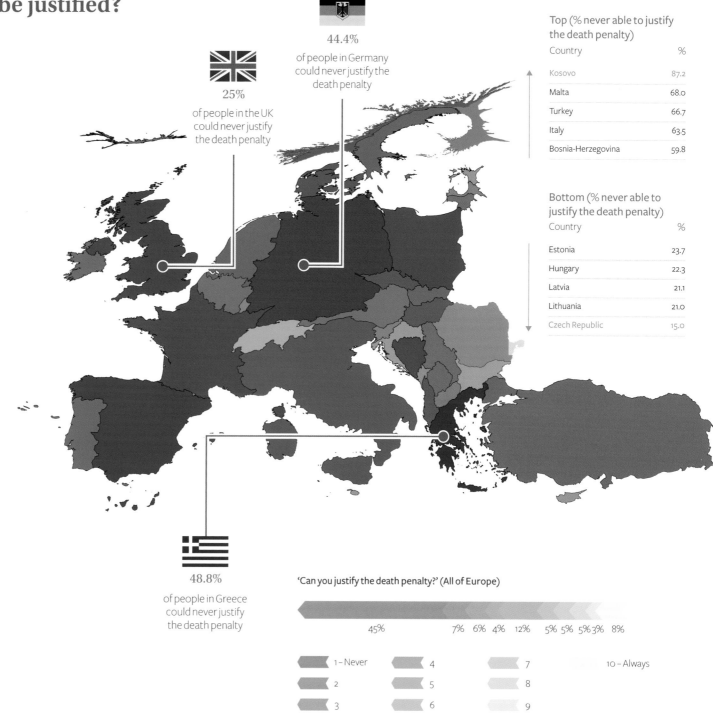

44.4%
of people in Germany could never justify the death penalty

25%
of people in the UK could never justify the death penalty

48.8%
of people in Greece could never justify the death penalty

Top (% never able to justify the death penalty)

Country	%
Kosovo	87.2
Malta	68.0
Turkey	66.7
Italy	63.5
Bosnia-Herzegovina	59.8

Bottom (% never able to justify the death penalty)

Country	%
Estonia	23.7
Hungary	22.3
Latvia	21.1
Lithuania	21.0
Czech Republic	15.0

'Can you justify the death penalty?' (All of Europe)

45%　　7%　6%　4%　12%　　5% 5% 5% 3%　8%

1 – Never	4	7	10 – Always
2	5	8	
3	6	9	

Belief in life after death

2008

Believing in life after death is a key aspect of many religions. This map shows estimates of people who do not believe in any form of an afterlife, and it is, to some extent, a mirror image of the map showing how important religion is in the lives of Europeans.

In relative terms, Albania is top of the list of non-believers, closely followed by three other countries which (like Albania) were once members of the communist bloc. Next highest is Germany, part of which was also in that bloc.

Across Europe, an estimated 56% of the population believe in life after death while 44% do not. The question appears to have been phrased in such a way as to discourage people from expressing the agnostic belief that there may be a life after death, but that they have no way of knowing.

Colour key, see Reference map A1, p 10

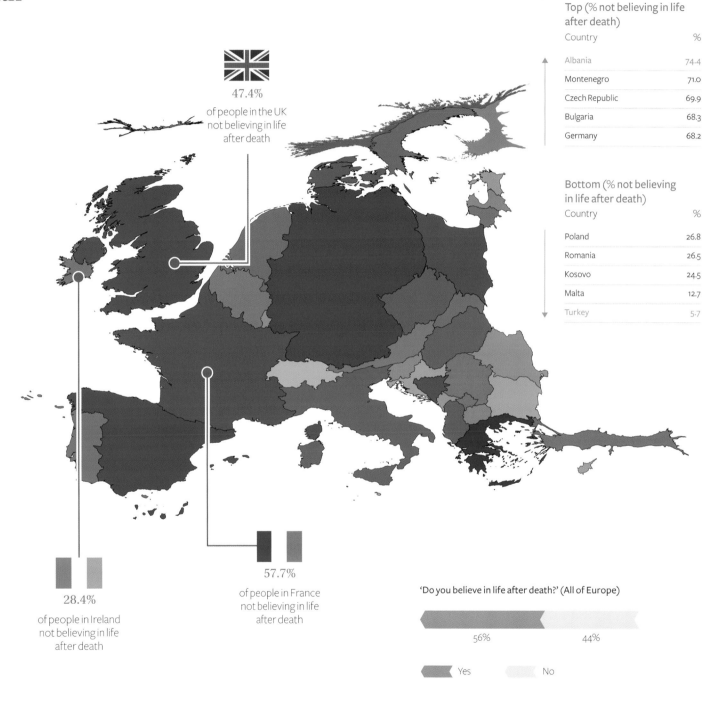

47.4%
of people in the UK not believing in life after death

28.4%
of people in Ireland not believing in life after death

57.7%
of people in France not believing in life after death

Top (% not believing in life after death)

Country	%
Albania	74.4
Montenegro	71.0
Czech Republic	69.9
Bulgaria	68.3
Germany	68.2

Bottom (% not believing in life after death)

Country	%
Poland	26.8
Romania	26.5
Kosovo	24.5
Malta	12.7
Turkey	5.7

'Do you believe in life after death?' (All of Europe)

56%   44%

Yes   No

Eurovision Song Contest

2015, TOTAL VOTES

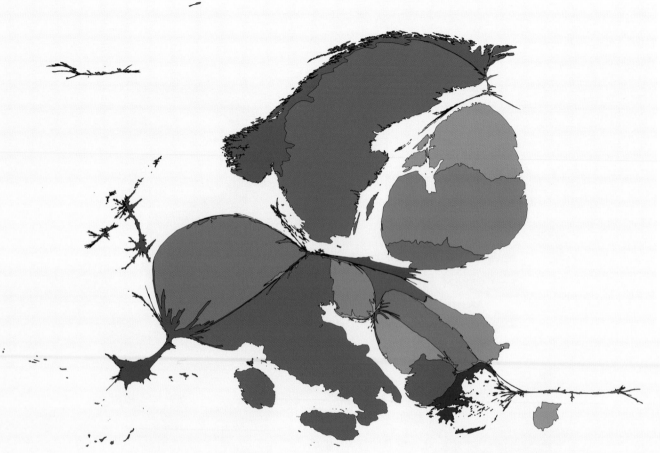

Top (votes for song)

Country	Points
Sweden	365
Italy	292
Belgium	217
Latvia	186
Estonia	106

Bottom (votes for song)

Country	Points
Cyprus	11
Poland	10
United Kingdom	5
France	4
Germany	0

Eurovision Song Contest voting patterns are popular for analysing European identity and culture. There are clear patterns based on geographical regions as well as cultural and language bonds, and typically groups of countries that give their votes to each other have been labelled as 'blocs' (the 'Scandinavian', 'Mediterranean', 'Western', 'Eastern', 'Balkan' bloc, and so on). Political considerations may also have an effect, and in the 2015 contest examined here, voting patterns were possibly influenced by the ongoing political and economic crisis in Europe.

Each competing country has to give 12 points to its favourite song, 10 points to the second favourite, 8 to the third, and 7 points to 1 point, in descending order, to the remaining seven ranked songs. These points are allocated via telephone voting, and all countries taking part in the final and two semi-finals are eligible to vote.

This map, of the total number of votes for each country's song, is dominated by the winner, Sweden, which received a total of 365 points, 73 more than Italy in second place. On the following map each country is sized according to the number of points that it gave to Sweden (with flags indicating all countries giving Sweden maximum points). Sweden was not, of course, allowed to vote for itself. The country inside Italy is San Marino, which gave Sweden 7 points.

Colour key, see Reference map A1, p 10

Eurovision Song Contest, votes given to Sweden

2015

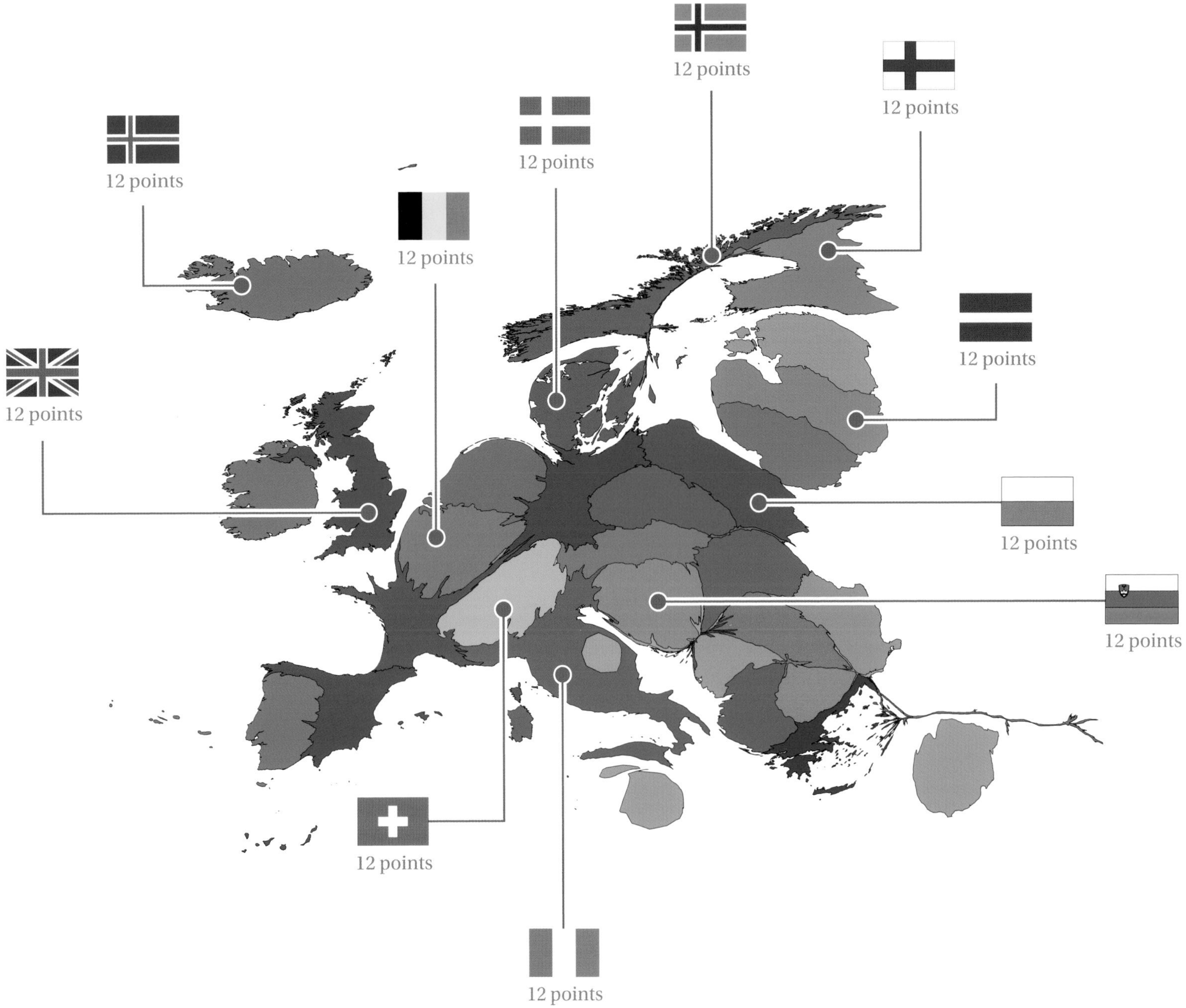

12 points

12 points

12 points

12 points

12 points

12 points

12 points

12 points

12 points

12 points

12 points

12 points

12 points

Colour key, see Reference map A1, p 10

J – EU Budget

The EU has an annual budget of over €140 billion, and can be seen as an economic power in its own right. However, it is important to highlight that the total EU budget is very small compared with the sum of the national budgets of all its member states.

At the time of preparing this atlas, the most recent EU budget data available were for 2013. In that year, the total EU budget was €148 billion, which represented less than 1/50th of the combined budgets of all EU member states, meaning that ***the EU spends much less than 2% of Europe's total public spending***!

This chapter focuses on current EU member states, exploring how far EU policy is being implemented and in particular how the EU budget is split up. The EU budget aims to promote the policy priorities agreed by all member states through a spending plan known as the 'Financial Framework', which specifies total EU spending over a fixed period for specified categories of expenditure. The current framework covers 2014–20, and ensures some security for planning the main areas of work towards the common political goals of the EU.

The contributions to the EU budget from each country are based on their economic power: each member state contributes a small proportion of its VAT receipts and 1% of its Gross National Income (GNI). However, because of various rebates, the EU's overall budget represents approximately 1% of the GNI of all member states.

- The data presented in this chapter show how the **net payments** by member states into the EU are spread geographically.
- They also show how the EU budget is split between different **spending categories**, such as preserving and managing natural resources, and administration.

EU budget: net contributors

2013

The amounts that member states pay into the EU budget can be very contentious. This map highlights the nine countries that pay more money into the EU budget than is spent within their borders. The figures are for 2013, with the amount varying year by year, according to a pre-agreed formula.

Germany was the biggest net contributor, paying €16.3 billion more into the EU than it received in return.

When looking at the net contributions in terms of GDP, the Netherlands topped the list in 2013, followed by Sweden, which has too small a population to appear in the top five total net payments. Germany is ranked third, followed by Denmark, with the UK appearing fifth, with a net contribution of 0.56% of GDP. The UK is a rich country, although it contains a relatively high percentage of people living in poverty (see also Chapter C), pushed up by the massive austerity measures imposed by domestic political parties since 2010. The size of the UK's contribution featured strongly in the debates leading up to the 2016 referendum on the UK's membership of the EU.

A third way of ranking takes into account the total population of the net contributors, and Sweden tops this list, followed by Denmark and the Netherlands.

Colour key, see Reference map A1, p10

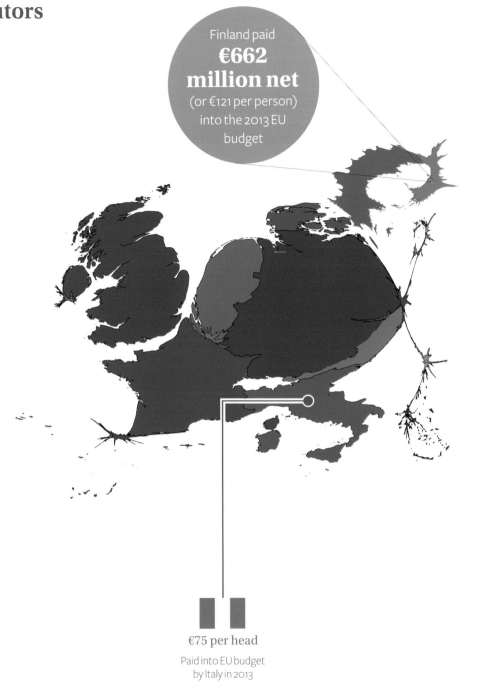

Finland paid
€662 million net
(or €121 per person)
into the 2013 EU budget

€75 per head

Paid into EU budget
by Italy in 2013

Top (net payments)

Country	€ billion
Germany	16.32
United Kingdom	10.76
France	9.05
Italy	4.61
Netherlands	4.29

Top (as % of GDP)

Country	%
Netherlands	0.70
Sweden / Germany / Denmark	0.61
United Kingdom	0.56
France	0.45
Austria	0.43

Top (€ per head)

Country	€
Sweden	263
Denmark	260
Netherlands	254
Germany	202
United Kingdom	167

EU budget: net receivers

2013

This map shows the countries that receive more money from Europe than they pay into the EU budget, sized by how much they benefit in terms of the total amount received.

Poland is the biggest net receiver. Here the difference between paying into the EU budget and spending within the country is nearly €12 billion. Greece is the second biggest receiver, followed by Hungary. It is interesting to note that in these countries in recent years there has been a significant rise of populist Eurosceptic parties.

When looking at these figures as a proportion of each country's GDP the order changes: Hungary tops the list, and the rest of the table is completed with other countries in Eastern Europe, from the Baltic States to the Balkan Peninsula.

Finally, when we consider the population size of each country, Luxembourg appears to benefit most although the high payments to Luxembourg and Belgium are largely explained by the central role they play in EU administration.

Colour key, see Reference map A1, p 10

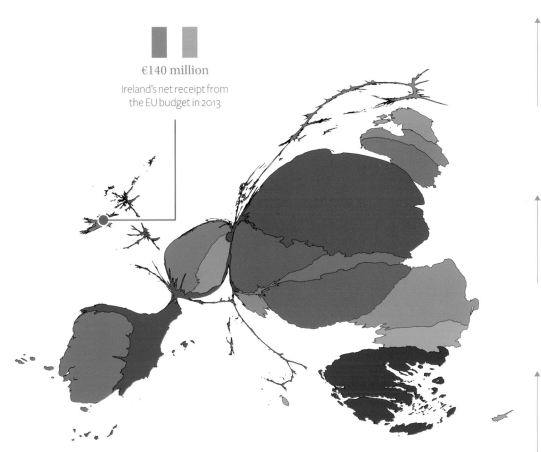

€140 million

Ireland's net receipt from the EU budget in 2013

Total spending of €7.21 billion
- Administration
- All other spending categories

Top (net amount received)

Country	€ billion
Poland	11.97
Greece	5.31
Hungary	4.90
Portugal	4.37
Romania	4.09

Top (as % of GDP)

Country	%
Hungary	5.10
Lithuania	4.42
Estonia	4.25
Bulgaria	3.82
Latvia	3.57

Top (€ per head)

Country	€
Luxembourg	2,295
Estonia	580
Lithuania	500
Hungary	497
Greece	484

How the EU budget is spent

2013

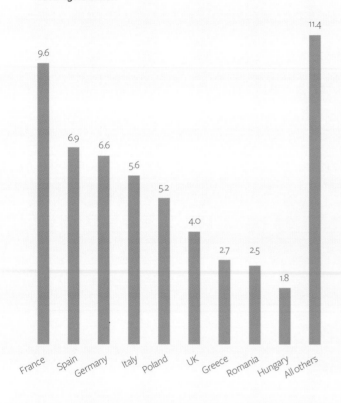

Preservation and management of natural resources (€ bn)

Total €58.0 billion

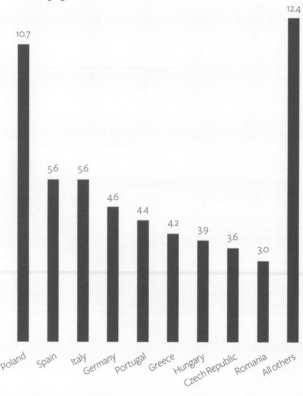

Cohesion for growth and employment (€ bn)

Total €56.3 billion

The EU budget is split between various spending categories, and spending within these categories varies widely between the member states.

'Competitiveness' includes spending on research and development, education and training, transport and energy networks, social policy, economic integration and accompanying policies to boost sustainable growth.

'Cohesion' includes spending to boost less developed EU countries and regions, to support sustainable development outside the least prosperous regions, and on inter-regional cooperation.

'Preservation and management of natural resources' is the largest category of spending and includes farm subsidies – increasingly geared towards paying farmers to manage

the land better, the Common Fisheries Policy, and rural development and environmental measures.

'Citizenship, freedom, security and justice' payments are spent on justice and home affairs, border protection, immigration and asylum policy as well as public health, consumer protection, culture, young people, and information and dialogue with citizens.

'The EU as a global player' covers spending on 'all external action ("foreign policy") by the EU' and is the smallest category in terms of total spending in EU countries (although additional payments are made from this budget to countries outside the EU). It is also the most skewed, with by far the highest payments made to Croatia, followed by Romania, Poland and Bulgaria.

Competitiveness for growth and employment (€ bn)
Total €12.6 billion

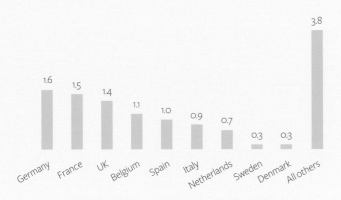

Germany 1.6, France 1.5, UK 1.4, Belgium 1.1, Spain 1.0, Italy 0.9, Netherlands 0.7, Sweden 0.3, Denmark 0.3, All others 3.8

Administration (€ bn)
Total: €7.6 billion

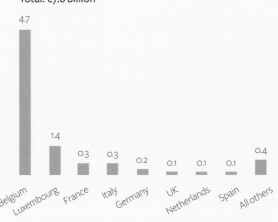

Belgium 4.7, Luxembourg 1.4, France 0.3, Italy 0.3, Germany 0.2, UK 0.1, Netherlands 0.1, Spain 0.1, All others 0.4

Citizenship, freedom, security and justice (€ m)
Total €1.7 billion

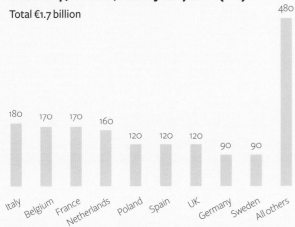

Italy 180, Belgium 170, France 170, Netherlands 160, Poland 120, Spain 120, UK 120, Germany 90, Sweden 90, All others 480

The EU as a global player (€ m)
Total €216 million

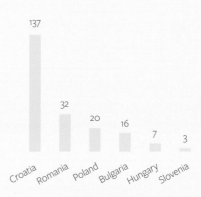

Croatia 137, Romania 32, Poland 20, Bulgaria 16, Hungary 7, Slovenia 3

Finally, spending on 'Running the EU' includes the administrative expenses of all the European institutions: buildings and staffing costs, including pensions and EU-run schools for staff members' children. Not surprisingly these are concentrated in Belgium (which houses the European Commission and the European Parliament), and Luxembourg (the European Court of Justice and Eurostat).

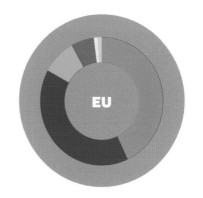

% spending in the EU in each category
Total: €148 billion

- Preservation and management of natural resources
- Cohesion for growth and employment
- Competitiveness for growth and employment
- Administration
- The EU as a global player
- Citizenship, freedom, security and justice

K – Conclusion

As we prepare to go to press Europe is at time of great crisis. While there has been an apparent rise of extremist and populist groups, at the same time there are widespread manifestations of support for the European project across the continent (including in the United Kingdom with the #marchforeurope events) with reported surges in EU support in many big European countries, especially after the Brexit vote and the election of Donald Trump as president of the United States.

Through the maps and infographics presented in *The Human Atlas of Europe* we have painted a picture of Europe, its people and its environment, which can further enhance such expressions of solidarity and transnational belonging across Europe.

We have tried to show how the places where we live are connected, are changing, are different, but are also all part of one whole. A perception of European identity and solidarity is growing in Europe especially among the increasing numbers of people who travel throughout the continent frequently, who have lived in more than one European country and speak more than one European language. The feeling of affiliation and belonging to something larger than the nation-state is at the heart of the modern-day European project. One day even this idea may appear quaint and outmoded as people all around the world see themselves more and more as part of one global entity, but that day is still hard to imagine. Europe – as a common home – is much more readily grasped.

Minimising borders

Looking at the maps in this atlas you can easily believe that you are looking at the cartography of a single large group of people living in a country called Europe: a country with few internal borders, a country with many cities,

mountains, rivers, the most complex of coastlines, and many more than a few islands. To draw a Europe dividing would require insertion of wide bands of white space between countries to show where new iron curtains were descending. We hope we never have to draw such a tragic map in the future. Walls, and fear of those who lived outside those walls, were a large part of our common European past. Our present is so different and our future could be just as different again. We firmly hope that the apparent revival of old divisions, national stereotypes and hatred currently experienced across many parts of Europe will have been conclusively reversed by the time this current decade ends. But we have no way of knowing: we can only hope, act and agitate.

The collection of demographic, social, economic and environmental maps presented here can be used to inform debates about prospects for the future of European identity and many other issues. We hope that our maps and graphics will enhance the chances that the current decade will be recognised as the start of an era in which the switch was made to sustainable, 'green' growth, and social cohesion began to grow again. The solidarity and solutions required to overcome the great economic crises of 2008 and to respond to the ongoing humanitarian crisis of the arrival of so many refugees and other displaced people by providing sanctuary in accordance with the underpinning ideals of the European Union could provide a good starting point.

A continent is not a continent until it is mapped and imaged as one whole; and its human geographical borders are far from fixed. As the population of Europe ages, and the numbers of young Europeans begin to shrink, the boundaries of Europe will continue to widen.

By the time you are reading these words one European country, the United Kingdom, may have started the process of leaving the EU. Other countries

may be further along the road to membership. Europe is, and always has been, changing.

Europe's responsibilities

Every year hundreds of thousands of people, mostly from Africa and Asia, risk their lives to reach the European Union. Every year thousands of people (including many babies and children) seeking refuge in Europe die, with the numbers of needless deaths rising to truly shocking levels in recent years. Not only do these deaths put many of the issues highlighted in this atlas into a far more important perspective, they also show how lucky Europeans are to be born and live in this very affluent continent.

This atlas highlights the responsibilities of Europe to live up to the ideals underpinning the EU and to welcome all refugees. In addition to the obvious humanitarian imperatives to do so, Europeans bear a disproportionate responsibility for the political turmoil in the rest of the world that has resulted in such large movements of people into Europe. Europeans are responsible for imposing many of the current arbitrary national borders, for impoverishing peoples through colonialism and for getting involved in proxy wars between superpowers that give rise to refugees (even though these are often presented as being merely local conflicts).

Europeans should also take far more responsibility for the pollution in our atmosphere that is accelerating climate change, because we were the first to burn coal in such huge quantities.

Europeans have many responsibilities, but living up to these responsibilities brings benefits. The average age and educational profile of immigrants and refugees boosts the potential contribution they can make to the economies and pensions systems of Europe's countries. There are also non-monetary benefits, as the integration of people with diverse backgrounds can be culturally enriching.

Where the differences actually lie

The maps presented in this atlas show how Europe and its diverse and newly arriving people can be seen as one entity, moving towards a European people, united in diversity. At the same time, they highlight very important, and sometimes extreme, social and spatial variations. Often the real differences are not found across national borders but between villages and cities, or between the rich and poor quarters of a town. Rich quarters generally have more in common with other rich quarters across Europe than with poorer areas in the same town.

Considerable efforts have recently been put into establishing socially and environmentally sustainable policies at the European level aimed at correcting economic and geographical imbalances and inequalities. Examples of such policies include the European Social Fund, the European Regional Development Fund and the Cohesion Fund. But are these enough? Do we need more and better policies of this kind? Is there a need for more European top-down policies, or more devolved powers to regions and local communities? No one knows for sure, but many people fear that divides in Europe may soon begin to widen again if we do not cooperate better in future.

A Europe of hope, not decline

There are some signs of a wider thinking emerging, with feelings of solidarity and common European identity being expressed more openly than before. This is all despite the revival of national stereotypes and the rise of the far-right, national populism and xenophobia. At the same time as the voices of division have become more vocal, from a more practical point of view there have been attempts to strengthen the feeling of pan-European citizenship and political action through the strengthening of institutions such as the European Parliament and the creation of the euro, the common currency used by the majority of Europeans today. We often forget just how far we have come in such a short space of time.

This atlas was drawn and written by three European geographers whose first languages are Greek, English and German respectively. We hope that the work presented within these pages will help to enhance feelings of social cohesion and solidarity among the people of Europe and to counter those alternative images that might be used to foster division.

We have tried to achieve this by highlighting important disparities and inequalities and, at the same time, reminding Europeans how much they have in common and the potential of what can be achieved if they move away from 'nation-state mentalities' of the past and work together towards a socio-economically and environmentally sustainable common European future.

The real social divides within Europe are more often within states rather than between them. Those divides are not products of being part of Europe. Europe contains some very steep local social and economic divisions but it is also home to almost all of the regions and countries with the highest levels of economic equality in the world, countries with some of the best health care, the best educational outcomes and schools, the best housing quality and services, many innovative scientists, the most productive workforces and the most enlightened of societies in terms of respecting and enhancing human rights. This is a continent full of diversity but it has only a small proportion of the world's land area and population, and its share of global population is rapidly shrinking.

It does not take many hours to travel from one side of the European continent to the other, if you have enough money and the right papers. And Europe does not appear that large or daunting when viewed in the ways we present it in this atlas, where all its peoples are given equal prominence and internal national boundaries are removed from many of the maps to show that they are not visible, natural boundaries. If you've taken a little time to get used to the maps in these pages you may have also begun to see the kind of Europe that we have been looking at for some time, the Europe that we see revealed by the facts and figures collected about us.

A continent united in diversity

The Europe we map here is more a Europe of cities, regions and people than of states. It is more a Europe of people united than of power dividing. And it should be more a Europe of hope than decline. After all, where else in the world is there such diversity, complexity, coherence and communality? Where else in the world do so many people live in a place where it is illegal for any government to execute any citizen, where people have so many rights, hopes, responsibilities and prospects? Where else in the world today do so many millions of people live within a whole they can't quite see, but can only imagine, whose borders they are not sure of, that is home to so many languages and cultures? Where else but in Europe do so many have so much without realising what they have? Europe is a continent that is truly united in such diversity.

Notes and sources

A – Introduction

REFERENCE MAP A1

- As of June 2014 Albania became an official candidate for accession to the EU, and therefore moved from the potential candidate to the candidate category.

TABLE 1

- World Bank data, 2014; except Vatican (from Vatican City State website).

MAPPING TECHNIQUE

- Population cartograms are based on a density-equalising approach proposed by physicists Michael Gastner and Mark Newman; for more detail, see: M.T. Gastner and M.E.J. Newman (2004) 'Diffusion-based method for producing density equalizing maps', *Proc. Natl. Acad. Sci. USA*, vol 101, pp 7499–504.
- For more detail on the gridded-population cartogram technique, see: B.D. Hennig (2013) *Rediscovering the World: Map Transformations of Human and Physical Space*, Heidelberg/New York/Dordrecht/London (Springer).

REFERENCE MAP A2

- Population data from World Bank, 2014.

REFERENCE MAP A3

- Gridded Population of the World data, 2013.

B – Population

POPULATION BY AGE AND SEX

- Eurostat data, 2014 (EU); 2012 (Germany and Albania).

ADULTS (WORKING AGE)

- Eurostat data, 2014.

CHILDREN

- Eurostat data, 2014.

OLDER PEOPLE

- Eurostat data, 2014.

GENDER

- Eurostat data, 2014.

ASYLUM-SEEKERS

- Eurostat data, 2015: asylum applications from United Nations High Commissioner for Refugees and International Organisation for Migration.
- For deaths at sea, see: http://missingmigrants.iom.int/sites/default/files/Mediterranean_Update_18_December.pdf

POPULATIONS OF CONCERN

- Eurostat data, 2013, from United Nations High Commissioner for Refugees.

ASYLUM HOLDERS

- Eurostat data, 2013, from United Nations High Commissioner for Refugees.
- Included are those officially recognised as refugees under the 1951 Refugee Convention, its 1967 Protocol and the 1969 OAU Convention governing the Specific Aspects of Refugee Problems in Africa, as well as those granted complementary forms of protection or temporary protection.

BORN ABROAD

- World Bank data, 2010; no data for Kosovo.
- The precise figure was stated to be 52,225,829.

BORN ABROAD, INCREASE

- World Bank data, 2000–10.

BORN ABROAD, DECREASE

- World Bank data, 2000–10.

FOREIGN CITIZENS

- Eurostat data, 2014.

ROMA PEOPLE

- Data from 'Romani diaspora' in Wikipedia; Minority Rights Group International, *World Directory of Minorities*, see http://minorityrights.org/directory/
- Poverty statistics from World Bank data, 2015, see: http://www.worldbank.org/en/region/eca/brief/roma
- The Vatican, Iceland, Malta, Andorra, San Marino, Liechtenstein and Monaco had no recorded Roma population.

INTERNATIONAL TOURIST ARRIVALS

- World Bank data, 2013.

POPULATION INCREASE

- World Bank data, 1990–2014.

POPULATION DECLINE

- World Bank data, 1990–2014.
- 'Wild wolves' westward spread continues across Europe as pack spotted in Germany', Justin Huggler in Berlin, *The Telegraph*, 2 February 2015.

PROJECTED POPULATION 2050

- UN Population Division data, 2014.

TOTAL BIRTHS

- World Bank data, estimated using Crude Birth Rate (births per 1,000 population in 2013) and Total Population (2014).

LIFE EXPECTANCY (NATIONAL)

- Eurostat data, 2013.

LIFE EXPECTANCY (REGIONAL)

- Eurostat data, 2013.

PRISONERS

- UN data, 2013.
- V. Justickis and K. Peckaitis (2001) 'Lithuania', in D. van Zyl Smit and F. Dunkel (eds) *Imprisonment Today and Tomorrow*, Martinus Nijhoff, pp 448–66.

HOMICIDES

- See www.cdc.gov/nchs/fastats/homicide.htm

C – Wealth and Poverty

GROSS DOMESTIC PRODUCT (GDP)

- World Bank data, 2014.

GDP INCREASE

- World Bank data, 2007–14.
- The figures used here have all been converted to what are called 'constant 2005 US$' to eliminate any distortions due to inflation or deflation.

GDP DECLINE

- World Bank data, 2007–14.
- The figures used here have all been converted to what are called 'constant 2005 US$' to eliminate any distortions due to inflation or deflation.

GDP PER INHABITANT

- Eurostat Regional Yearbook, 2013.
- The Purchasing Power Standard (PPS) is an artificial currency set in 2011, theoretically equivalent to the amount of money which would be needed to buy the same amount of goods and services in each country.

DISPOSABLE INCOME

- Eurostat data, 2011.
- Note also that there were no data for Turkey and the Western Balkan countries, which include some of the poorest regions in Europe.

DISPOSABLE INCOME CHANGE

- Eurostat data, 2007/08–2011.

GOVERNMENT DEBT

- World Bank data, 2012.
- The World Bank defines government debt as the entire stock of direct fixed-term contractual obligations of the state to others outstanding on a particular date, which includes domestic and foreign liabilities such as currency and money deposits, securities other than shares, and loans. It is calculated as the gross amount of government liabilities reduced by the amount of equity and financial derivatives held by the government.

STOCK EXCHANGE LISTED COMPANIES

- World Bank data, 2012.
- Business failure in the UK is estimated from the number of companies no longer paying VAT.

MARKET VALUE OF STOCK EXCHANGE LISTED COMPANIES

- World Bank data, 2012.

STOCKS TRADED

- World Bank data, 2012.

INTERNET ACCESS

- World Bank data, 2014.
- Although services using encryption technology may not be completely secure (following revelations in the summer of 2013 about encryption having been broken by various security services, and possibly other agencies), they are most probably of a high specification and fast.

TELEPHONE LINES

- World Bank data, 2014.

MOBILE PHONES

- World Bank data, 2014.

VULNERABLE EMPLOYMENT

- World Bank data, 2013.
- Bar chart estimates are based on data from various years: EU 2011, India 2010, Brazil 2009, Australia 2008, New Zealand 2008.

RELATIVE POVERTY (NATIONAL)

- Eurostat and World Bank data, 2014.

RELATIVE POVERTY (REGIONAL)

- Eurostat and World Bank data, 2014.
- This map is drawn with regions resized in proportion to the population living within them, and then shaded to show the numbers of people living on an income that is less than 60% of the national median.

POVERTY BELOW US$2 A DAY

- Eurostat and World Bank data, 2012.

- Prices are made comparable using established 'purchasing power parity' (PPP) ratios – essentially this is a measure of how many people cannot afford to buy a meal that might cost $2 in the US with the money they receive a day, given the cost of a similar basic meal where they live.
- Bar chart estimates based on 2012 data for EU; 2011 data for other countries/regions.

BILLIONAIRES

- Data from *Forbes* magazine, 2015.

INCOME INEQUALITY

- Eurostat and World Bank data.
- On this map countries have been sized according to population and then shaded to show their Gini coefficient (the extent to which distribution of income varies from being perfectly equal).
- See N. Stotesbury and D. Dorling (2015) 'Understanding income inequality and its implications: Why better statistics are needed', *Statistics Views*, 21 October (www.statisticsviews.com/details/feature/8493411/Understanding-Income-Inequality-and-its-Implications-Why-Better-Statistics-Are-N.html)

GENDER INEQUALITY

- Eurostat and World Bank data, 2013.
- For more details on the GII, see http://hdr.undp.org/en/content/gender-inequality-index-gii

HUMAN DEVELOPMENT INDEX

- Eurostat data, 2013.
- For more details of Professor Sen's work see http://hdr.undp.org/sites/default/files/hdr2015_technical_notes.pdf
- For more details on the HDI, see http://hdr.undp.org/en/content/human-development-index-hdi

D – Health

MORTALITY RATE

- WHO data, 2012.

- As mortality rates will be higher in countries that have greater life expectancy and therefore greater numbers of older people, an age-standardisation method was used to take account of the age structure and make the rates comparable between countries.

DEATHS FROM NON-COMMUNICABLE DISEASES

- WHO data, 2012.
- Each country is drawn in proportion to total population and then shaded to show the age-standardised mortality rate for this cause per 100,000 people (see note under *Mortality rate* above).

DEATHS FROM INJURIES

- WHO data, 2012.
- Each country is drawn in proportion to total population and then shaded to show the age-standardised mortality rate for this cause per 100,000 people (see note under *Mortality rate* above).

DEATHS FROM COMMUNICABLE DISEASES

- WHO data, 2012.
- Each country is drawn in proportion to total population and then shaded to show the age-standardised mortality rate for this cause per 100,000 people (see note under *Mortality rate* above).

DEATHS FROM DISEASES OF THE CIRCULATORY SYSTEM

- Eurostat data, 2011.
- Regions are sized in proportion to the number of people living there, and then shaded to show the total regional rate of deaths from circulatory system diseases per 100,000 of the population.

DEATHS FROM CANCER

- Eurostat data, 2011.
- Regions are sized in proportion to the number of people living there, and then shaded to show the total regional rate of deaths from cancer per 100,000 of the population.

DEATHS FROM DISEASES OF THE RESPIRATORY SYSTEM

- Eurostat data, 2011.

- Regions are sized in proportion to the number of people living there, and then shaded to show the total regional rate of deaths from respiratory system diseases per 100,000 of the population.

DEATHS FROM ALCOHOL USE

- UN and WHO data, 2008.
- Countries are sized in proportion to their total population, and then shaded to show the geographical pattern of alcohol consumption-related deaths per 100,000 people. The rates shown here were adjusted to take into account differences in the age structure of the population between countries.
- Alcohol consumption figures are based on litres of pure alcohol consumed by the total adult population (aged 15+).

DEATHS FROM DRUG USE

- UN and WHO data, 2008.
- Countries are sized in proportion to their total population, and then shaded to show the geographical pattern of drug-related deaths per 100,000 people. The rates shown here were adjusted to take into account differences in the age structure of the population between countries.

OBESITY

- UN and WHO data, 2008.
- The rates shown here were adjusted to take into account differences in the age structure of populations between countries.

FEMALE SMOKERS

- WHO data, 2015.
- The definition of smoking used here includes daily and occasional use of all forms of tobacco among females aged 15+.

MALE SMOKERS

- WHO data, 2015.
- The definition of smoking used here includes daily and occasional use of all forms of tobacco among males aged 15+.

SUICIDES

- WHO data, 2012.

- The data are age-standardised to take account of differences in the age structure of populations between countries.

- For more on suicide statistics and work capability assessments in the UK, see: www.centreforwelfarereform.org/uploads/attachment/456/work-capability-assessment-deaths-and-suicides.pdf

TOTAL HEALTH SPENDING

- World Bank data, 2014.

- Each country is resized on the map in proportion to total health spending (both public and private).

PUBLIC/PRIVATE SHARE OF HEALTH SPENDING

- World Bank data, 2013.

- For mortality rates in private hospitals, see https://chpi.org.uk/wp-content/uploads/2014/08/CHPI-PatientSafety-Aug2014

DOCTORS (NATIONAL)

- Sources: The Guardian data blog (Rogers, 2012), citing WHO, 2010; World Bank and WHO data.

- Each country is resized on the map in proportion to the number of doctors working in that country.

- Bar chart data for the EU is for 2011.

DENTISTS

- WHO data, 2009/10.

HEALTHCARE PROFESSIONALS

- Eurostat data, 2014.

- Note that statistics were only collected for nurses, not midwives, in Ireland, although the 1,193 total for nurses there may include some midwives.

DOCTORS (REGIONAL)

- Eurostat data, 2012.

- All regions are sized in proportion to the number of people living there, and then shaded to show the numbers of practising physicians measured as a proportion of the population.

HOSPITAL BEDS

- Eurostat data, 2012.

- Regions are sized in proportion to the number of people living there. In the UK data were only available at national level, as the current Westminster government has been cutting the availability of statistical data.

- Bar chart data is for 2014; see NHS Confederation (2016) *Key statistics on the NHS*, last updated 15 November 2016, www.nhsconfed.org/resources/key-statistics-on-the-nhs

E – Education

INTRODUCTION

- For Europe 2020 Strategy, see http://ec.europa.eu/europe2020/index_en.htm

NO SCHOOLING

- Barro-Lee educational attainment dataset (2013), data for 2010, but missing for Andorra (estimated using rates for Spain), Bosnia and Herzegovina, FYR Macedonia and Montenegro (estimated using rates for Serbia), Liechtenstein (estimated using rates for Switzerland), Monaco (estimated using rates for France), San Marino (estimated using rates for Italy) and the Vatican City.

- This dataset was created by Robert J. Barro and Jong-Wha Lee of Korea University (2013) to analyse educational attainment across the world from 1950 to 2010, using UNESCO's International Standard Classification of Education (ISCED), widely considered to be one of the most suitable for international comparisons of education statistics. (While educational comparisons are never ideal, some are better than others.) See further R.J. Barro and J.W. Lee (2013) 'A new data set of educational attainment in the world, 1950–2010', *Journal of Development Economics*, vol 104, pp 184–98 (www.barrolee.com/).

PRIMARY ONLY EDUCATION

- Barro-Lee educational attainment dataset (2013), data for 2010, but missing for Andorra (estimated using rates for Spain), Bosnia and Herzegovina, FYR Macedonia and Montenegro (estimated using rates for Serbia), Liechtenstein (estimated using rates for Switzerland), Monaco (estimated using rates for France), San Marino (estimated using rates for Italy) and the Vatican City.

SECONDARY ONLY EDUCATION

- Barro-Lee educational attainment dataset (2013), data for 2010, but missing for Andorra (estimated using rates for Spain), Bosnia and Herzegovina, FYR Macedonia and Montenegro (estimated using rates for Serbia), Liechtenstein (estimated using rates for Switzerland), Monaco (estimated using rates for France), San Marino (estimated using rates for Italy) and the Vatican City.

TERTIARY EDUCATION

- Barro-Lee educational attainment dataset (2013), data for 2010, but missing for Andorra (estimated using rates for Spain), Bosnia and Herzegovina, FYR Macedonia and Montenegro (estimated using rates for Serbia), Liechtenstein (estimated using rates for Switzerland), Monaco (estimated using rates for France), San Marino (estimated using rates for Italy) and the Vatican City.

GRADUATES (AGED 30-34)

- Eurostat data, 2014.

- Regions are sized in proportion to the number of people living there.

RAISING GRADUATE NUMBERS

- Eurostat data, 2008–14.

- Regions are sized in proportion to the number of people living there.

STUDENTS

- Eurostat data, 2010.

- Regions are sized in proportion to the number of people living there, and are then shaded to show numbers of students as a percentage of the total population aged 20–24.

VOCATIONAL PROGRAMMES

- Eurostat data, 2013.

- Regions are sized in proportion to the number of people living there.

EARLY LEAVERS FROM EDUCATION AND TRAINING

- Eurostat data, 2014.

- Regions are sized in proportion to the number of people living there.

CHILDREN IN PRE-SCHOOL

- Eurostat data, 2013.

- Children in pre-school may be older/younger than 4 which explains rates greater than 100%.

- Regions are sized in proportion to the number of people living there.

STUDYING ABROAD: INCOMING STUDENTS

- Eurostat data, 2012.

- Each country is sized according to the numbers of European students coming from elsewhere to study at university there.

STUDYING ABROAD: OUTGOING STUDENTS

- Eurostat data, 2012.

- Each country is sized according to the numbers of students who left that country to study elsewhere at university.

F – Work

LABOUR FORCE

- World Bank data, 2013.

- Every country is resized in proportion to the number of people aged 15 and over in the labour force in 2013. Data were missing for Andorra, Liechtenstein, Monaco and San Marino.

WOMEN IN LABOUR FORCE

- World Bank data, 2013.

- Every country is resized in proportion to the number of women aged 15 and over in the labour force in 2013. Data were missing for Andorra, Kosovo, Liechtenstein, Monaco, San Marino and the Vatican.

UNEMPLOYMENT (NATIONAL)

- World Bank data, 2013.

- Every country is resized in proportion to the estimated total number of unemployed people registered as out of work or looking for work in 2013.

CHANGE IN UNEMPLOYMENT

- World Bank data, 2007–13.

- Each country is sized in proportion to the increase in numbers of unemployed people over this period.

- What is being shown here is the net change in the total numbers officially recorded as being out of work or looking for work at two particular points in time. People will still have experienced unemployment where unemployment fell, but more people will have gained jobs than lost them. Similarly, in areas where unemployment has risen, many more people will have lost jobs than the number shown, but some will have since gained jobs.

- Germany only appears on this map because of the size of some of its neighbours – if it did not matter to keep them separated, it would not appear at all! Montenegro's decrease was negligible – just 16 fewer unemployed people – so has been rounded to zero.

YOUTH UNEMPLOYMENT

- World Bank data, 2013.

- Every country is resized in proportion to the estimated total number of young unemployed people aged 15–24 registered as out of work or looking for work in 2013.

- For information on unemployment in Rwanda, see: www.newtimes.co.rw/section/article/2015-08-18/191656/

CHANGE IN YOUTH UNEMPLOYMENT

- World Bank data, 2007–13.

- Each country is sized in proportion to the increase in numbers of young unemployed people (aged 18–24) over this period.

- Numbers of young people growing up in Germany have been declining steadily over time, and this might have contributed partly to the fall. Numbers of all young people fluctuate due to changing numbers of births in every area over the relevant period.

UNEMPLOYMENT (REGIONAL)

- Eurostat data, 2014.

- All regions are sized in proportion to their population and then shaded to show the unemployment rate in 2014.

PEOPLE WORKING IN AGRICULTURE

- World Bank data, 2012.

- Agriculture is defined here to include hunting, forestry and fishing.

- Countries are resized in proportion to the total estimated population working in agriculture there. Data were missing for Andorra, Kosovo, Liechtenstein, Monaco, San Marino and the Vatican.

PEOPLE WORKING IN INDUSTRY (NATIONAL)

- World Bank data, 2012.

- Countries are resized in proportion to the total estimated population working in industry there. Data were missing for Andorra, Kosovo, Liechtenstein, Monaco, San Marino and the Vatican.

PEOPLE WORKING IN SERVICES

- World Bank data, 2012.

- Countries are resized in proportion to the total estimated population working in services there. Data were missing for Andorra, Kosovo, Liechtenstein, Monaco, San Marino and the Vatican.

PEOPLE WORKING IN INDUSTRY (REGIONAL)

- Eurostat data, 2012.

- Note that this map shows employment in industry as a share of the total non-financial business economy, defined as covering industry, construction and non-financial services, ; whereas the national map on p112 shows employment in industry as a share of total employment.

- Regions are sized in proportion to the number of people living there and then shaded to show employment in industry as a share of the total non-financial business economy.

PEOPLE WORKING IN CONSTRUCTION

- Eurostat data, 2012.

- Regions are sized in proportion to the number of people living there and then shaded to show the employment in construction as a share of the total non-financial business economy, which is defined as covering industry, construction and non-financial services.

PEOPLE WORKING IN THE SERVICE SECTOR

- Eurostat data, 2012. Regions are sized in proportion to the number of people living there and then shaded to show employment in non-financial services as a share of the total non-financial business economy, which is defined as covering industry, construction and non-financial services.

PEOPLE WORKING IN HIGH-TECH SECTORS

- Eurostat data, 2014.

OCCUPATIONAL CATEGORIES (ALL PAGES)

- EU-SILC data, 2011.

SKILLED AGRICULTURAL, FORESTRY AND FISHERY WORKERS

- For trade figures, see http://ec.europa.eu/agriculture/sites/agriculture/files/trade-analysis/map/2014-1_en.pdf

G – Environment

CARBON DIOXIDE EMISSIONS

- World Bank data, 2011.

- For details of the EU's 2020 climate and energy package, see http://ec.europa.eu/clima/policies/strategies/2020/index_en.htm

NITROUS DIOXIDE EMISSIONS

- World Bank data, 2010.

METHANE EMISSIONS

- World Bank data, 2010.

OTHER GREENHOUSE GAS EMISSIONS

- World Bank data, 2010.

MOTOR VEHICLES

- World Bank data, 2012.

- Motor vehicles here are defined as cars, buses and all road-going freight vehicles (excluding motorbikes). Cars are vehicles 'intended for the carriage of passengers and designed to seat no more than nine people (including the driver)'.

RAILWAY LINES

- World Bank data, 2012.

- This map shows how the total length of railtrack is distributed across countries, with every country resized so its area is drawn in proportion to the total length of track within its borders.

VULNERABILITY OF EUROPEAN REGIONS TO CLIMATE CHANGE

- European Commission data, 2010.

- The composite index, taking values from 0 to 100, is based on estimates of: the total number of people in each region who are expected to be affected by increased river flooding; the total population living at less than 5 metres above sea level; the regional gross value added in agriculture and fisheries and in tourism and summer tourism; expected changes in precipitation and temperature; and the impact of the total extent of mountainous areas in each region.

- Regions are sized in proportion to the number of people living there and then shaded to show vulnerability to climate change.

ENERGY PRODUCTION

- World Bank data, 2010.

- 'Energy' is defined as all forms of petroleum (crude oil, natural gas liquids and oil from non-conventional sources), natural gas, solid fuels (coal, lignite and other derived fuels), combustible renewables and waste, and all energy used in primary electricity generation, from both renewable and non-renewable sources.

ENERGY USE

- World Bank data, 2010.

ENERGY USE: FOSSIL FUELS

- World Bank data, 2010.

- Each country is sized in proportion to total population and then shaded to show fossil fuel use as a percentage of total energy consumption.

ENERGY USE: COMBUSTIBLE RENEWABLES AND WASTE

- World Bank data, 2010.

- Combustible renewables and waste comprise solid and liquid biomass, biogas and industrial and municipal waste.

- Each country is drawn in proportion to total population and then shaded to show combustible renewables and waste energy use as a percentage of total energy consumption.

FRESHWATER WITHDRAWALS

- World Bank data, 2013.

- Agricultural withdrawals include withdrawals for irrigation and livestock production, and direct industrial use includes withdrawals for cooling thermoelectric plants.

RENEWABLE FRESHWATER RESOURCES

- World Bank data, 2013.

TERRESTRIAL AND MARINE PROTECTED AREAS

- World Bank data, 2010.

- Terrestrial-protected areas are defined as 'scientific reserves with limited public access, national parks, natural monuments, nature reserves or wildlife sanctuaries, protected landscapes, and areas managed mainly for sustainable use', whereas the marine-protected areas include 'intertidal or subtidal terrain-and overlying water and associated flora and fauna and historical and cultural features – that have been reserved by law or other effective means to protect part or all of the enclosed environment' (see http://data.worldbank.org/indicator/ER.PTD.TOTL.ZS).

- Each country is drawn in proportion to the total population and then shaded to show the terrestrial and marine protected areas as a percentage of its total territorial area.

FOREST AREA

- World Bank data, 2012.

LONELY EUROPE

- From B.D. Hennig (2016) 'Visualising spaces of global inaccessibility', in S. Carver and S. Fritz (eds) *Mapping wilderness: concepts, techniques and applications of GIS*, Heidelberg/New York/Dordrecht/London (Springer), pp 103–16.

H – Politics

HOW IMPORTANT IS POLITICS?

- European Values Survey, 2008.

IS DEMOCRACY THE BEST POLITICAL SYSTEM?

- European Values Survey, 2008.

For statistics on recent far-right voting figures, see www.nytimes.com/interactive/2016/05/22/world/europe/europe-right-wing-austria-hungary.html?smid=fb-nytimes&smtyp=cur&_r=0

IS ARMY RULE A VERY GOOD POLITICAL SYSTEM?

- European Values Survey, 2008.

HOW MUCH INTEREST IN POLITICS?

- European Values Survey, 2008.

VOTING PREFERENCES – LEFT, RIGHT OR CENTRE?

- European Values Survey, 2008.

- Quote from Peter Mandelson, Business Secretary for New Labour government in 1998.

ATTENDING LAWFUL DEMONSTRATIONS

- European Values Survey, 2008.

- See further: www.nytimes.com/interactive/2016/05/22/world/europe/europe-right-wing-austria-hungary.html?smid=fb-nytimes&smtyp=cur&_r=0

JOINING UNOFFICIAL STRIKES

- European Values Survey, 2008.

BELONGING TO WELFARE ORGANISATIONS

- European Values Survey, 2008.

BELONGING TO PEACE MOVEMENTS

- European Values Survey, 2008.

OCCUPYING BUILDINGS/FACTORIES

- European Values Survey, 2008.

TRUST IN NATIONAL GOVERNMENT

- UN data, 2007–12.

- See Human Development Report statistical tables (http://hdr.undp.org/sites/default/files/hdr14_statisticaltables.xls)

WOMEN IN PARLIAMENT

- The size of every country is drawn in proportion to total population.

QUALITY OF GOVERNMENT

- Index calculated by Nicholas Charron, Lewis

Dijkstra and Victor Lapuente (for the European Commission); see N. Charron, L. Dijkstra, and V. Lapuente, (2014) 'Regional governance matters: Quality of government within European Union member states', *Regional Studies*, 48(1), 68–90.

- All regions are sized in proportion to the number of people living there, and then shaded to show index scores.

I – Identity and Culture

GENERAL HAPPINESS

- European Values Survey, 2008.

LIFE SATISFACTION

- Gallup World Poll questionnaire, UN data, 2007–12.

- The actual question was worded: 'Please imagine a ladder, with steps numbered from 0 at the bottom to 10 at the top. Suppose we say that the top of the ladder represents the best possible life for you, and the bottom of the ladder represents the worst possible life for you. On which step of the ladder would you say you personally feel you stand at this time, assuming that the higher the step the better you feel about your life, and the lower the step the worse you feel about it? Which step comes closest to the way you feel?' The size of every country is drawn in proportion to total population, and countries are then shaded to show the average national response to this question.

FEELING 'EUROPEAN'

- European Values Survey, 2008.

FEAR OF LOSING NATIONAL IDENTITY

- European Values Survey, 2008.

HOW IMPORTANT IS LEISURE TIME?

- European Values Survey, 2008.

HOW IMPORTANT IS WORK?

- European Values Survey, 2008.

HOW IMPORTANT IS FAMILY?

- European Values Survey, 2008.

HOW IMPORTANT ARE FRIENDS?

- European Values Survey, 2008.

ATTITUDE TO COMPETITION

- European Values Survey, 2008.

TRUST IN OTHER PEOPLE

- Gallup World Poll questionnaire, UN, 2009–11.

THE IMPORTANCE OF RELIGION

- European Values Survey, 2008.

BELONGING TO RELIGIOUS ORGANISATIONS

- European Values Survey, 2008.

CAN THE DEATH PENALTY BE JUSTIFIED?

- European Values Survey, 2008.

BELIEF IN LIFE AFTER DEATH

- European Values Survey, 2008.

EUROPEAN SONG CONTEST

- Eurovision data, 2015.

- Not all countries included in this atlas took part in the final round of the contest or in the voting in 2015.

J – EU Budget

EU BUDGET: NET CONTRIBUTORS

- European Commission data, 2013.

EU BUDGET: NET RECEIVERS

- European Commission data, 2013.

HOW THE EU BUDGET IS SPENT

- European Commission data, 2013 (see further http://ec.europa.eu/budget/figures/2007-2013/index_en.cfm).